THE
GREASE
MACHINE

THE GREASE MACHINE

David Boulton

HARPER & ROW, PUBLISHERS
New York, Hagerstown, San Francisco, London

To Anthea, Kate and Nell

A sordid tale of bribery, and of shadowy figures operating behind the scenes ... a cast of characters out of a novel of international intrigue.

Senator Frank Church

Contents

Acknowledgments

I wish most warmly to thank the following friends for their assistance: David Plowright and the management of Granada Television, who made it possible for me to write this book despite my heavy television commitments; all who helped me make the TV programme 'How To Sell An Airforce', in particular George Jesse Turner and Alan Bale; Alan Brothers of Lockheed's London office; the staffs of the Church Committee and Donner Commission; Pam Adshead and Angela Street, who did the typing.

Most of all, however, I want to record my special debt to my colleagues John Blake and Andrew Cockburn. They were responsible for all the original research that went into 'How To Sell An Airforce', and together they went on to help me put this book together. Blake had a major hand in chapters 6 and 8, and Cockburn was largely responsible for chapter 7. Though the final versions and thus the shortcomings of these chapters, as of the rest of the book, are my own, the whole book owes much to their resourceful efforts.

DAVID BOULTON

Belmont, Lancashire

'kick-backs', 'pay-offs', or simply 'questionable payments'. In May 1977 Lockheed acknowledged that the figure of $22 million was a gross underestimate and that 'questionable payments involved more than $30 million and possibly as much as $38 million'. Even that figure did not include the millions paid in the 1950s and 1960s.

The Church Committee's public questioning of Lockheed executives was supplemented by the release, as official Congressional documents, of several hundred pages of subpoena'd Lockheed records: letters, interdepartmental memos, contracts, telexes, receipts, audit reports—office minutiae spawned over a full decade. Buried in this indigestible and seemingly random collection was evidence which would soon ruin reputations and rock governments. But it was all couched in a jumble of corporate double-speak: the lawyer's recondite phrase, the spy's mysterious allusion, the bagman's euphemism, and plain code.

As one reporter—Jim Hougan in *Harper's*—put it:

> The material was impossible to interpret on a short deadline, and its publication in full was absurd to contemplate. In the absence of indictments, the shortage of time, the interest of space, and the prevailing confusion, the story tended to be reduced to a single headline: WOGS TAKE BRIBES. Which was hardly news.

Freed of those cramping deadlines, it has proved possible to penetrate the maze, expose the euphemisms, break the code and unlock the hidden secrets to discover who bribed whom, how, when and why. In our journey of discovery through Lockheed's filing cabinets and related papers we find ourselves face to face with a cast of characters whom John le Carré wouldn't and Harold Robbins couldn't invent: a prince with an expensive taste for the wild life and—according to Dutch press stories—a Paris popette improbably but delightfully known as 'Pussy' Grinda; a samurai warrior with low fascist sympathies and high Liberal connections; a survivor of Nazi medical experiments and a White Russian retainer at the court of the House of Orange; a former priest carting currency from Hong Kong to Tokyo in Californian orange boxes; the general who planned the attack on Pearl Harbor, and a porno-actor turned kamikaze pilot; a Bavarian godfather and a Saudi pirate; 'la donna Lockheed' and her bizarre entourage of octogenarian down-and-outs—all backed by a massed male chorus of Indonesian widows and orphans. Linking them all, an endless parade of dummy corporations, underground banks, numbered accounts, charitable fronts: the ingenious

Introduction

1

'RUSH RUSH RUSH STRONGLY SUSPECT MACHINERY STALLED FOR L
OF GREASE ... '

So ran the cable from one of Lockheed's salesmen in Saudi Ara
to company headquarters in Burbank, California. And comp
treasurer Robert Waters didn't need his little black codebook to
him what that was all about.

This book, recording one multinational corporation's do
diplomacy, sets out to tell for the first time the full story of the Lo
heed bribery scandal. How the biggest defence contractor in
western world indirectly raided the public coffers of a dozen gove
ments, destabilised the democratic process in three of Americ
major allies, subverted aircraft procurement in NATO and SEA
corrupted world trade and the free market, bought the favours
princes and premiers, and systematically bamboozled America's o
regulatory agencies, legislators and taxpayers.

Parts of the story have been told before, though few, even amo
those that have made headlines, have been explored in detail. Son
parts have hitherto been no more than hinted at, and left in an u
explored jungle of allegation or innuendo, denial or evasion. Ar
some of the best parts have simply never surfaced before, lying buri
under mountains of arcane documentation, creative accountancy ar
artful code.

The Lockheed scandal first began to surface in the summer of 197
when the US Senate Sub-committee on multinationals under th
chairmanship of Senator Frank Church opened a series of hearing
on the company's affairs. These hearings lasted well into 1976 an
provoked further investigations which promise to drag on into th
1980s.

The company acknowledged paying $202 million in 'consultanc
fees' and 'commissions' from 1970 to 1975, at least $22 million o
which went in bribes which Lockheed preferred to characterise a

creations of shadowy lawyers and accountants, each as flexible as a Yuri Geller spoon.

And the Lockheed papers released by the Church Committee, richly rewarding as they are, by no means exhaust the documentary source material. The two Congressional investigations (there were also hearings by Senator Proxmire's Banking Sub-committee) and the more rigorous but less exposed enquiries launched by the Securities and Exchange Commission (SEC) were followed by major investigations around the world, and several of these—notably the Dutch, Italian and Japanese—produced their own wealth of detailed evidence. The Dutch enquiry even released American material not available in America, such as transcripts of the closed sessions of the Church hearings and the text of SEC interrogations. Finally, with the completion in June 1977 of the report of Lockheed's own Special Review Committee, coupling admission of past misdemeanours with the promise of perfect probity for the future, the way was clear to a comprehensive study of the billion-dollar grease machine—the story of ruthless businessmen on the take and greedy politicians on the make.

Where possible I have supplemented my documentary researches with meetings and interviews with some of the leading characters Some have asked to remain anonymous, and some have not asked but will nevertheless be so. I would like, however, to thank Dan Haughton and Adnan Khashoggi for helping to clarify my mind. Both did so while I was engaged in making the television documentary 'How To Sell An Airforce', the world-wide interest in which led to this book. Neither man—the great giver nor the great taker—was prepared at the time to talk freely and without qualification, but Dan Haughton in particular, then the chairman and absolute monarch of the Lockheed empire, made me understand the immense political, economic and social pressures which nudged Lockheed along the road to bribery and corruption. It is no part of my task to defend Haughton's exercise of 'business judgment' in authorising or condoning bribery—a practice which, in any case, he inherited rather than initiated—but it is very much my intention to show that it wasn't a simple question of ugly Americans squaring greedy foreigners. Haughton and his men—good, patriotic, God-fearing Republicans, most of them—bribed recklessly because they came to fear the alternative was the collapse of their company, with catastrophic consequences for employment and their country's defence capability. And within their own lights, taking the short view, they

Dramatis Personae

The action of this drama spans a dozen countries spread across the world, and covers a period of more than twenty years. Inevitably the number of characters who have their exits and their entrances is large, and it may help the reader keep a grasp of the principals, at least, if they are introduced here at the start in a manner which makes for ready reference.

ALLEN, James — Vice-president and director, Northrop. Convicted of involvement in illegal domestic political contributions.

ANDERSON, Roy A. — Chief financial officer, Lockheed corporation, during the period investigated. Now chairman of the board.

'BAARN, Victor' — A fictitious name in which a bank account was opened to receive payments intended by Lockheed for Prince Bernhard of the Netherlands.

BERNHARD, Prince of the Netherlands — Consort to Queen Wilhelmina, inspector-general of the Dutch armed forces and a director of KLM during the period investigated.

CHURCH, Frank — Democratic senator for Idaho and chairman of the Senate Sub-committee investigating multinational corporations (the Church Committee).

CLUTTER, Jack — President, Lockheed Aircraft (Asia) Ltd, registered in Hong Kong to sanitise Far East commissions.

COWDEN, William — Senior sales executive, Lockheed corporation.

CROCIANI, Camillo — Industrialist, and Lockheed undercover agent in Italy.

DASAAD, August — Lockheed's agent in Indonesia in the 1960s and early 1970s.

DE FRANCIS, Frank — Washington lawyer, Northrop agent and lobbyist.

ELLIOT, Al — Lockheed public relations officer in Tokyo on the TriStar campaign.

FANALI, General Diulio — Head of the Italian air force under prime minister Rumor. Code-named by Lockheed 'Pun'.

FINDLEY, William G. — Partner in Arthur Young and Co., Lockheed's auditors.

FRORIEP, Andreas — Swiss lawyer and head of Northrop 'front' company, the Economic and Development Corporation.

FUKUDA, Taro — Associate and interpreter of Yoshio Kodama. Lockheed public relations consultant on Starfighter and TriStar campaigns.

GENDA, Minoru — Japanese general who planned Pearl Harbor raid, Lockheed Starfighter supporter and member of the Diet (Parliament).

GERRITSEN, Teengs — Dutch wartime resistance leader, friend of Prince Bernhard and agent for Lockheed and Northrop.

GONZALEZ, 'Manny' — Northrop sales executive, Middle East.

GROSS, Courtlandt — Deputy chairman, Lockheed corporation, 1933–61, chairman 1961–9.

GROSS, Robert — Chairman, Lockheed corporation, 1933–61.

GUI, Luigi

Italian minister of defence during the Hercules campaign. Arrested 1976.

HASHIM, General

Head of the Saudi Arabia air force during the Hercules campaign, code-named by Lockheed 'Trumpet'.

HAUGHTON, Daniel J.

Lockheed corporation president, 1961-7, and chairman, 1967-76.

HAUSER, Ernest F.

Lockheed's customer relations manager, Koblenz, Germany, 1960-4, and liaison with defence minister Franz Josef Strauss.

HAUSMAN, Ed.

Lockheed's Georgia-subsidiary contracts director during early Indonesian campaign.

HIYAMA, Hiro

President of Marubeni, Lockheed's official sales agent in Japan. Arrested 1976.

HULL, John Kenneth

Lockheed sales executive, Far East, in the late 1960s.

ITOH, Hiroshi

Director of Marubeni. Arrested 1976.

JOHNSON, Clarence 'Kelly'

Lockheed ace designer of many planes, including the Starfighter.

JONES, Thomas V.

Chairman and chief executive, Northrop. Convicted of illegal domestic political payments, 1974.

KHALID, bin Abdullah, Prince

Member of the Saudi royal family and undercover sub-agent for Lockheed and Northrop.

KHASHOGGI, Adnan

Lockheed and Northrop agent in Saudi Arabia.

KISHI, Nobusuke

Friend and former cell-mate of Yoshio Kodama. Prime minister of Japan during Starfighter campaign.

KODAMA, Yoshio

Lockheed's secret agent in Japan in the 1960s and 1970s.

KOTCHIAN, Carl — President, Lockheed corporation, 1967–76. Headed campaigns in Italy and Japan.

LEFEBVRE, Ovidio — Lockheed's agent in Italy for Orion and Hercules campaigns.

MAENO, Mitsuyasu — Japanese porn-film actor and one-time follower of Yoshio Kodama.

MARTIN, John H. — Chief counsel, Lockheed corporation.

MEUSER, Frederick C. — Lockheed's European sales director and link with Prince Bernhard.

MITCHELL, Robert — Lockheed's corporate vice-president, international operations.

MYERS, Gifford — Lockheed corporate vice-president, marketing.

OHNO, Bamboku — Vice-president, Japanese Liberal Democratic Party during Starfighter campaign.

OKUBO, Toshiharu — Managing director, Marubeni.

ONI, Yoshiyoshi — Former espionage agent and Lockheed's office manager in Tokyo during Starfighter campaign.

OSANO, Kenji — Lockheed's secret sub-agent in Japan during TriStar campaign.

PANTCHOULIDZEW, Col A. E. — White Russian retainer to Prince Bernhard of the Netherlands and nominal recipient of payments intended by Lockheed for the prince.

RIDINGS, Ned — Lockheed sales executive, Far East.

ROHA, Clarence 'Lefty' — In charge of Lockheed's Paris office during Italian Hercules campaign.

ROOSEVELT, Kim — Former CIA operative, Northrop agent in Iran and Middle East.

RUMOR, Mariano — Italian prime minister consulted by Lockheed on Hercules sale. Code-named by Lockheed 'Antelope Cobbler'.

RUSMIN, Air Marshal — Head of AURI, the Indonesian air force.

SAVY, William — Former intelligence officer, 'bag-man' for Northrop slush fund.

SMITH, Roger Bixby — Former Lockheed counsel, later consultant, and link with Prince Bernhard and Italian payments.

STEHLIN, General Paul-Marie — French deputy and secret Northrop consultant.

STRAUSS, Franz Josef — West German defence minister during Starfighter campaign, and leader of the Bavarian CDU party.

SULTAN, Prince — Saudi defence minister.

TANAKA, Kakuei — Japanese prime minister during the TriStar campaign, now on trial for receiving bribes.

TANAKA, Shoji — Japanese member of the Diet during the Starfighter campaign.

TANASSI, Mario — Leading member of the Italian Social Democratic Party, former defence minister, now on trial.

TURKI, Prince — Saudi deputy defence minister.

VALENTINE, Charles — Director of contracts, Lockheed's Georgia company.

WATERS, Robert — Lockheed corporate treasurer to 1975. Killed himself when scandal broke.

WEISBROD, Hubert — Swiss lawyer, consultant to both Lockheed and Northrop, and link-man for Lockheed with Prince Bernhard.

WILDER, Don — Lockheed's vice-president, marine sales, during Orion campaign in the Netherlands and Italy.

ZUHAYR, General — Saudi head of air force, succeeding General Hashim. Code-named by Lockheed 'Geranium'.

1
Cover-up

I thought the least said about these matters the better.
Dan Haughton, chairman, Lockheed corporation

1

Mr Findley was puzzled. He was almost through with his routine check of Lockheed's overseas sales ledger for 1970. He sat in a modest office on the second floor of the corporation's sprawling and faintly run-down administrative headquarters in downtown Burbank, California, gazing through the window across line upon line of automobiles to the even more run-down terminal buildings of Burbank Airport, which Lockheed owned but were trying to sell. Lockheed had money troubles. But what puzzled Mr Findley had nothing whatever to do with the current threat of bankruptcy.

William G. Findley was a partner in the prestigious international firm of Arthur Young and Co., auditors to Lockheed since 1933. What puzzled him, on this February morning of 1971, was a curious entry which, when matched up with explanatory memos and correspondence, seemed to indicate that Lockheed was making generous contributions to a widows' and orphans' welfare fund in Djakarta, Indonesia.

Like most private corporations conscious of their public image, Lockheed often donated to popular charities. But in recent, leaner years the donations had been modest, well publicised and local. Those that were now puzzling Findley involved several hundred thousand dollars, considerable secrecy and a curiously remote beneficiary.

Although he disclaimed the role of guardian of his clients' morals, it was Findley's job to question any payment or receipt which seemed curious, abnormal, or, perhaps because of inadequate documentation, simply inexplicable. Fraud, dishonest diversion of funds, tax-dodging, bribery—this is what he was trained to sniff out. The Securities and Exchange Commission and the Internal Revenue Service (IRS) rely on independent auditors to police the financial affairs of private companies. Who, Findley needed to know, were these far-off widows and orphans, and why had a handful of Lockheed executives so suddenly and generously concerned themselves with their welfare?

He put the questions bluntly to the appropriate divisional vice-president, M. H. Greene. Greene told him that the 'donations' had been paid to a bona fide consultant who in turn assigned the money to the head of the Indonesian air force. The payments were 'a private matter between the consultant and the air force head'[1] and — according to Greene — had nothing to do with Lockheed. The air force chief, for reasons of his own which again didn't concern Lockheed, chose to designate his cash a welfare fund for widows and orphans. Who was to know and whose business was it to pry into what he did with his money? This was Djakarta, not Los Angeles.

So Lockheed was diverting money to this general for services rendered or to be rendered, prompted Findley. Greene gave a dead-pan answer. There was 'no indication the assignment related to the performance of any Lockheed contract with the air force'.

The auditors, not entirely reassured, had come across cases like this before. Way back in 1959 Findley's predecessor had picked up some mysterious cash payments in yen to a consultant in Japan. His concern then was that these might conceal kick-backs to Lockheed employees, but enquiries were dropped when it became apparent that Lockheed's senior management knew of and approved this unusual method of paying their consultant. Then, in the 1960 audit, the auditors had queried a $300,000 cheque signed, most unusually, by the then Lockheed chairman, Robert Gross. Findley's colleague W. J. Mayhugh was told by Gross that the payment was 'in connection with the company's European marketing effort'. Mayhugh 'did not recall whether he asked or was told who had received these funds'. Fifteen years later it became clear that the name he didn't recall being told was none other than Prince Bernhard of the Netherlands.[2]

In the 'widows and orphans' case, Findley decided the payments

1 Except when otherwise indicated, all quotations in this chapter are from the Lockheed Special Review Committee Report lodged with the SEC and Washington district court in May 1977. Names of consultants and countries, omitted from the report and the exhibit, have been added here where they can be confidently deduced from other Lockheed documentation. Although I rely on the report for much of the narrative of this chapter, comments and conclusions are of course my own.

2 The Dutch 'Commissie van Drie' which investigated Bernhard's involvement concluded that Lockheed *intended* the payment for the prince, though he denied having received it. See chapter 5.

were 'sensitive' and told Greene it was essential that the corporation's chief financial officer, Roy A. Anderson, was given all the details. Greene later stated that he had done so, and when Findley made a discreet check, Anderson confirmed that he knew of 'the problem'. On the strength of this assurance (of which Anderson said later he had 'no recollection'), Findley apparently decided it was unnecessary to pursue his investigations further. He was not to know that the Indonesian general's welfare fund was but the tiniest tip of an immense submerged iceberg, and that he had missed an opportunity to uncover and smash perhaps the world's most sophisticated network of bribery and corruption. And missed opportunities, misunderstandings and executive amnesia soon laid the groundwork for one of the most dazzling cover-up operations since Watergate, planned at the very top and subsuming directors, accountants — and even auditors.

2

Two years later Findley was back in the same office conducting the 1972 audit. This time his interest was aroused by the highly unusual nature of receipts collected by Lockheed salesmen for 'marketing expenses' for the TriStar jumbo jet in Japan. One which baffled him read simply:

'I received One Hundred Peanuts. (signed) Hiroshi Itoh.'

Others referred to the receipt of 'pieces'. Few were on formal, printed receipts, and some were scrawled on the torn-off corners of what appeared to be newspaper wrappers. Some were unintelligible because in Japanese, others unintelligible although in English. What staggered Findley, once he was told that 'peanuts' and 'pieces' represented one million Japanese yen (approximately $3,300), was that the 'marketing expenses' accounted for in this somewhat casual and innovative fashion appeared to total nearly $5 million — and were clearly continuing at an ever-accelerating rate.

Findley shared his bafflement with his Arthur Young colleague Bill Mayhugh and together they decided to go straight to the top. On February 25, 1973, they met Lockheed chairman Dan Haughton in his office to convey their concern at the amount of money that was being handled this way. Both recall asking Haughton whether he knew the purpose of the payments and the reason they were paid in mittee. Mayhugh was given the unenviable job of breaking the bad news to Haughton, who responded angrily:

> You have spoken to your counsel and if you go to the audit committee they will speak to their counsel and their counsel will tell them to tell the board. Why don't you just go put it in the *Los Angeles Times*? You will destroy our ability to do business there [in Japan].

Haughton then resourcefully 'requested permission' of Jack Horton to attend the next audit committee meeting on March 4 together with Kotchian. (This was even more irregular than Kotchian's attendance at the earlier meeting but Horton did not object.) Then, at the conclusion of normal business, Dan Haughton asked that the committee go into 'executive session', with the minutes secretary excused and no record kept.[1] Again no one argued. Thereafter, every time the audit committee discussed apparent irregularities in sales commission payments they went into 'executive session'. It is not clear who was at these secret sessions. Everyone remembers that, besides Haughton, Kotchian, Findley and Mayhugh, the independent directors present at the March 4 meeting were Jack Horton, Dwight M. Cochran and L. J. Hector. Horton and Findley remember that chief financial officer Roy Anderson was there too; but Anderson again has 'no recollection' of being present or taking any part in the discussion. (His imperfect memory was not a factor when, in 1977, he was chosen to succeed to the chairmanship of the company.)

Mayhugh told the committee there had been 'large, unusual and partially unauditable transactions', and described the records, which indicated that several million dollars had gone to one consultant, $200,000 to another, and $400,000 had been disbursed by Asia division executive Jack Clutter to unknown parties. Another executive had written that he 'needed receipts' for $100,000 which was unaccounted for. Arthur Young was not in a position to pass judgment on the 'legality or morality' of the payments, said Mayhugh, though there was evidence that some of the records were 'deliberately deceptive'. They had 'no hard evidence as to the ultimate disposition of the funds', and were particularly critical of the fact that there was no written contract with Yoshio Kodama, recipient of by far the greatest part of the money.

---

1 Findley, however, kept notes which he later used as the basis for his testimony to the Church Committee.

Haughton countered with his by now familiar argument: such payments were necessary, confidentiality had to be observed, and 'any public knowledge of the payments and relationships could have a significant adverse effect on the company's ability to do business overseas'. As he put it later: 'I thought the least said about these matters the better.'

A decision to report the facts to the full board of directors or press for the enquiry Arthur Young wanted would be a direct and possibly fateful challenge to the authority of the corporation's two most powerful officers. The audit committee backed away from such a conflict. It concluded that, 'considering Haughton's and Kotchian's comments and the information in hand', the payments were 'proper sales costs in advancing the L-1011 (TriStar) program and that it was not necessary to make any report to the Board'.

The committee did recommend, however, that the management take steps to regularise its relationship with Yoshio Kodama by obtaining a signed contract for his services. Accordingly, later in the year Arthur Young were shown a copy of a signed agreement — back-dated 'as of 1969'. Apparently, the auditors did not comment on this irregularity. Findley simply reported the existence of the document to the board's audit committee.

As Lockheed's own Special Review Committee, reporting to the SEC in 1977, noted in its report, 'there appears to have been no other substantive work or investigation by Arthur Young regarding the currency payments in Japan (which continued until July 1975)' until the Church Committee's hearings raised the matter publicly.

Meanwhile, for Haughton and Kotchian it was business as usual.

3

There is a third tier to Lockheed's audit structure. Quite apart from Arthur Young and the audit committee of the board, the corporation has an internal audit organisation composed of resident staffmen at its California and Georgia companies and at its various divisions — missiles, electronics, shipbuilding and the smaller divisions and subsidiaries. This third tier, too, stumbled across 'improper payments' abroad — and looked the other way.

In the 1960s, when Lockheed was in its heyday, the internal audit organisation numbered some 120 people. But the corporation's financial misfortunes in the 1970s forced staff cutbacks here as elsewhere.

It is ironic that the slide towards bankruptcy which resulted in a huge expansion of secret bribery overseas also resulted in the progressive strangulation of the audit organisation whose job it was to seek out and prevent such abuses.

Bud Inman, director of internal auditing, wrote to Jack Horton on April 16, 1973 — six weeks after Horton's audit committee had skirted the Japanese affair — and complained about the dwindling staff at his disposal. The resultant 'reduction in the coverage of regular operations', he wrote, coupled with pressure of 'high level special work assignments' arising from the company's cash-flow crisis, was 'tending to change the nature of the audit function from a control concept to a troubleshooting role'. This, suggested Inman, merited 'consideration by management as to its ultimate effect on the overall control system'. In plain English, Bud Inman's department was too understaffed to do its job properly and he wanted to know what management was going to do about it.

Horton passed his letter to Roy Anderson with a covering note:

> I assume that you and Dan [Haughton] are fully aware of this change and may have some comments on the overall control system.

Anderson (whose memoese was even more arcane than Inman's) replied to Horton on May 11:

> Rest assured we are concerned about the trend ... Now that we are getting some of our specific problem situations better under control, we intend to reverse the audit trend to one of more normal overall control system coverage. While the precise amount of audit effort for optimum control is not determinable, we would hope to maintain the audit coverage of operations at a practical level as an effective part of the overall control system. We would like to do this and still permit the assignment of audit effort to special problem situations where Internal Audit capabilities are particularly applicable and of direct benefit to management.

What in practice seemed to be 'of direct benefit to management', however, was not a reversal but an acceleration of the process by which the internal audit department was emasculated. Internal audit man-days suffered a 9 per cent cut in 1973, a 10 per cent cut in 1974 and a 6 per cent cut in 1975, by which year Bud Inman's staff was little more than half its strength in the 1960s. Small wonder, then, that corrupt practices in overseas marketing, though spreading rapidly, were almost entirely undetected by the department. With the exception of one 'special purpose audit' in 1973, the department left consultants' commissions and payments wholly unaudited from 1970 to June 1975.

Even the one 'special purpose audit', in the Georgia division, was curiously inconclusive. It arose from a suspicion that two company employees were taking kick-backs, and a wide-ranging investigation was ordered into commission payments in Saudi Arabia, Italy, Spain, Indonesia and two other countries which cannot be identified with certainty.

No evidence of employees' kick-backs emerged, but the Georgia division's staff audit team did come across a range of irregular practices which were listed in a memorandum of August 16, 1973, from the audit manager, F. G. Gaugh, to the finance director of Lockheed-Georgia, A. H. Lorch. They found payments into secret numbered Swiss bank accounts and payments of 'special compensation in recognition of extra personal services, expenses and advice' over and above contractual commission fees. And the Indonesian widows' and orphans' fund was uncovered again.

This was the clearest indication yet that the practices which disturbed Arthur Young in Japan were much more widespread than was admitted. Yet, astonishingly, the memo reporting these findings was never permitted to be sent from the Georgia division's base in Marietta to corporate headquarters in Burbank. Contrary to normal procedures, no copy was sent to corporate head of internal audit, Bud Inman, and, as a consequence, no report was made to the board's audit committee or Arthur Young and Co.

When, months later, Gaugh's memo was superseded by a formal final report, the report made no mention of the audit team's specific findings. It contained the vaguest of summaries:

> Overall, we consider the conditions we found indicative of some general weakness in the current system of controls provided by [the Georgia company] over the payment of sales commission ... Inasmuch as this review was made at the special request of [Lockheed-Georgia] management, a reply is not required.

Not surprisingly, in view of so singular a lack of urgency, the Special Review Committee investigating Lockheed's affairs could find 'no indication of any other follow-up regarding this matter by any Lockheed management personnel'.

4

By the end of 1973, then, all three tiers of Lockheed's audit system —Arthur Young, the board's audit committee and the management's internal audit organisation—were aware of major irregularities. Yet the practices continued unabated.

There was one more discovery which might have prompted an investigation but didn't. In the 1972 audit of Lockheed's Hong Kong division, carried out by the Hong Kong office of Arthur Young, the auditor noted that 'an amount of $100,000 was transferred out from a [company] bank account to another bank account under another party's name which was not disclosed by Mr. Andrew [F. J. Andrew Jr, then finance director and later director-general of Lockheed Aircraft International Ltd, Hong Kong]'. The auditor minuted his understanding that 'this amount might have been paid under-the-counter to someone for the procurement of a sale contract which is at present being negotiated'. He also noted another 60 million Japanese yen unaccounted for.

His report has a curious, anonymous note scrawled in the margin: 'OK, Mr. C. R. Warman is aware of this item.' But Warman, the partner in charge of Arthur Young's Hong Kong office, can cast no light on this: he has since died. And Mr Andrew can no longer recall discussing the matter with Warman. In any case, the report seems never to have found its way to Los Angeles. It was left to gather dust in a filing cabinet in Hong Kong.

5

After the March 4 meeting at which Haughton and Kotchian successfully persuaded the audit committee to go along with the view that the payments questioned by Arthur Young were proper marketing expenses, a full year passed before any serious concern was again expressed about the dubiety of some of these transactions. On March 3, 1974, the audit committee—which had met only once in the meantime—was sufficiently worried to press Haughton and Kotchian for a full list of all the corporation's consultants, together with details of commissions paid and the sales to which such payments were said to relate.

On May 7, Horton, Cochran and Hector of the audit committee

and Findley and A. J. Feiffer of Arthur Young met Haughton, Kotchian and Anderson of Lockheed management to review the tabulation. Although it omitted grand totals, a quick totting up showed that commissions paid or promised totalled $140 million on sales of about $1·3 billion in twelve countries.

The audit committee, at last beginning to show its teeth, decided the magnitude of the payments was so great, and the ultimate destination of much of the money so uncertain, that the company should take outside legal advice on the permissibility of such payments both under US law (including the Internal Revenue Code) and under applicable law in the countries where the payments were made. The task of consulting outside counsel was delegated to the company's own chief legal officer, John H. Martin. The choice, as we shall see, was an ironic one.

Seven weeks later, on June 28, Martin reported progress to Roy Anderson. He had selected four countries, including Saudi Arabia and Japan, whose contract arrangements he had submitted to outside counsel. The firm of Miller and Chevalier in Washington would give an opinion relating to US law and a Paris-based firm, Coudert Frères, had been asked to examine applicable law in each of the four selected countries. The opinions of both firms would be based on Martin's own representations as to how Lockheed paid its consultants, and these representations in turn would be based on his own 'personal examination of all our consultant files' and his 'general knowledge regarding the background of certain of the more significant contracts'.

On September 10 Roy Anderson transmitted to the audit committee a status report from Martin. Miller and Chevalier were of the opinion that the payments reported to them by Martin 'do not contravene any law of the State of California or the United States' and were 'properly deductible by Lockheed under Section 162(a) of the Internal Revenue Code'. Coudert Frères had still to deliver a final report, but a preliminary opinion from one of their correspondent firms was equally reassuring: Lockheed's payments, as described to them by Martin, 'appear[ed] to be consistent with local practices and law'. Another of Coudert's correspondent counsel advised that 'no substantial problem exists regarding foreign exchange control or domestic tax'.

Astonishingly, none of the members of the audit committee was shown the actual text of the legal opinions they themselves had commissioned. Instead they were content with the most generalised assurance from Martin that his soundings had produced 'all-clear' signals. This was at best no more than half true since there was a great deal that Martin concealed in his report.

First, the committee was not told that Miller and Chevalier had added a rider to their opinion recommending that payments to Swiss numbered accounts be discontinued. More important, the committee was not advised of concern expressed by another firm, Musick, Peeler and Garrett, which Miller and Chevalier had consulted for specialist advice on local Californian law. The Musick opinion stated:

> We have assumed that no director, officer, agent or employee of Lockheed ... has knowledge of the disposition of the payments made to the consultants or representatives; furthermore, such payments have been assumed to be generally commensurate with those being paid for services similar to those required by the Agreements, involving the same territory and similar United States or foreign made products. The latter assumption is relevant in determining whether knowledge of the high levels of compensation being provided to the representatives or consultants places the directors and officers of Lockheed on notice that something unusual is occurring, and thus requires that they investigate to ascertain whether the representatives or consultants are making illegal rebates or other payments. In other words, assuming that the directors and officers of Lockheed have no knowledge of any illegal rebates or other payments, an issue may still exist as to whether they will be held responsible despite this lack of actual knowledge if indeed illegal rebates or other payments are being made.

Martin, whose representations to independent counsel were based, as he said himself, on his own 'personal examination' of the files and 'general knowledge' of commission payments, must have been aware that some of these assumptions were artful, if not false. Most members of the audit committee also would have guessed that such assumptions were over-optimistic. But they were never made aware of Musick's cautionary opinion.

Again quite unknown to the audit committee, there were other reasons why the 'all-clear' signals from Miller and Chevalier and Coudert Frères were virtually valueless. These opinions, as we have seen, were based entirely on Martin's representations, and not all his representations were accurate. For instance, Martin told them that:

... no employee or official of any foreign government, or any director, officer or employee of a customer is a party to any of these agreements.

This may have been strictly true in that there were probably no formal agreements with government officials on file. But it is surprising if Martin did not know, or guess, that some of the agreements he studied in his 'personal examination' of the files were with intermediaries fronting for government officials.

Another of his representations to counsel was that:

... no director, officer, agent or managerial employee of Lockheed or an affected subsidiary has knowledge of the disposition of the payments made to the consultants.

Martin may not have known the ultimate recipients of these payments. But, as we shall see, he himself had been one of a handful of managerial employees who had controlled a secret 'off-the-books' fund from which payments were made to consultants. And what's more, among his co-signatories controlling the secret account were two partners in the law firm of Coudert Frères—the very firm to which Martin now looked for independent legal advice on the payments in question.

6

Back in 1968, Martin's predecessor as Lockheed chief counsel, Roger Bixby Smith, had told Charles Torem, a partner in the Paris office of Coudert Frères, that Lockheed was setting up a Swiss bank account 'to meet the requirements of a European sales effort'. Torem agreed to be a co-signer with certain Lockheed executives, including Smith and Martin. The account was opened in the name of a Swiss lawyer, Hubert Weisbrod, and operated with the express intention that payments made from it would not be readily identifiable as Lockheed money. Martin's participation in the control of the fund increased when Smith left Lockheed—to join Coudert Frères.

Lockheed paid $325,000 into the secret account. In September 1968 $100,000 was withdrawn for 'Victor Baarn', apparently a fictitious name for Prince Bernhard.[1] Early in 1969 $25,000 was paid to

1 See chapter 5.

an official of KLM. On July 8, 1970, $10,000 was paid to 'an intelligence-gathering organisation' in London.

Some time in 1971 the account was closed and the remaining $190,000 placed in cash in a safe-deposit box under the control of Smith and Torem of Coudert Frères, and Martin, A. G. Otsea and apparently Robert Mitchell of Lockheed.

Soon after, according to Martin, he was asked by corporate executive vice-president T. F. Morrow (now dead) to bring $20,000 back to the United States. He collected the money in $100 bills at the Coudert Frères office and took it to Los Angeles. There he was told that it was intended for 'obligations in Washington', which he rightly took to mean illegal domestic political contributions. According to his own account, he refused to hand the money over. When Haughton and Kotchian, in a discussion of political contributions, declared themselves 'opposed to using any such money', Martin returned the cash to the safe-deposit box in Geneva, apparently evading currency control by taking it in instalments from mid-1972 to mid-1973.

In July 1973 Martin was requested by Lockheed treasurer Robert Waters to go to Geneva and transfer the $190,000 to a box at another bank. (The reason for the switch is not clear, but Lockheed sources have said it was to eliminate the then corporate vice-president, commercial aircraft marketing, Robert Mitchell, from the select list of authorised signatories.) Martin and Roger Smith, then with Coudert Frères, carried out the transfer, placing nineteen packets of $100 bills in two briefcases and carrying them across the street to the second bank.

Over the next few months nearly $400,000 in cash was added to the box, all of it, according to the Special Review Committee's report, 'accumulated in the form of bearer checks outside the Company's customary financial controls'. Withdrawals included $80,000 for 'a senior official of one of the company's foreign customers' — this turned out to be the Hong Kong based private airline Cathay-Pacific — and $45,000 'given to a special consultant as compensation for preparation of false receipts'.[1] Much of this must have been done with Martin's direct participation because he was one of the signatories controlling access to the box where the money was held. And suddenly in 1974, he was the man charged with the task of reassuring the worried auditors that all was legal and above board.

1 See chapter 10.

7

The audit committee was not to know that the corporation's chief legal officer, busily soliciting independent legal advice on their behalf, was himself a signatory on off-the-books accounts and safe-deposit boxes. (Puzzlingly, Martin told the Lockheed Special Review Committee that 'at that time I had no concept of an off-the-books account'.) Still less were they aware that members of the ostensibly 'independent' firm of Coudert Frères, whose preliminary opinion they had found so reassuring, were in fact co-signatories with Martin. Senior management, however, cannot have been so ignorant. Carl Kotchian authorised payments from the deposit box and certainly knew that Martin was one of the co-signatories. It must have been a singular convenience that the review of questionable practices was itself in such practised hands.

On October 3, 1974, Martin drafted for W. R. Wilson, vice-president, international marketing, a set of 'Guidelines for the Selection of Consultants'. As a result of the 'legal audit' of the more significant commission agreements, he wrote, 'we have concluded that there is no legal impropriety (either with respect to foreign law or domestic law) with respect to either the agreements themselves or the administration thereof'. Fourteen recommendations followed, including that no payments be made 'off the books', or to numbered bank accounts, or to government or customer officials. Martin's draft concluded:

> While, at first glance, some of the foregoing may seem to be somewhat onerous, the fact is that in practice we have generally been conforming to these requirements in the past.

This was, of course, untrue; but that was not why Wilson returned the draft to Martin for rewriting. Wilson's worry, which presumably reflected the attitude of other senior management men with whom he discussed it, was that it was 'too prospective' in tone. It carried an implication, for those who would seek it, that all had not been well in the past. If there had to be guidelines, Wilson and his colleagues wanted them to be framed so that they would seem to be not so much establishing new rules as reinforcing old, unquestioned procedures.

The redraft that won Wilson's approval for circulation to all divisional presidents and marketing directors omitted the words 'While at first glance some of the foregoing requirements may seem to be somewhat onerous', and left out completely the crucial recommendation that the company satisfy itself that its consultants were not acting as conduits to government officials. The revised document no longer claimed that Lockheed had 'generally' conformed in the past to the recommendations, but robustly converted the half-truth into a full-blooded lie by concluding:

> In practice we have been conforming to these requirements in the past, and I am enumerating them at this time only because I believe it important that we be careful to continue to conform in the future.

Many of the salesmen in the front line, to whom this was circulated, must have known it to be a lie. But the message was clear: carry on regardless.

8

Lockheed's multi-million-dollar business bribes would evidently have continued unchecked by effective audit scrutiny had it not been for a time-bomb ticking away in Washington.

The revelations of illegal contributions by other corporations to Nixon's 1972 re-election fund set in motion a series of Congressional and SEC investigations into the hidden financial affairs of multinational corporations. On May 5, 1975, Carl Kotchian told the board of directors that a letter had been received from the SEC requesting details of foreign sales commissions.

There was no problem, Jack Horton assured the board. There would be no Lockheed scandal like those which were engulfing the oil multinationals and had so damaged ITT and United Fruit. The audit committee had taken steps to obtain the best available legal opinion (from Coudert Frères, of course) and had been assured there was no legal impropriety in the company's system of payments. Arthur Young had 'reviewed the accounting' for these payments. And the department of defense itself had issued a document endorsing the use of paid consultants for overseas sales.[1] Lockheed had nothing to hide.

A month later, Frank Church's Senate Sub-committee on multinational corporations opened hearings on Lockheed's rival, Northrop,

---

1 Presumably the Hoenig paper, see chapter 9, page 217.

and Northrop chairman Tom Jones admitted publicly that his consultancy agreements, which included bribes, were modelled on those of Lockheed. One immediate result was a sudden surge of activity from Arthur Young and Co. which had done no substantive work on Lockheed's sales commissions since raising (and dropping) the Japanese payments in 1973. Amid a spate of press speculation following Jones's bombshell, Arthur Young requested that Kotchian, Martin, Duane Wood (president of Lockheed-California) and L. T. Barrow (vice-president, international finance) sign a letter stating that, to the best of their knowledge and belief,

> All [consultancy] payments are made in accordance with the agreements and are duly recorded on the books of Lockheed ...
>
> No employee or official of any foreign government, or any director, officer or employee of a customer is a party to any of the agreements.
>
> No director, officer, agent or managerial employee of Lockheed or an affected subsidiary has knowledge of the disposition of the payments made to the consultancy.

Arthur Young were hoping to leave the buck with Lockheed. But the Lockheed men were not prepared to be made sole scapegoats in the event of a scandal. They refused to sign. Arthur Young in turn refused to certify the annual report. An investigation, staffed jointly by the company and Arthur Young, was launched to resolve the impasse. But it was too late.

Haughton was subpoena'd to appear before a Senate Subcommittee. He was tough, resilient and used to dealing with censorious politicians. But some of his subordinates were less thick-skinned. On August 24, the day before the hearing, corporation vice-president and treasurer Robert Waters, who had helped administer Martin's 'off the books' account and its transformation into a currency slush fund, locked himself in his home in Valencia, California, wrote a note mentioning business problems, and shot himself dead through the temple.

The Lockheed scandal had broken.

2

The Making of the
Grease Machine

Had Lockheed been a British company it would have sent
out a hen-pecked salesman with some superficial brochures
to try to sell a product that didn't exist and that his own
country didn't want. This is hardly the way to get results. In
contrast, Lockheed flooded the market with overwhelming
confidence, generously offering to let friendly nations have a
part of the world's greatest airplane.

Bill Gunston, *Early Supersonic Fighters
of the West* (Ian Allen, London, 1976)

1

Every corporation, national or multinational, likes to look back to the hard times, the early days of hope and struggle, often embodied in a single rugged, romantic pioneer who set out with a dime in one trouser pocket and a hole in the other to conquer adversity and found a mighty empire. Lockheed's pioneer and paterfamilias was Allan Haines Loughead of San Francisco, California, who adopted a phonetic spelling for his name and his company in the 1920s. We shall adopt it from the start.

Allan Lockheed was one of thousands of adventurous, mechanically-minded young Americans for whom the modern age began when the Wright brothers made a 100-foot powered flight lasting twelve seconds at Kill Devil Hill, Kitty Hawk, North Carolina, on December 14, 1903. Teenagers then, Allan and his younger brother Malcolm immersed themselves in the infant science of aerodynamics and the mysteries of power-to-weight ratios, cadging flights wherever they could and teaching themselves to fly. They made several attempts to build their own plane before the first successful Lockheed model took shape in 1912. It was a trim wood-and-fabric biplane with a curious, squared-off look — but it flew. The *San Francisco Call* noted its 'clean-cut appearance' as the Model G swooped over the bay early in 1913. The plane even made money. At a dollar a time, Allan transported over 600 passengers in fifty days at the 1915 Panama-Pacific International Exhibition.

A year later, with an architectural draughtsman named John K. Northrop, the brothers set up business in a disused garage on the waterfront at Santa Barbara. There the three men handbuilt a small sports biplane, two seaplanes for the navy — their contribution to the war effort — and, for its day, the largest flying boat on the California coast, a twin-engined ten-seat monster called the F–1. On April 12, 1918, the F–1 flew the 211 miles from Santa Barbara to San Diego in 181 minutes, 'a new American endurance record', claimed the company extravagantly, confident that no one would challenge them. A year later the F–1 was on charter service in Europe, attracting the attention of King Albert and Queen Elizabeth of the Belgians, whom Allan piloted on a tour of the Channel Islands. The pilot-designer took good care to have his illustrious patrons photographed with the plane: the first known example of a Lockheed promotional partnership with European royalty.

Lockheed's misfortune, however, was that it was too small and under-capitalised, as well as being too remote in its west coast location, to take advantage of the war boom. The Model G was one of about thirty planes built in the whole of the United States in 1913. In 1918 the American industry turned out 14,020. This colossal expansion left a glut of surplus aircraft when the armistice was signed. In 1920 the Santa Barbara garage closed its doors and went out of business. Malcolm Lockheed left the aircraft industry altogether to develop and sell one of his spin-off inventions, the Lockheed four-wheel brake system for automobiles. It made him the fortune that was denied his brother.

For six years the Lockheed company ceased to exist. Then in 1925 the celebrated Air Mail Act, intended 'to encourage commercial aviation and to authorise the Postmaster General to contract for air mail services', gave the industry its second wind. New manufacturing companies sprang to life and old ones re-formed, among them the partnership of Allan Lockheed and John Northrop. In 1926 a revived Lockheed Aircraft Company found elbow room again in a garage, this time in Hollywood, squeezed by the expanding floorspace of another growth industry, the movies.

Here Lockheed and Northrop together designed and built the plane which would give the company an international reputation, the sleek, high-winged Vega. In a characteristically imaginative piece of promotion, Lockheed persuaded newspaper tycoon George Hearst to buy the first Vega and enter it in the 1927 Dole race from California to Honolulu. The exceptionally modern, aerodynamic shape of the Vega attracted considerable interest, which fortunately survived the catastrophic loss of Hearst's prototype during the last stage of the race. When in 1928 a Vega became the first plane to fly over both the North and South Poles, a flood of orders followed as infant airlines and go-ahead businesses rediscovered the romance and sheer practicality of air travel in the post-1927 'Lindbergh boom'.

As the orders rolled in, Lockheed was forced out of its cramped Hollywood quarters to a more spacious site in Burbank. The Vega was followed by the parasol-wing Air Express for Western Air Express; the low-wing Sirius, which Lindbergh flew from Washington DC to Japan in 1931; the two-seater Altair; and the seven-seater Orion, the first production transport aircraft to have a retractable undercarriage. Trail-blazing pilots such as George Hubert Wilkins, Amelia Earheart, Rosco Turner and the company's test-pilot, Wiley Post, all set and re-set speed and distance records in Lockheed planes. The company boasted in its advertisements: 'It takes a Lockheed to beat a Lockheed!'

But all was not as well as it seemed. First, the very success of the Vega encouraged Allan Lockheed to concentrate on too limited a market, that of the private enthusiast. It was left to Boeing and then to Douglas to make heavy inroads into the potentially high-profit, long-range commercial market. Secondly (and ironically in view of later developments) Lockheed was blind to the opportunities opened up by large-scale military procurement. The 'Five Year Program' Acts of 1926 authorised the navy to procure 1,614 aircraft and the army 1,800 between 1927 and 1931, but Lockheed virtually ignored the military field.

These flaws were not apparent in 1929 to the Detroit Aircraft Corporation, a holding company with grandiose ideas of becoming a General Motors of the air. Early that year, Detroit bought its way into twelve aircraft companies, including Lockheed. Allan himself left the reorganised company which still bore his name. But within months the stock market crash of 1929 ended Detroit's expansionist dream and put it into receivership. For nearly three years the Lockheed subsidiary struggled on, but the small-plane market in which it specialised was drying up and Lockheed didn't have the reach to hoist itself into the bigger league. The trickle of orders stopped and employment dropped to four. In 1932 a federal receiver took inventory, valued Lockheed's assets at $129,961, and put them up for sale.

Ironically, one interested potential buyer was Allan Lockheed. But he could only put his hands on $50,000 and this seemed to him an insultingly low offer for the company that bore his name. He was trying to raise $100,000 for a realistic bid when he heard that the receivers had accepted another offer—for $40,000.[1]

The new buyer—the man whose drive and flair would make

1 Allan Lockheed was subsequently hired by the corporation as a 'consultant', which he remained until his death in 1969.

Lockheed one of the biggest corporations in America—was a thirty-four-year-old investment banker, Robert Ellsworth Gross. He first heard that the company was for sale when general manager Carl B. Squier telephoned him with an inside tip-off: the receiver was willing to accept an offer as low as one-third of valuation, something around $43,000. Gross rounded it down to $40,000 and prepared to haggle. The receiver settled without argument, and a banker with no knowledge whatever of flying found himself the instant owner of an aircraft factory.

Robert Gross and his younger brother Courtlandt, who joined the new enterprise as deputy chairman, were the sons of a well-to-do Boston family with business interests sprinkled along the north-east coast. The family affected 'English' manners and Robert was privately educated by a family governess till 1908 when, ten years old, he was sent to the fashionable St George's School, Newport. At Harvard he developed a passionate interest in automobiles, buying and discarding in turn a Mercedes, Voisin, Hispano-Suiza and a Panhard-Levassor. He graduated with only average grades, took a commission in the army just as the war was ending, found it dull, bought himself out and joined the prestigious investment banking house of Lee, Higginson and Co. on the recommendation of a family friend.

It was quickly apparent that he had a flair for playing the market. By his thirtieth birthday in 1928 he was a dollar millionaire, much admired for his champagne parties and the nucleus of what was to become an impressive collection of Klees, Braques and the works of other fashionable modern painters.

When Wall Street crashed in 1929 Gross lost much but by no means all of his million dollars. His investments were well spread and he avoided the ruin which befell richer but less well-connected friends. He had what his admirers, not to mention Lockheed's salaried hagiographers, chose to describe as an instinct for market fluctuations, ascribed by his enemies to a well-developed network of inside connections which amounted to a private intelligence system. With the severely depressed prices that followed the crash, the fortunate minority who managed to hang on to their money actually found themselves richer in spending power if not in paper value. Gross used his affluence to move to the west coast, buy a magnificent apartment in exclusive Bel Air, Los Angeles, and lend his financial expertise to a small and ailing airline (which he soon sold off at a substantial profit).

He knew nothing of aircraft and the aviation industry, and next to nothing—despite his youthful passion for exotic automobiles—about mechanics and engineering. It was his aesthetic senses which were aroused by flying machines, and when his airline took delivery of a sleek, plywood-moulded Lockheed Orion he coveted it as he would a new Paul Klee. He visited the little factory at Burbank to watch Lockheed's joiners gluing and nailing the fuselages together. Not long after, the thirty-four-year-old financier, short, well built, with pink face, grey-brown hair and piercing blue eyes, took the call from Carl Squier which changed his life and Lockheed's.

Gross characteristically changed the name of the company to the grander Lockheed Aircraft Corporation and appointed himself chairman and treasurer. What he got for his $40,000 was floor-space, several boxes of spare parts, a number of blueprints and a labour force totalling four. What he put into the venture was a shrewd ability to take the long view and to assess the needs of the market over the next ten years. It was an ability which Donald Douglas and William Boeing, Gross's early rivals, shared—and which Allan Lockheed had lacked.

Gross saw that the future of aviation lay with long-distance flight by 'airliners' capable of carrying several passengers at a time. Lockheed had concentrated on the dwindling small-plane market, unemancipated from the romantic vision of the pre- and early post-war era when flying was perceived as a kind of aerial equivalent of private motoring rather than a potential means of mass travel. Boeing had been more far-sighted and his all-metal ten-seater Boeing 247 had won a $4 million order from United Airlines in 1931, making possible the first scheduled coast-to-coast flights in less than a day. Douglas followed immediately with the twelve-seater DC–1 and DC–2, luxuriously appointed with galley, lavatory and even reading lamps and ventilation systems. The twenty-passenger DC–3 took over in 1935 and gave Douglas a long pre-eminence in the commercial field. Lockheed had a lot of catching up to do.

To join the race, as Gross was determined to do, considerable capital had to be raised quickly. Gross began by restarting Orion production and blitzing the neglected overseas market. Swissair was the corporation's first foreign customer and they were followed by an increasing number of Europe's smaller airlines. Eighteen months after the take-over, Lockheed rolled out its answer to Boeing and Douglas, the all-metal twin-engine Elektra Model 10, a ten-seater with the modern refinements of retractable undercarriage, flaps and variable-pitch screws. Lockheed spent the then considerable sum of $139,400 on research, development and production and by the end of 1935 had sold forty, half of them on the export market. A junior version, the six-seater Model 12, ensured that the corporation's new ambition to join the big-airliner race didn't mean an over-hasty abandonment of the small charter market.

By 1936 Lockheed was making money for the first time since 1929. The eleven-passenger Model 14 Super Elektra followed and sales boomed when Howard Hughes and a crew of four established a new world record in 1938 by flying one round the world in three days nineteen hours.

The last of the family, and Lockheed's biggest to date, was the fourteen-seater Model 18 Lodestar, later reborn in a heavy bomber version known as the Ventura. This was the plane that hoisted Lockheed into the big time. For if Gross pulled up the company by its boot straps in chasing the commercial airline market, he showed himself no less shrewd in foreseeing and preparing for the rapidly expanding demands of the military. Where the Lockheed brothers had been too small and too remote in location to share in the aircraft boom of the First World War, and Allan Lockheed had shown no interest in chasing the army and navy contracts which followed the 'Five Year Program' Acts of 1926, Gross recognised the potential and as events moved towards war in Europe he grabbed his opportunities.

Aircraft companies have never liked being considered part of the international arms industry, modern merchants of death. James McDonnell, founder of the only company to rival Lockheed as a 'defence' contractor and builder of what was commercially the most successful military plane of all time, the Phantom Two, always liked to describe his occupation as 'waging peace'. Gross and his colleagues at Lockheed were never so squeamish or hypocritical. War meant defence, defence meant planes and planes meant profit. Lockheed headed that way in 1937 and never looked back.

At first the corporation, along with the rest of the industry, was inhibited by President Roosevelt's Neutrality Act which banned the export of all armaments, including aircraft, to countries at war. But Gross pinned his commercial judgment to a bold, because hitherto untested, proposition that war meant a formal declaration of hostilities. By this legalistic definition there were few wars in the martial decade of the 1930s: Italian fought Abyssinian, Japanese fought Chinese, and Spaniard fought Spaniard with no declaration of anything except perhaps an undying devotion to peace. There were other tensions, moreover, that were clearly leading up to war but hadn't yet achieved it. Gross exploited them all to the full and was undismayed by the peace scare of 1937 when Standard Statistics noted gloomily that 'any trend toward better international relations would thus reduce earning power substantially'. In Gross's book, the fear of peace was much exaggerated. And he was soon proved right.

Early in 1937 Gross sent his brother Courtlandt to London to try to interest the British in the potential of the Model 14 as a medium-range bomber. Lockheed's deputy chairman returned disappointed and empty-handed; the British had told him there wasn't going to be a war, and if there was, the British aircraft industry was 'quite adequate' to cope with demand. The Germans, to whom, with a super-salesman's studied impartiality, he also tried to sell, also pointed (with better cause than the British) at their own self-sufficiency.[1] So Robert Gross decided to concentrate on the home market. A Model 10 was adapted to high-altitude flying and, as the XC–35, was turned over to the US Army Air Corps for a rigorous testing programme. Although it was the world's first successful pressurised substratospheric plane and won the coveted Collier Trophy, no orders were forthcoming. But a breakthrough wasn't long delayed.

Lockheed had engaged the services of the man who was soon to make his reputation as the most brilliant aircraft designer of his generation. Clarence 'Kelly' Johnson, a bulky, bullet-headed engineer, shared Robert Gross's aesthetic or romantic view that a plane 'must look good before it will fly good'. That ran contrary to the hard-nosed scientific view of practically all Johnson's rivals, who held that the technical requirements of the machine must determine its character and cosmetics should come later. Johnson first designed *beautiful* planes and then devised ways of making them do the job required of them. It was crazy – but it worked.

In February 1937 the Army Air Corps (precursor of the US Air Force, which wasn't created until 1947) invited the aircraft industry to submit designs for a new high-speed multi-engine fighter. Johnson, doodling on his note-pad, produced a simple, revolutionary design which extended the engine mountings backwards to meet and join a wide, raised tail, while so shortening the fuselage as to make it little

---

1 Lockheed had better luck with Japan. They concluded a contract with the emperor on the eve of war in 1939.

more than a stubby bubble in the middle of the wings. It looked like no other plane that had ever flown: it was beautiful, and (as Johnson was soon to prove) it worked. The Air Corps awarded a contract for the P–38 and the famed Lockheed Lightning went into production. Nearly 10,000 rolled off the assembly lines before the war was over.

Then in 1938 Gross learned that a British military mission was on its way to the States, having apparently reassessed requirements and the capacity of British industry to meet them. The mission was due in California in five days. According to Lockheed legend, it took precisely that time to build from scratch a wooden mock-up of a Model 14 converted to a bomber. The British were impressed. There followed a $25 million order for 175 bombers which the British called the Hudson.[1] It was the biggest order any single aircraft manufacturer had ever received – but it didn't remain so for long. A few months later British orders for more Hudsons, Venturas and Lightnings totalled $65 million. Lockheed formed two subsidiaries to help deal with this phenomenal expansion of demand, the Vega Airplane Company with thirty acres of land next to Union Air Terminal, Burbank (merged with Lockheed in 1943), and a British Reassembly Division at Speke, near Liverpool. Later in the war, more reassembly bases were set up in Northern Ireland, Scotland and Australia. Lockheed had become a kind of multinational.

Where there had been four employees in 1932 there were 2,500 by the end of 1938, 7,000 by the end of 1939 and more than 90,000 at the height of the war. Lockheed rolled out 2,900 Hudsons, 2,700 Flying Fortresses,[2] 2,600 Venturas and 10,000 Lightnings. Production surged to 23 planes a day: total value, more than $2 billion.

These are the statistics. But it was more than the luck of the war which turned a major manufacturer into the biggest defence contractor in the western world, for there were other, bigger companies in the field before war broke out which seemed better placed to scoop the pool. What won Lockheed its pre-eminence was, in large part, the personal style and charisma of its chairman. Robert Gross relied on systematic intelligence: on finding out what plans customers and potential customers were making, and setting out to meet the need,

1 So fearful were Lockheed that war would overwhelm Britain before they could deliver that the contract was worded to require payment 'for materials ordered, labour expended and planes completed in full or in part', whether delivered or not.

2 A Boeing-designed machine built by Lockheed under a 'pooled production' arrangement.

whether by innovation, adaptation or improvisation. And he cast his net wide, recognising the potential of export orders long before most of his competitors. Intelligence-gathering and courting the overseas customer: these were to be Lockheed's chief hallmarks in the post-war period.

2

Luck, too, was a vital ingredient in Lockheed's success. It was a combination of luck and foresight which saved the corporation from the consequences of the huge contraction which followed the war. A similar contraction had put the young Allan Lockheed out of business in 1920. But the huge corporation of the 1940s, which by its very size had further to contract and fall than any of its competitors, survived and prospered.

This luck-and-foresight combination is most clearly seen in the famous Constellation programme. As far back as 1939, Lockheed announced a project to develop what it called the L–44 Excalibur, planned as a thirty-passenger answer to the big Boeing Stratoliner and the DC–3. In April 1939 the Excalibur project was merged with preliminary design work by 'Kelly' Johnson for an even larger air-liner to a specification by Transcontinental and Western Air (later Trans-World Airlines), which wanted to inaugurate regular trans-continental flights at up to 300 m.p.h.

TWA had just come under the control of multi-millionaire Howard Hughes, heir to a tool company fortune, Hollywood impresario, sponsor and escort of Jean Harlow and Jane Russell, ace flier, and a very different man from the misanthropic recluse he became in later years. Hughes urged forward the new project which became the hugely successful Constellation. While the plane was little more than a doodle on 'Kelly' Johnson's note-pad, TWA ordered nine and increased this to forty when Pan-American placed a rival order. In 1941 and 1942 construction of the prototype went ahead as fast as military commitments would permit, and on January 9, 1943, it made its first test flight. Just over a year later, on April 17, 1944, Hughes flew the first production model from Burbank to Washington DC in the record transcontinental time of 6 hours 47 minutes 30 seconds.

Pearl Harbor and American entry into the war might have been expected to put a brake on the Constellation's development. All that happened was that TWA and Pan-American waived their rights to the first production batch in favour of the Army Air Corps, which converted them into troop-carriers. As a result of this military take-over, production of the world's biggest, fastest and most expensive airliner was uninterrupted by the war, an astonishing stroke of luck which left Lockheed with easily convertible models in stock when peace came in 1945. By the end of the year, twenty had been sold to TWA, six to BOAC and five to other airlines. In the pipeline were orders for 105 more, valued at $75 million, buyers including Pan-American, American and Eastern at home and Air France and KLM abroad. The USAF ordered more military versions and stuffed them full of electronic scanning equipment. Continually updated versions of the civil airliner sold all over the world through the 1940s and 1950s. The Constellation was the big success story of early post-war commercial flying.

The same combination of good luck and shrewd judgment gave Lockheed a head start in the revolutionary field of jet development. In 1942 'Kelly' Johnson tried to interest the Army Air Corps in his plans for the world's first jet fighter. When military chiefs showed themselves somewhat sceptical that a plane without props would ever get off the ground, Robert Gross nevertheless backed his own judgment and put development work in hand. By the following year when the Air Corps had tested a de Havilland Goblin turbojet engine, found it worked, and urgently wanted a fighter to fit it, Lockheed was already halfway there. The Air Corps wanted the prototype in 180 days. Johnson's 'special projects team', working in a camouflaged lean-to prefab which was the lineal ancestor of Lockheed's famous 'Skunk Works', did it in 143. By the end of the war the F–80 Shooting Star was in production, soon to be followed by the F–94 Starfire. They were the newest generation of fighters, America's first operational jets, and that meant they would be the last to be scrapped—and the first to see active service again as the cold war hotted up.

So while scores of their rivals shut up shop altogether (40 out of 66 airframe plants operating in 1944 had disappeared by December 1945) or diversified out of aircraft into washing machines, Lockheed actually stepped up its wartime production of Constellations, Shooting Stars and P–2 Neptune patrol bombers for the navy. Once again Robert Gross had successfully overcome the threat of world peace. He was all the better prepared, therefore, when war broke out again on an obscure peninsula of Asia called Korea.

North Korea's invasion of South Korea in June 1950 was just what the aircraft industry needed to lift it out of recession. The US air force, independent at last from the army and navy, asked Lockheed to reopen a massive Second World War factory in Marietta, Georgia, to overhaul and refurbish 120 B–29 bombers which had been mothballed in 1945. Within a year the work-force at Marietta had grown from 150 to 10,000 with a new air force contract for Boeing-designed B–47 Stratojets, the first plane designed specifically to carry nuclear bombs, made by a temporary consortium of Lockheed, Boeing and Douglas. But Marietta was also to see the birth of another pure Lockheed design, a plane which would become the corporation's single biggest moneymaker – and the centrepiece of Lockheed scandals around the world.

The giant C–130 Hercules troop transporter was Dan Haughton's baby. The man who would eventually succeed the Gross brothers as sole ruler of the Lockheed empire won his first big break when he was despatched to the newly-formed Lockheed-Georgia subsidiary to be given charge of the complex B–47 production line. By 1952 he was clearly one of the corporation's rising stars, a reputation he confirmed by his coup in winning Hercules production for Georgia rather than the parent company in California. After that, he never looked back.

Daniel Jeremiah Haughton was born in 1911, the son of a poor Alabama farmer who also ran a village store and worked as timekeeper in the local mine. Like Robert Gross, but for very different reasons, he was late in starting school: Gross was taught by a governess, Haughton by real hardship and deprivation. At eight he was supplementing the family income by selling newspapers and cutting pit props. When he did start school he developed an aptitude for figures and is said to have exploited his talent by lending money to his school friends at shrewdly calculated rates of interest. His mathematical ability took him at the age of seventeen to the University of Alabama, where he studied accounting and business administration. When he graduated in 1933 in mid-Depression he headed for the Californian coast where, after a succession of undistinguished jobs, he landed a $3,300-a-year post as a systems analyst with Lockheed. The year was 1939 and with Lockheed on the verge of unprecedented expansion, Dan Haughton could hardly have made a better move. With America's entry into the war, the number of young men with top-management potential who were still in civilian clothes dropped fast, and Haughton's star rose accordingly. He was soon spotted by the Gross brothers and marked for bigger things. Courtlandt Gross described him as an ideal company man, always willing 'to subordinate his own time and rest to the overall good of the company'.

Accordingly, in 1949 Dan Haughton was rewarded with the presidency of two small Lockheed subsidiaries which manufactured service equipment for customer airlines. Both were languishing for lack of orders, but Haughton proved himself a master salesman, barnstorming the length and breadth of America, daringly undercutting his competitors here, rashly promising near-impossible delivery dates there and utilising his Alabama-bred folksy charm everywhere. One airline was reportedly dazzled into placing an order for equipment to service planes it didn't possess. Within a year, president Haughton's subsidiaries were back in profit. Haughton was promoted to corporate assistant general manager — and then came the Korean war, Marietta and the Hercules coup.

The modern airplane is usually born in travail. Planemakers like to picture themselves forever advancing the frontiers of man's knowledge, a romantic, idealised self-portrait which explains away the embarrassing and costly failures which so often drive them back to the testground or the drawing board. The Hercules was different. It was an immaculate conception, a design that worked perfectly from the start, though it took five years to complete. 'Kelly' Johnson's team made the blueprints in 1951. Their object was to provide US forces in Korea with a rugged, versatile troop and cargo carrier which could be rapidly loaded and unloaded through a vast rear cargo door and could take off in less than 900 feet of runway. Even though the Korean war ended in 1953 before the prototype was ready, the USAF continued to back the project, even increasing its order. The prototype first flew on August 23, 1954, the first production model on April 7, 1955, and the first delivery batch in December 1956. There was just one snag. As the labours of Hercules spread over five years, costs overran initial estimates by several million dollars. Initial USAF orders alone, big as they were, didn't pay for the plane. Haughton's prestige and, indeed, his chances of making it to chairman of the board depended on his ability to repeat on a far larger scale the successes of his salesmanship of 1949.

How he met the challenge, selling 1,400 Hercules to no fewer than thirty-seven countries at an eventual profit to Lockheed conservatively estimated around the $300 million mark, will be a recurrent theme as our story develops.

3

Another recurrent theme also has its roots in the Korean war, which gave birth to the most controversial fighter plane ever made: the Starfighter.

When the United States, flying the United Nations' flag, launched its air offensive against the Soviet-aligned North Koreans, it did so with an ageing Second World War generation of jets, including Lockheed's pioneer Shooting Star. American statistics show that in three years of air-to-air combat US aircraft destroyed 1,108 Communist planes for the loss of only 114 of their own. But the figures conceal a grim fact of which every American combat pilot was only too well aware: while the Americans had overwhelming pilot superiority, the Soviets, in the MiG–15, possessed a fighter that could outdistance, out-gun and out-manoeuvre any machine the Americans could put into the sky.

In 1951 a number of military aircraft designers, Clarence Johnson among them, made it their business to talk to pilots with combat experience of the deadly MiGs. The pilots were unanimous on what they wanted: a machine which would fly faster and higher than the Soviet plane and would prove more manoeuvrable and responsive than the Sabre and Shooting Star. But the designers were not unanimous on how to do it.

North American and McDonnell believed it could be done by building bigger jets with bigger engines: speed and manoeuvrability would hinge largely on increased power. This formula was followed successfully in the F–100 and F–101. Other makers explored a scaling-down process but backed out when they hit what seemed insuperable thrust–weight ratio problems. Only Clarence Johnson and Lockheed started on this latter course and pursued it to the bitter end, tackling the problems head-on.

On a trip to Korea to find out on the spot how his F–80 was doing and what changes the pilots wanted, Johnson found the demand for dramatically improved flight performance had reached such a pitch that pilots were prepared to abandon all 'unnecessary' refinements in search of a lighter plane, and among the items regarded as expendable were ejector seats, parking brakes, duplicated flying-control systems, armour and radar. Col. 'Gabby' Gabreski, a Second World War ace, is said to have told Johnson that radar was a waste of time: 'I'd rather sight with a piece of chewing gum stuck on the windscreen.' Pilots wanted to fly higher and faster than the enemy and make tighter turns, and most of them were prepared to sacrifice everything but the wings and the tail to do it.

These demands from the front line ran directly counter to work already in progress in Lockheed. Johnson's first major attempt to find a replacement for the F–80 Shooting Star and the F–94 Starfire was a project designated XF–90, which was a big step *up* the scale of size and complexity. It is likely that Lockheed would have taken the same road as North American and McDonnell, ignoring Gabreski and his comrades, had Westinghouse not fallen down on the XF–90's propulsion. That put Lockheed back at square one – and Johnson began producing the doodles from which the Starfighter would grow.

The doodles were backed by a wealth of research. Lockheed had been given access to classified supersonic flight data produced both by the air force and the navy, and could also draw on its own current programme of flight trials up to Mach 4 at over 150,000 feet using unmanned rockets. This programme showed that at speeds above Mach 2 a short, stubby, unswept, very thin wing was ideal. It was the extreme difficulty of making such a wing without unacceptable loss of strength which stopped other manufacturers from proceeding further down this road. It didn't stop 'Kelly' Johnson. Nor did other problems that were thought insuperable. As he commented later:

> The large airplane exponents claimed that equal speed, range and fighting power could not be obtained in a smaller airplane because such fixed items as the pilot size, canopy size, engine thrust per square foot of frontal area, and fixed equipment item weights, were a smaller percentage of the large airplane weight than of the smaller one. Likewise, the fuselage cross-section and size, in general, would be unfavourable for the smaller airplane, resulting in lower ratios of lift to drag and thrust to drag, even if the same percentage fuel weight could be carried. There was not in existence a small engine which had as good thrust–weight ratios or specific fuel consumption as the larger engines then available. These factors were all true at the time; so it was necessary to make some rather major advances on practically all of these fronts before a successful light-weight fighter could be developed.[1]

There followed a year of research and design development as intensive as anything in aviation history, at the end of which there existed

---

1 Quoted in *Early Supersonic Fighters of the West*, by Bill Gunston, much the best account of the Starfighter's development.

on paper a revolutionary fighter with wings no more than $7\frac{1}{2}$ feet long, and a large body housing cockpit, engine and fuel. In March 1953 the air force placed a contract for two prototypes required to exceed Mach 2 and have a combat ceiling of at least 60,000 feet. The prototypes were designated XF–104 and in July Lockheed gave them the name Starfighter. In the same month the Korean war ended: but Lockheed and the air force predicted more of the same, and work continued uninterrupted.

Taxying trials began with the first prototype at Edwards USAF Base in February 1954, and the first flight followed on March 4. Problems were immediately apparent. Johnson had given the Starfighter a high T-tail to counter pitch-up, but it didn't counter it enough. The tail was modified several times but pitch-up — a problem common to all, but especially small, high-speed aircraft — persisted. Eventually Johnson was forced to load the Starfighter with complex electronics to provide automatic pitch control — just the kind of thing the Korean veterans had wanted to get rid of and the Starfighter was created to do without.

This turned out to be the first of several such compromises — and it still fell short of what was needed. The high tail also made it necessary to fit downward rather than the usual upward ejector seats (the USAF insisted on ejector seats of one kind or the other, however blasé their pilots affected to be about them) but these had the evident disadvantage that, in case of trouble on take-off or landing, the pilot would be hurtled at high speed straight into the concrete runway. Worse was the realisation that, having dispensed with heavy pressurising equipment, the pilot would be likely to have to wear a space-suit to protect him from rapid decompression following engine flame-out at high altitudes. Pilots described the suit as torture to wear for anything much over half an hour.

More ludicrous, and much more culpable because the problem was obvious from the start, was the absurd inadequacy of the radar sight system. Lockheed's difficulty was that a light system which fitted into the pointed nose without overweighting it was totally inadequate in range and power for a subsonic interceptor, let alone one designed to fly at Mach 2. On the other hand, the kind of radar demanded by the very high flight performance was too big and heavy for the Starfighter. The result was that a plane designed largely for an air-to-air search and tracking role at up to twice the speed of sound had a radar sight range of no more than five to ten miles. Gabreski's chewing gum on the windscreen would have been as effective.

The USAF didn't wait for these problems to be cured, or in some cases even diagnosed, before rushing ahead with more orders. Two months before the maiden flight of the first prototype, an order was placed for a further fifteen test aircraft, designated YF-104A. The first of these was rolled out from Shop B-1 at Burbank on December 23, 1955, and made its first flight on February 17, 1956. A new problem was soon apparent, one which hadn't shown up on the prototypes. The YF-104A was fitted with new General Electric J-97 engines which made no provision for modulated afterburning. Pilots quickly found that bringing in the afterburner took them straight from Mach 1 to Mach 2·2 with no ability to stabilise at any speed in between! Moreover, when they did reach Mach 2 the engines began to overheat and they had to plunge all the way down to Mach 1 again.

In the circumstances, perhaps Lockheed's greatest achievement with the early Starfighter was to hold the interest of the USAF in a plane which was becoming immensely expensive and more, rather than less, trouble-prone with each test. By the end of 1955 the corporation had an order for 155 F-104As for Air Defense Command. The Pentagon, of course, was as reluctant as Lockheed to admit they were in for a bum, and it was the air force which provided most of the $30 million cost of the four-year flight test programme. Not until January 1958, when the first delivery was made, did the F-104A receive service clearance, and even then it soon became apparent that the problems of the all-or-nothing J-97 engines were as far from solution as ever. Three months after going into service all Starfighters were grounded for three months while a new General Electric 3B engine was fitted. A re-engined test aircraft momentarily lifted the heavy hearts of Lockheed's executives by taking new world height and speed records, but other problems proved intractable. A year after taking the F-104A into service the USAF cut its losses and abandoned it, selling most to whatever sections of the reservist Air National Guard could be persuaded to buy. The Puerto Rican ANG was an enthusiastic customer, provoking one wag to suggest they should paint their initials prominently on every plane. Others were sold to such undiscriminating nations as Nationalist China, Pakistan and (as late as 1968-9) Jordan. By the time the Starfighter had logged its 100,000th flight hour (in April 1961) 49 of those in use by the USAF had been destroyed and 18 pilots killed, not one of them in combat — the worst record of any comparable fighter.

That the F-104A was on a disaster course was apparent — despite their public optimism — both to the USAF and to Lockheed by the mid-1950s. The air force wanted planes to outfly MiG–15s in the Korean war. The war had ended in 1953, and deliveries did not begin until 1958. Even then, the plane delivered bore little resemblance to 'Kelly' Johnson's paper miracle. It turned out to be the antithesis of what the Korean veterans wanted in 1951, a plane designed to fly light but which wouldn't perform at all unless stuffed with heavy aids and correctional devices. Even as modified it met virtually none of the USAF's specifications. It was an unforgiving, dangerous machine, aesthetically as magnificent as anything in Robert Gross's art collection, but as suited to modern air combat as a hot-air balloon.

But the USAF, of course, had other irons in the fire. Lockheed did not — at least not on the fighter front. While the US taxpayer had borne most of the cost of the Starfighter programme, Lockheed's urgent need was to keep the California company's gigantic production lines busy and save the jobs of some 15,000 workers. Lockheed calculated at the outset that they needed to sell between 2,500 and 3,000 Starfighters to give them the kind of profit which would enable them to stay among the Big Three. By 1956 they had managed, by a mixture of arm-twisting and artful cajolery, to step up the USAF's order from 15 to 170, and it was clear they couldn't expect much more from that quarter.[1] That left them more than 2,300 short of their target.

Their only hope was the export market. But how do you persuade the air forces of other nations to spend a fortune buying planes which your own air force clearly doesn't want?

And, as it turned out, that wasn't the half of Lockheed's problem. By the mid-1950s the pendulum had swung decisively against the kind of light, simple plane the Starfighter was supposed to be. Air forces in Europe and across the world, all beginning to plan replacements for their clapped-out Second World War machines, were looking for all-weather, all-purpose, multi-mission planes. The Starfighter's ludicrously inadequate radar alone meant that it could perform only in daylight hours in fine weather, and then only a limited mission.

It was exactly the kind of plane the world's military aircraft buyers were not looking for. But Lockheed needed to sell it to them, and in quantity. Their only chance was to take the F–104A, already wrapped

1 The USAF ordered no more F–104As, but it did order 26 F–104B trainers 77 F–104C fighter-bombers and 22 F–104D trainers.

about and weighed down with modifications, and modify it further, pouring yet more aids and devices into 'Kelly' Johnson's overloaded shell to produce something that could claim to meet the market's requirements. The Super Starfighter (though the name never caught on), designated F–104–7 and later F–104G, weighed 28,780 lb – almost twice the 15,000 lb aimed at by Johnson in his original design.

To sell their lamb in wolf's clothing, Lockheed naturally looked first to where the need was greatest. Japan and West Germany, disarmed after the war but now firmly allied to the West, were both embarking on the reconstruction of their national air forces.

It was to Japan that Robert Gross sent his first Starfighter sales mission.

3

Japan: The Black Mists

I don't say that all these distinguished people couldn't be
squared; but it is right to tell you that they wouldn't be
sufficiently degraded in their own estimation unless they
were insulted with a very considerable bribe.

Pooh-Bah, The Mikado (W. S. Gilbert)

1

A few minutes before midnight on December 22, 1957, John Kenneth Hull climbed wearily into the transit bus at Tokyo airport at the end of the long haul from Los Angeles. His irritation at missing a family Christmas at home had begun to evaporate over the Pacific Ocean, and now, as the bus trundled its load of bleary-eyed business executives from the aircraft steps to the garishly-lit airport buildings, he tried to concentrate his mind on the all-but-impossible assignment which had brought him to Japan.

When Lockheed chairman Robert Gross had put it to him at corporate headquarters in Burbank, the assignment had seemed at first almost routine: set up an office, hire yourself some expert help — and sell the Japs the Starfighter. But there was one problem which loomed so large that to those in the know it must have seemed futile to waste company resources on further sales efforts. The problem was that the Japanese had already arrived at a decision — and not the decision Gross wanted. They had looked at the Starfighter's credentials and rejected them in favour of the rival Grumman F–11A Super Tiger. John Kenneth Hull's job was to show the Japanese government that they had made a mistake, and somehow persuade them to switch to Lockheed.

As he checked into his reserved suite at the Palace Hotel, Hull reflected over a stiff nightcap that Gross had ordered him into a race on which the chequered flag had already fallen, with the opposition already gloating over its trophy.

But he had not been sent to Japan without resources. Gross himself, and other executives down the line, had been free with suggestions, culled from corporate selling experience, on what needed to be done and how to do it. There was in Japan a wide network of expatriate American businessmen, operators, ex-administrators from the occupational era and even diplomats of both overt and covert varieties who knew whom to talk to and how to help the conversation along. Not least, Hull knew he had ample financial resources: Gross had left him with the impression that the company was prepared to spend a small fortune on chasing the contract—and a large fortune on winning it.

Time was short. Some time in the new year, Japan's National Defence Council would meet to rubber-stamp the military's choice of the Super Tiger and put the final signature to the contract with Grumman. Lockheed's slender hopes rested on Hull's skill or luck or influence in preventing this final slamming of doors against them. He knew what to do. First, he opened a Lockheed office in Tokyo. Then he began to look for ways of by-passing the Daiichi trading firm which had represented Lockheed's interests in Japan until outsmarted by Grumman's agents.

He talked to the US air force men in the embassy's military mission. They could be expected to know more than most why the Starfighter had lost out to the Super Tiger in Japan's procurement process for they, rather than Daiichi, had made the running—albeit discreetly—in pushing sales. The Starfighter was a USAF plane, the Grumman rival a protégé of the US navy. Each force had a vested interest in the success of its own fighter, not only for reasons of pride and prestige but primarily because a major overseas order would reduce unit costs on domestic purchases. Whether Hull learned much from the USAF men in Tokyo is doubtful. If he did it was of negative value: how not to proceed. But from other, evidently better-informed contacts, possibly the intelligence community, he seems to have picked up a great deal more. By the end of January 1958 he had found his way to the fringe of an extraordinary underworld of fixers and string-pullers whose methods would have scandalised the embassy cocktail set, but whose value to Lockheed was to prove virtually incalculable.

Hull's first positive contact was a man as far removed as possible from the respectable world of military and diplomatic lobbying. He was an American-born Japanese named Taro Fukuda (not to be confused with Takeo Fukuda, a later prime minister). Fukuda had been deprived of his American citizenship for working for the Japanese government in occupied Manchuria during the war. In 1946 he had been jailed for war crimes. On his release three years later he started a public relations company, and it was this company which, despite its owner's criminal record and anti-American antecedents, Hull hired to run Lockheed's eleventh-hour win-or-bust campaign to rescue the Starfighter from oblivion in the overseas market.

Fukuda introduced Hull to a wider circle of contacts. One of them, Yoshiyoshi Oni, a former espionage agent who had worked first for the Japanese in China and then for the American occupation, was hired as Lockheed's local office manager.

The list of Lockheed's allies was to grow more bizarre yet, taking in before long the pilot who had planned the Japanese attack on Pearl Harbor, an ultra-nationalist publisher purged by the American occupation, a member of parliament who was convicted of embezzlement and a former cell-mate of Fukuda who, within ten years of his release from jail, became Japan's prime minister.

But the most powerful of Hull's recruits was an underworld king whose astonishing and barely credible exploits mark him as a principal without rival among what Senator Church called the 'shadowy figures operating behind the scenes' who came to populate the 'novel of international intrigue' which makes up our story.

Yoshio Kodama, short, powerfully built, with a hammer face and a disarmingly soft, seductive voice, was quite simply the most influential man in post-occupation Japan—a master operator in what the Japanese call 'the black mist', the dark, undefined world of big-business wheeling and dealing. He too had lodged in the same prison block as Taro Fukuda, who had become his disciple and English-language interpreter. It was from Kodama's fabulous private fortune that Fukuda's public relations firm was funded. Within days of his first meeting with Hull in February 1958, Kodama was enrolled as Lockheed's secret agent in Japan, and the battle to achieve a miraculous change of mind in the Japanese cabinet was under way.

2

What was it about Yoshio Kodama that qualified him as Lockheed's choice miracle maker?

Born in 1911, he was orphaned in infancy and left in the care of distant relatives. At eleven, tricked by his guardians into believing that he was being sent away to get an education, he was sold to the Korean owners of a primitive iron foundry who kept him and a score of similarly luckless youths in virtual slavery, imprisoned in company barracks, forbidden to leave and paid only in food and workclothes. Kodama certainly picked up an education, if not an academic one, learning early how to live by his own wits and resources.

It was perhaps the foreign status of his Korean masters – *owners*, for all practical purposes – which turned the young Kodama to Japanese nationalism and immersion in the nation's martial tradition. At fifteen he was a romantic ultra-nationalist, heading a secret cell in the foundry. He was wont to boast that his family was a noble one, temporarily fallen upon hard times, but linked by blood to a tradition of samurai glory. At seventeen he broke from his servitude, fled to Tokyo and joined the official nationalist movement Kenkoku Kai and a score of conspiratorial societies with names like the Blood Brotherhood and Holy War Execution League. These were part nationalist clubs, part terrorist cells and part street-gangs, not very different from Hong Kong's Triads and Belfast's politicised sectarian murder gangs.

They fought mainly with each other. Then, as depression bit into the economy and provoked a wave of left-wing protest, they united spasmodically to fight 'the Communists', a label loosely applied to all non-nationalist radical dissent. In this they were both funded and manipulated by wealthy industrialists who used them as private armies of strike breakers, equipped to deal mercilessly with any sign of revolt or revolution. Kodama joined the ultra-rightist Federation of Radical Patriotic Workers, an early Japanese equivalent of the blackshirt movements of Europe, and in negotiating terms for his services as a strike-breaking leader with the federation's industrial bankers he had his first taste of big business and caught his first whiff of big money. He was not yet out of his teens.

Soon, at twenty-one, he became impatient of both established and underground nationalist movements and formed Dohuristu Seinen Sha, the Independence Youth Society, under his personal control. DSS's distinctive brand of ultra-nationalism was planned to take the form of the ritual assassination of Japan's 'enemies within', which included Communists, trade unionists and all who were perceived from an ultra-rightist view as soft on the Left. To Kodama, the Left included the entire Japanese government and most of the emperor's court, excluding only the divine person of the emperor himself. Never one to do anything by halves, Kodama and the DSS leadership determined to start with a bang by blowing up the prime minister, Admiral Saito. But the attempt was bungled, there was a battle with armed police, and Kodama was shot and wounded. The authorities jubilantly reported him killed and an American reporter elaborated with an imaginative description of his 'magnificent funeral conducted by Shinto priests and attended by nearly a thousand members of patriotic and political societies'.[1]

Kodama was not dead but in jail, where he was held for three years awaiting trial, incommunicado for much of the time. He finally appeared in court in December 1935 and despite the gravity of his crime was given only a further year in prison. The leniency of his judges may have had something to do with Japan's expansionist war with China, which had the effect of making Kodama's brand of ultra-nationalism more fashionable and acceptable. Again, it may have had something to do with friends and influence, for Kodama had already begun to develop his political connections.

A glimpse of the romantic and mystical element which was the other, but no less traditionally Japanese, side of his cultural and philosophical make-up is afforded by Kodama's own later reflections on this his first extended period in jail. 'My greatest pleasure', he recalled in a quaintly translated post-war autobiography, 'was to gaze upon the sparse grass and flowers [of the exercise yard]. In season, when the cosmos were flowering, strong winds used to blow, breaking the stems of the flowers. On such occasions, I felt so badly at the sight of the windblown cosmos as if I had my own arms broken. Often, I used to put splints on the broken stems of the flowers.' Apparently concerned lest anyone should equate such tender thoughts with degenerate liberalism, he added: 'But on such occasions there were no leftist thoughts – only a deep love and a feeling of adoration of nature welled in my heart.'

His sentence served by the end of 1936, Kodama the conspirator resumed ascendancy over Kodama the poet. Japan was now in control of Chinese Manchuria and had established a puppet kingdom, Manchukuo, where Kodama could indulge his ruthless fantasies to the full. He began to move regularly between China and Japan, attracting the attention of US army intelligence which was soon crediting him with organising a China-wide network of Manchurian spies and collaborationists. Years later, when he found it expedient to repair his fences with the Americans, Kodama claimed to have been sickened by the atrocities which made a mock of the chivalric code professed by the samurai.

Perhaps his curious mode of idealism really was blunted by the

---

1 Hugh Byas in *Government by Assassination*, published in 1942. Mr Byas was formerly *New York Times* correspondent in Tokyo. He is quoted by Jim Hougan in an article, 'The Business of Buying Friends', in *Harper's Magazine*, December 1976.

discovery of what happened in practice when his precious racist-nationalism was unleashed against the defenceless Chinese. Certainly Kodama seems over the next few years to have become less concerned with mystical politics and more preoccupied with feathering the nest of Yoshio Kodama. Whatever the truth of those intelligence reports suggesting his role as super-spy, an ever-increasing portion of his time and artful energies was devoted to what the Japanese would have regarded as entrepreneurial business but the luckless Chinese recognised as simple looting. Manchukuo was a paradise for ultra-nationalists. They dominated its administration and Kodama had friends everywhere. By the end of 1937 he was one of the Orient's most successful clandestine operators, wheeling, dealing, appropriating and fixing. The same year he undertook a series of missions throughout China and Vietnam—the next target of Japanese expansionism—for the Japanese army intelligence and for Kempei Tai, the secret police.

Kodama's multiplying business interests were now consolidated in an agency called the Kodama Organ, or KO, operating from a suite of rooms in Tokyo's Shin-Asia Hotel. In 1941 the KO was entrusted with the vast task of supplying the Japanese naval air force with its entire complement of wartime equipment, making Kodama the supplier, among other things, of some of the Kamikaze planes which were soon to provide the most spectacular demonstration of the ritualised fanaticism close to his heart. (Some of Japan's air fleet had been bought from Lockheed in 1939, but Lockheed's path was not yet to cross Kodama's.)

According to a report of the US army's Counterintelligence Corps, Kodama equipped the Imperial navy by using his own private army to force the Chinese villagers to sell him the goods he demanded at a pittance, reselling them at large profits to naval procurement officers who were almost certainly in on the racket. Systematically looting occupied China of its raw materials, he amassed a stupendous fortune. He is said to have bought heroin on the black market in Tokyo, traded it for precious tungsten in Shanghai, sold the tungsten for yen, used the yen to buy guns, sold the guns in Borneo for gold, and exchanged the gold for industrial diamonds which he kept in sacks in his home—a bizarre touch which anticipated his practice, years later, of receiving currency from Lockheed in wooden packing cases and stacking them in his locked cellar.

As if all this was not enough, US intelligence also had him cornering the Shanghai radium market by emptying the hospitals of their supplies; operating salt mines, iron mines, farms, fisheries, a molybdenum mine, secret munitions factories and even, oddly, an orphanage, throughout central China; minting his own yen; financing the Shanghai office of the Kempei Tai in return for its 'physical support'; and, possibly, murdering one of his business partners.

But in August 1945 two atomic bombs dropped from aircraft made by a consortium which included Kodama's future benefactor, Lockheed, ended the Allies' war with Japan, hastened the liberation of China and put an end to the Kodama Organ. Kodama had all incriminating papers burnt but hid away his diamonds, half a roomful of platinum, and cash worth 3·5 billion yen (about US $175 million at the time, or more than £40 million sterling). For a few brief months it seemed that his precautions might be unnecessary. Not only was he untouched by the first purges of General MacArthur's occupation, he retained the rank of brigadier-general and was briefly appointed a financial adviser to the cabinet. Then, in 1946, the US administration caught up with him and he was interned without trial for suspected war crimes.

Even without the partisan evidence, supplied by US intelligence, of his violent record in occupied China, Kodama would almost certainly have been purged by the American forces of occupation. The total annihilation of all remnants of Japanese militarism, particularly the samurai variants with which Kodama had been associated, was the avowed first objective of the supervisory regime established by MacArthur. Ultra-nationalists were removed from their posts in central administration, local government, education and business. Kodama could scarcely have survived so extensive a comb-out.

But even had he contrived to keep secret his deepest convictions and affiliations, he could not have hoped to escape the next purge: an assault on big business and Zaibatsu, the interlocking super-corporations which had financed the war machine and still controlled the Japanese economy. MacArthur's avowed intention was to smash Japan's war potential and create a neutral 'Switzerland of the Far East', incapable either of military adventure or of economic competition with American industry, sections of which were demanding reparations which only the disappropriation of the Zaibatsu could finance. To underline the point, post-war Japan was given a 'peace constitution' which expressly outlawed Japanese participation in any future war and prohibited the maintenance of an army, navy, or air force. Japan was to be restructured as a liberal democracy in the Western and particularly the American mould, but with pacifism grafted on by force. Kodama and his friends were properly treated as the enemies of this process, being perceived as the embodiment of an old, dead Japan that had been, and must remain, defeated.

So, condemned on three counts – as a Class A war crimes suspect, a potentially subversive and unregenerate nationalist and simply as a rich businessman – Yoshio Kodama was locked up in Tokyo's Sugamo Prison. And among the friendships and contacts he made there were the two men with whom he would one day work to secure the Lockheed Starfighter contract: Taro Fukuda, his disciple, interpreter and eventual public relations frontman; and Nobusuke Kishi, imprisoned for his responsibility as a wartime cabinet minister, and soon to become, with Kodama's help, Japan's prime minister.

It has generally been the privilege of the left-wing prison graduate to bide his time behind bars and wait for the world outside to shift in his favour. But this time it was the turn of Kodama and his fellow-martyrs of the Right. MacArthur's drive towards a neutral or emasculated Japan began to falter. Fears of Soviet expansionism, Communist advances in China and, temporarily, Vietnam, coupled with a resurgence of leftist militancy in the Japanese labour movement, sowed seeds of doubt in the minds of some US policy-makers as to the wisdom of leaving Japan weak and defenceless before the red menace. So began a split in occupation policy which was promptly exploited by nationalist elements, particularly among former Imperial army officers, and, of course, the Japanese business community, threatened as it was by dismemberment. Secret alliances began to be forged between hawks in the US military occupation and 'traditional' Japanese. Major-General Charles Willoughby (called 'my lovable fascist' by MacArthur) succeeded in protecting and fostering two groups of the defeated Japanese military: an intelligence sector concerned with spying on America's former ally, the Soviet Union, and a group in charge of the 'demobilisation boards' which were supposed to place officers in safe civilian jobs out of harm's way, but in fact used their powers to build a formidable police force staffed by and under the control of right-wing officers. As a sideline, Willoughby's protected groups served US intelligence by spying on the blossoming labour movement.

Such trends were good news to Yoshio Kodama. Apart from other considerations, it meant that pressures began to be exerted for his release. By May 1947 these pressures were strong enough to provoke MacArthur's G–2 intelligence section to respond with a strongly worded report (classified until 1976) arguing for Kodama's continued internment. The anonymous author proved prescient. He concluded:

In summary, Kodama appears to be a man doubly dangerous. His long and fanatic involvement in ultra-nationalistic activities, violence included, and his skill in appealing to youth make him a man who, if released from internment, would surely be a grave security risk. In addition, there is the outstanding probability to be reckoned with that, as a result of his hearty co-operation with the war effort, he has a large fortune to back up whatever activities he might see fit to undertake. His success in the difficulties of securing supplies in wartime for the Navy mark him as one who could very easily become a big-time operator in Japan's re-constructional period. Persistent rumours as to his blackmarket profits in his Shanghai period, plus his known opportunism, are forceful arguments that he would be as unscrupulous in trade as he was in ultra-nationalism. Kodama's past performance indicates that he is the sort of man G–2 considers more dangerous than either the superannuated ideologists or the professional men who aided Japan's war-time effort for reasons of patriotism or survival of their professional interests ... Dangerous potentialities for the future.

Six weeks later a progress report on Kodama by his chief inquisitor, Lt Frank O'Neill, concluded: 'I am satisfied that Kodama or his associates for whom he is responsible committed numerous acts of violence in China in the acquisition by foul means or fair of commodities and goods [belonging to] the Chinese.' The fact that it was thought necessary to reassert the charges against Kodama suggests that friends outside were vociferous in calling his continued internment into question.

Kodama, characteristically, was not content to leave his fight to others. He spent his evenings writing the self-serving record of his life which was published later as *I Was Defeated*. This laid special stress on the one characteristic the Americans could be expected to admire in him: his fanatical anti-Communism. It was translated into English by his comrade and ally-for-Lockheed, Taro Fukuda, and quickly found its way to the right quarters in occupied Tokyo. 'Who in this age of ideological confusion, is capable of bringing the labouring masses, influenced completely by Communist ideals and rampaging like a wounded beast, under control?' he asked. It was a question designed to reconcile him to his captors, newly dedicated as they were to the cold war against the Soviet Union.

> The bestial roar of the Communist Party [reaches] into my cell through the barred windows of Sugamo Prison ... I can hear the dull thud of the marching feet of thousands of Communists advancing toward the bolshevisation of Japan ... Who will fight the last fight with them? Behind the steel bars of Sugamo this young life of mine, burning with the passionate ardour of a love of my country and of justice, strains against the bars that hold it in ...

The questions were not rhetorical. Who would lead the anti-Communist crusade? None other of course than Yoshio Kodama, veteran of the Federation of Radical Patriotic Workers. It took one more threatening push by the socialist left and one more answering pull by Kodama's friends and backers and he was a free man. Released with him in 1948 were his friend Nobusuke Kishi and seventeen other associates, most of whom would rise to prominence in the new Japan.

World events and Japanese developments were kind to them. Mao's triumphant victory in China in 1949 decisively swung the balance against the neutralist faction in Japan's occupation forces and in favour of those manoeuvring for a shift to the right. As George Kennan and his Policy Planning Staff wrote at the time, Japan was suddenly seen as 'the sole great potential military-industrial arsenal of the Far East'. MacArthur too, virtual dictator of Japan, announced:

> Now the Pacific has become an Anglo-Saxon lake and our line of defense runs through the chain of islands fringing the coast of Asia. It starts from the Philippines and continues through the Ryukyo archipelago which included its broad main bastion, Okinawa. Then it bends back through Japan and the Aleutian island chain to Alaska.

So much for the 'peace constitution' and the 'Switzerland of the Far East'. Within three and a half years of a war which had ended in a double nuclear cataclysm, Japan was being remade as the eastern bastion of the American alliance and the Free World.

It was hardly the new Japan of which the young Kodama had dreamt in his samurai fantasies. But it was better than Communism, not bad for business and, as it turned out, very good indeed for Yoshio Kodama.

Business was the first beneficiary of this policy turn-about. The dissolution of the Zaibatsu was slowed, then stopped, then put into reverse. Purged businesses reappeared, their wealth and power miraculously intact. If Japan was to be reshaped as an American ally, she might as well be a strong ally, and that meant allowing her to rebuild her economy, replacing reparations by aid. So ceilings formerly placed on production levels in strategic industries were abandoned, including those with direct war potential. The 'peace constitution' was either ignored or cynically circumvented by doublespeak. As historian John Dower put it, 'What had been officially identified as "Japanese Industrial War Potential" in the early stages of the occupation ... now passed through the rhetoricians' steam room and emerged benignly as Japan's "peaceful industries".'

The process accelerated with the outbreak of the Korean war in June 1950. MacArthur's authorisation of a 75,000-strong paramilitary National Police Reserve was claimed by his critics, and by the Japanese left, to violate Article 9 of the constitution which still forbade the creation of 'land, sea and air forces, as well as other war potential'. These 'police' reserves were unique: they were trained in tanks, renamed 'specialised vehicles' by the busy wordsmiths of the occupation, and were taught to use carbines, machine-guns, mortars, and bazookas. By 1952 this well-protected constabulary boasted naval and air sections, while the original authorisation of 75,000 had more than doubled — and was to go on rising till it was pushing the quarter-million mark. By 1954 the NPR had been renamed the Self-Defense Force, abandoning the pretence that the new Japanese military was composed solely of policemen, but still not facing the evident fact that 'peace constitution' or no, Japan once again boasted an army, navy and an air force, in fact if not in name.

From all this Yoshio Kodama benefited directly. The new forces needed supplies and Kodama made sure he secured a share of the contracts. From the Korean war years date his first regular business contracts with US arms manufacturers and salesmen. But it wasn't simply as a businessman that Kodama made his comeback. Along with the revival of Japanese industry came another revival even more beneficial to his peculiar talents. Deeply rooted in Japanese tradition is the role of the kuromaku, the secret mediator or power broker, the go-between who discreetly arranges the innumerable negotiations, compromises and deals on which Japanese business, and much of its social life, depend. Kuromaku means, literally, 'black curtain', and comes from the stylised kabuki theatre where the essence of the action occurs unseen in the wings. The kuromaku tradition reflected a view that power should not be brandished openly but applied with finesse and discretion from behind a veil. In theory or fable, the kuromaku laboured selflessly on behalf of his friends, resolving their problems and bringing a disinterested wisdom to bear on their quarrels. Needless to say, the practice was different. Behind the black curtain often lurked a fixer on a percentage or a crude greaser of palms.

The nobility of the original concept had no doubt appealed to the mystic in the young Kodama. He later discovered its practical rewards. He made himself the most accomplished kuromaku in pre-war Japan. And now that, after a short disruption, the offices of fixer and power-broker were again in demand, he was ready and only too willing to pick up where he had left off. By the time the US occupation ended and Japan resumed sovereignty in 1952, it was becoming increasingly hard to do business in Tokyo, particularly if it involved government participation or approval, without going through Yoshio Kodama.

That may well have been the assessment of the CIA. The formal transference of power from American officials to approved Japanese politicians brought a change in the way American influence was exerted. Where manipulation had been open and legal, legitimate fruit of the victories of war, it had now to be covert. The CIA quietly took over from MacArthur and, as they were to do in other parts of the world where Americans looked to the protection and advancement of their own interests against Communism, they smoothed the paths of approved politicians, thwarted the unreliable and subverted left-wing elements in the trade unions. If they needed a 'black curtain', Kodama was their man.

Against the slowly growing strength of a labour movement with leftist and neutralist leanings, those who had determined that Japan would be held for the 'Free World' preached the virtues of freedom and democracy. And while they preached, their agents smashed strikes and workers' demonstrations. Their instruments were the 'patriotic youth' of the *yakuza*, Japan's organised street gangs, and the *uyoku*, the ultra-rightist sects. Kodama, with his vast wealth and influence, had the undisputed allegiance of both.

But the threat from the left refused to go away and when, in 1954, the factionalised socialist opposition in the Diet united to form a single party which looked set to win the next election, the CIA was almost certainly behind answering moves to encourage countervailing mergers on the conservative right. This was a huge undertaking since conservatives were divided not so much by ideology as by bitter personal feuds and ancient rivalries. To overcome murderous hostilities required ruthless threats of violence against recalcitrant faction leaders (and the wherewithal in manpower and hardware to make good such threats), jobbery on a bold scale, and bribery running into millions of dollars.

What part Kodama played in all this is unclear. The details of his tangled relationship with US intelligence have never been fully unravelled. What is a matter of record is that at forty-three the former samurai and war-crimes internee became midwife to the cynically-named Liberal Democratic Party which was to rule Japan without a break for more than twenty years, and remained undefeated even in the 'Lockheed election' of December 1976.

It should not, and by now will not, be supposed that Yoshio Kodama spent his cash and energies to create the LDP out of simple affection for the Americans or love of liberal democracy. Kodama's *quid pro quo* was of an altogether different order. He calculated, quite simply, that the man who welded the party together would become its kingmaker. And every king and petty crown princeling would be beholden to the power exerted on his behalf from behind the black curtain. Yoshio Kodama, without ever holding a single political or administrative office, would become the most powerful man in Japan.

His instrument within the party was the Seirankai, a cell of like-minded ultra-nationalists-turned-businessmen. It was with Seirankai backing that Kodama's old prison-mate Nobusuke Kishi was elected party leader and prime minister in 1957. It would be simplistic to assert that Kodama accomplished Kishi's selection by straightforward bribery. Fairer to say that money in Japanese politics was (and remains) the arbiter of factional and personality disputes within the governing party, and Kodama just had more of it than anyone else.

So when John Kenneth Hull arrived in Tokyo in December 1957 to sell the Lockheed Starfighter, Kodama was at the zenith of his career. Grumman, first in the field, may have had the unanimous support of the defence chiefs but Lockheed had Yoshio Kodama, and Yoshi Kodama had his line to prime minister Kishi. Suddenly the impossible seemed not quite so impossible after all.

3

Kodama's first step was to advise that the Daiichi trading firm which still held Lockheed's sales franchise in Japan be replaced by Marubeni, a much more aggressive company intent on carving out an empire to rival those of the established giants Mitsubishi and Mitsui. So Marubeni became Lockheed's official agent, possibly in total ignorance of Kodama's secret connection with their client and his behind-the-scenes activities. Completing the team which went in hot pursuit of the Starfighter contract were Kodama's protégé and interpreter, Taro Fukuda, in charge of public relations; Yoshi-yoshi Oni, the wartime master-spy whom Fukuda had recommended to Kenneth Hull as Lockheed's Tokyo office manager; and finally, two top Seirankai politicians – the LDP's veteran vice-president, Bamboku Ohno, and Ichiro Kono, strong-man of one of the party's most powerful factions.

Since the Japanese service chiefs had already made known their decided preference for Grumman's F–11A Super Tiger, the first and most urgent task was to stop the National Defence Council from formally approving their choice. Precisely what part the Lockheed team played in this remains unclear, but they certainly won the breathing space they needed. The council, headed by prime minister Kishi, unexpectedly announced that there would be a delay in the final choice of plane 'pending further study'. Kodama later publicly claimed credit for engineering this crucial turn-about, though he said nothing of how it was accomplished.

Then, just as things seemed to be going well for Lockheed, Kodama met his first major setback. At the end of 1958, Kishi's position as premier – still crucial to any hope of a Starfighter victory – came under heavy pressure within the ruling party. Among his bitterest critics were Ohno and Kono and virtually the whole of the Seirankai faction on whose support Yoshio Kodama counted. The right plotted to oust Kishi in the January 1959 election for party president which would automatically topple him from the premiership.

The crisis was a classic test of Kodama's manipulative skills. Somehow he had to save Kishi without losing Ohno and Kono. The problem was tackled with breathtaking audacity and panache. First he met with the Ohno faction, promising Ohno that the entire resources of the Kodama machine would be thrown behind him to ensure his election as party leader and premier when Kishi had run his term. Then he promised Kono the premiership after Ohno. The two men dropped their opposition, the Lockheed forces were reunited, and Kishi was re-elected party president on January 24, 1959.

By now, of course, Grumman must have been aware that their rivals were enjoying something more than a run of good luck. They were not without their own supporters, including the formidable LDP secretary-general, Shojiro Kawashima. But when Kawashima fell ill and took a three-month rest cure in Hawaii, Kodama moved to exploit his absence. Through Taro Fukuda, he had comparative data on the Starfighter and Super Tiger fed to a member of the Diet, Shoji Tanaka, for an intensive parliamentary blitz. Much was made, reasonably enough, of the Starfighter's new world records, for altitude (91,243 ft on May 8, 1958, raised to 103,396 ft the following year) and speed (1,404·9 m.p.h. on May 16, 1958).

But the circulating of highly selective data was by no means Tanaka's most telling contribution. Much more damaging to the Super Tiger was his charge that Grumman had won Japanese air force support by bribery. Politicians supporting the Starfighter no doubt professed themselves deeply shocked by the suggestion of such dishonourable tactics. Later, Shoji Tanaka's political career collapsed when he was jailed for embezzlement in an unrelated business deal. Meanwhile, the damage to Grumman was done.

Then in July 1959 Kodama's intrigues paid off with what was to prove the decisive blow struck for the Starfighter. The crucial job of chief of the air staff had fallen vacant and Kodama, Ohno and Kono canvassed the virtues of General Minoru Genda, a somewhat odd candidate since he was a navy rather than an air force commander. Kishi hesitated, but for quite a different reason. Genda was the man who had planned and executed the devastating attack on Pearl Harbor on December 7, 1941. Kishi thought his appointment would be resented by the Americans. But Kodama was persuasive and Kishi gave way.

As if to show there were no hard feelings, Genda's first action as the new chief of staff was to lead a mission to the US. He visited Lockheed in California and there, at his own request, piloted a Starfighter and declared it the best fighter the world had ever seen. Back in Japan he pressed its selection, and the issue was no longer in doubt. A few months later General Genda was awarded the US Legion of Merit by the USAF — seventeen years after he had annihilated its planes in Hawaii. When, shortly after, he retired from his air force post, he was elected with Kodama's backing to the upper house of the Diet.

With Genda's advocacy, Lockheed's triumph was assured. Early in 1960 the Japanese defence ministry signed a contract which eventually led to the purchase of 230 F–104Js, 23 purchased direct and 207 made under licence in Japan. The Super Tiger, so long the favourite, had been finally ditched. Just how much Lockheed paid Kodama, and how much Kodama disbursed to other parties, remains something of a mystery. But it was certainly in excess of $1·7 million, since receipts for that amount in yen (Y629 million), bearing his rubber-stamped signature and 'chop' mark or seal, were kept by Lockheed.[1] And there is good reason for believing that not all payments were receipted, and not all receipts retained.

Kodama insisted on having much of his cash in yen, which necessitated a somewhat cumbersome delivery process. W. Hammond, then treasurer of Lockheed Aircraft International, instructed his manager of cash operations, A. G. Eley, to have cheques prepared payable to a Los Angeles foreign exchange house, Deak and Co., for the purchase of yen. The cash was then flown out to Tokyo and delivered direct to Kodama. Eley was told by Hammond to 'keep the matter quiet'.[2] Later it proved more practicable to use the Bank of America in Hong Kong, where a special account was opened in the names of Lockheed executives Erle Constable, T. L. May Jr, R. G. Todd and Eley. Any two of them could draw on the account, and over a four-year period following the Starfighter campaign, 138 million yen (approximately $360,000) passed through it. This money – presumably part of the total $1·7 million – was given to Jack Clutter, president of Lockheed's Asia subsidiary, for passing on to Kodama.[3]

Lockheed's official agents, Marubeni, say they didn't know what was going on; Kishi has disclaimed any involvement in the affair; Ohno and Kono are dead; and Kodama, in ill-health and under judicial investigation, is keeping his silence. But it is clear that Lockheed money subverted the political process and helped make a mockery of Japan's frail experiment in democracy, an act of manipulation which was to remain wholly secret for fifteen years. It was not

1 Special Review Committee report, exhibit 8, page 11. The report avoids mentioning consultants by name, but Kodama is clearly the recipient referred to.
2 Ibid., exhibit 8, page 12.
3 Ibid.

the first secret intervention by an international corporation in the affairs of a sovereign nation-state, nor was it the last. For Lockheed, however, it was the start of a pattern.

And the process cost Lockheed and its shareholders not a penny. The $1·7 million paid to Kodama was simply added to the purchase price. It was the Japanese taxpayers who finally footed the bill.

Ironically, perhaps, what seems most to have shocked the Church Committee when Lockheed's links with Kodama first came to light on February 4, 1976, was the corporation's cynical lack of patriotism. 'Most disturbing of all', commented Church, was Lockheed's decision to employ as agent 'a prominent leader of the ultra-Right-wing militarist political faction ... In effect we have had a foreign policy of the US Government which has vigorously opposed this political line in Japan and a Lockheed foreign policy which has helped to keep it alive through large financial subsidies.'

Shocking, but hardly surprising. The arms trade — of which the sale of military aircraft is a major part — is by its nature conservative. Those who run large corporations tend to be conservative, and those who run large corporations specialising in armaments have a vested interest in the good health of those political factions at home and abroad which preach the need for an ever-increasing supply of weapons. When Lockheed looked to sell the Starfighter in Japan, its natural allies were on the right. The moderate liberals and newly converted democrats cultivated by the State Department had the advantage of respectability but the disadvantage of political impotence. Lockheed was more concerned with winning a lucrative contract than with keeping respectable company.

4

Yoshio Kodama dips out of our story for the best part of a decade. But he was far from inactive in that time, and his activities are by no means irrelevant to Lockheed's progress. First, his contract was renewed (2 per cent commission on sales of aircraft and parts, excluding 'extraordinary special expenses') and extended to cover South Korea as well as Japan. Then, within weeks of his secret service to Lockheed, he found himself called upon to render open service, though of a very different nature, to no less a person than US President Eisenhower.

Kishi was again in difficulty. Kodama's manipulations had saved him once before but could not protect him indefinitely against mounting popular unrest, still focused on his avowedly pro-American policy. After the U–2 fiasco of May 1960, when Eisenhower was forced to concede that he had lied about the spy-plane's mission, virulent anti-American protests erupted in Tokyo and other Japanese cities. Eisenhower's hasty plan to repair strained relations with his Far East allies by a personal tour only made matters worse. When the date of his proposed state visit to Japan was announced, Tokyo's powerful trade union and student movements threatened to paralyse the city by mass strikes and street demonstrations. Fearing that his paramilitary police force would be too stretched to cope alone, Kishi turned for help to the veteran of organised street violence against the left.

Kodama quietly took charge of what was officially called 'Operation Protect Ike' – though the nature of the 'protection' offered seems to have been somewhat ambiguous. He is estimated to have collected more than $2 million from businessmen with property to protect, using his network of nationalist clubs and paramilitary societies to prise out the money. He spent it on hiring a huge army of paid thugs, an 'anti-Communist militia' equipped with its own riot gear, armoured trucks and helicopters. But Kodama's private army never saw action. Faced with the prospect of a bloodbath, US embassy officials persuaded Eisenhower at the last moment to call off his trip.

Kishi could not survive this humiliation and resigned in July 1960. Kodama's influence ebbed with that of his former cell-mate and he failed to make good his promise to install Ohno as Kishi's successor. Neither the new premier, Hayato Ikeda, nor his successor, Eisako Sato, were obligated to Kodama and when Lockheed competed for a new fighter contract their secret agent no longer had the political muscle to overcome the powerful claims of the McDonnell Douglas F–4 Phantom.

So for a time he turned his energies towards Korea. One of his associates, yet another fellow-veteran of Sugamo, was Ryoichi Sasagawa, chairman of the Japan Shipbuilding Association, patron of the martial arts, and leader of a Korea-based organisation called 'Win over Communism'. WOC was the secular, fund-raising arm of the Unification Church founded by the colourful Rev. Sun Myung Moon, who proclaimed President Park's South Korea the anti-communists' new Jerusalem. Park's paradise could only be sustained by massive US aid, however, and as a Senate investigation subsequently discovered, US aid was secured in part by a huge programme of Korean bribes to selected US congressmen.

Kodama's association with WOC—he was the movement's financial adviser for a time—proved to be no more than a stop-gap outlet for his talents. By 1969 he was back in the big time with Lockheed, the corporation's secret weapon in the murderous jumbo-jet war that would dominate the early 1970s.

Meanwhile, Lockheed was busy in Europe.

4

Germany: The Godfather

These salesmen are everywhere. I can't open a drawer in my desk without a Lockheed man falls out of it.

Franz Josef Strauss, West German defence minister, 1958

1

Lockheed's wooing and winning of Japan for the Starfighter did much to wipe out the baleful consequences to Lockheed of the USAF's lack of interest in the plane. But Japan was only one of two prime targets. Robert Gross knew that it was in Europe, and particularly in Germany, that the real killing was to be made.

Like Japan, the Germany of the 1950s was a vacuum waiting to be reinvaded by foreign industry. Here, too, the post-war allied occupation had become a vehicle for industrial and commercial penetration and, in particular, for a substantial American–German industrial sector, America being the only one of the three western allies with the resources to take full advantage of its opportunities. In 1950 the debate on German rearmament began, soon to grow into the dominant political issue of the decade. As in Japan, the rearmament question led to an alliance between the American business community and German conservatism. The alliance coalesced under the leadership of Konrad Adenauer, who, with his fellow Christian Democrats, saw rearmament as the symbol of the sovereignty they aspired to recover.

The three western occupying powers, the US, Britain and France, had at first disallowed any form of German militarism, only reluctantly authorising the creation of a native police force as a counterpart of the 'People's Police' of the Soviet zone. But the consolidation of Soviet control through eastern Europe, culminating in the Communist coup in Czechoslovakia and followed by the outbreak of the Korean war, strengthened the hand of the rearmers just as it had in Japan. Churchill, Pleven and Adenauer began to wonder aloud whether the risks of reviving German militarism were not preferable to the risk of Soviet westward expansion. In Washington DC the pro-rearmament lobby candidly canvassed the view that 'controlled normalisation' of German defence could provide 100,000 American jobs in the aircraft industry.

The European left — not least the SDP in Germany — campaigned passionately against rearmament, arguing (long before Hungary and Czechoslovakia rammed the point home) that the Soviets were already over-extended and more preoccupied with holding down their new imperial possessions than acquiring new ones. Churchill and Eisenhower professed themselves content to leave the decision to the German people, and when Adenauer won the 1953 elections with a sweeping two-thirds majority it was clear that Germany would soon be on the march again. The Paris agreements of October 1954 restored full sovereignty to the Federal Republic, and opened the way the following year to full membership of the North Atlantic Treaty Organisation, which gave Germany not only the right but the positive duty to maintain a standing army — and to rebuild the Luftwaffe.

The arrival in the market place of a new shopper with an empty basket and (thanks to American aid) a full purse soon had the salesmen in full cry. NATO was, in any case, ripe for American military aircraft penetration. Most member-countries, still struggling to rebuild their shattered economies after the war, ran air forces which varied from the shabby to the ludicrous. Planes which had done veteran service in the early 1940s were still flying — when they were not in the repair shop. Europe's air defences, if not quite obsolete, were plainly in need of wholesale renewal. This, moreover, was the age of determined talk of standardisation: the need to impose some cohesion and uniformity on a chaotic situation where every member of the alliance was flying a different machine and firing a different weapon. Whichever aircraft manufacturer in the United States (or Britain, or France, but the US was best placed to compete) could come up with a good, modern, reasonably priced multi-role plane would scoop the pool. Lockheed saw the opportunity and jumped.

From the start, they had to fight hard in an intensely competitive market. Grumman was in there, pitching for the excellent Super Tiger, and Northrop had the early designs of the F–5 on offer. There were two competitors from Britain, two from France and one from Sweden. But Lockheed had one significant advantage. Clarence Johnson had dreamed up the Starfighter as far back as 1951. The prototype had flown in February 1954. By the time West Germany joined NATO and laid itself open to offers, a production line was in the process of being organised, and even before German defence minister Strauss had fired the starting pistol, the Starfighter had been given a Hollywood-style public unveiling at Palmdale. Lockheed offered not just blueprints and promises but an existing product. Whether it was the right product was a matter of opinion. And the most important opinion was Strauss's.

Just how important it was to Lockheed to win that German order and open up a breach to a wider European market only becomes apparent when we examine the mounting difficulties the corporation was facing. For the Starfighter programme was not their only problem area. Lockheed's commercial plane business, the basis of the company's post-war prosperity, was also beginning to hit trouble.

The Constellation, in its various stretched and improved versions, had done the company proud for more than a decade, but in the early 1950s Lockheed set its sights on a dramatic goal which would mark a watershed in international flight: regular scheduled non-stop transatlantic flights *in both directions* all the year round. The first generation of Constellations had pioneered Atlantic flights to Britain and France with refuelling stops at Gander, Newfoundland, and Shannon. Then stretched versions with more fuel capacity had cut out the Gander stop on the eastward route, and by 1953 the Super Constellation was flying from New York to Amsterdam for KLM without even calling at Shannon. But a non-stop westward journey, in the teeth of the Atlantic's strong westerly headwinds, was beyond even the Super Constellation's capacity.

Lockheed's designers were convinced as early as 1948 that no piston-engined plane would ever achieve the prize. So the company poured huge resources into financing development of a jet airliner. Douglas had already begun a similar programme and Boeing was soon to follow. But by 1952 the Gross brothers were seriously alarmed at the huge sums, variously estimated up to a billion dollars, which the company was pouring into the bottomless pit labelled jet research without any indication of the necessary break-through. They sounded the US government for development aid and when it was not forthcoming they pulled out of the airline jet race to lick their roasted fingers. Douglas abandoned their jet programme the following year and the wry comment of president Donald Douglas fits both companies: 'I have always held the conviction that aero-planes should make money as well as headlines.'

But in 1954, in pursuit of the money and the headlines which would accrue to the first planemakers to smash the two-way non-stop transatlantic barrier, both Lockheed and Douglas started the design of new non-jet long-range models. Lockheed went for a radically redesigned version of the Super Constellation powered by turbo-props, where conventional propellers were powered not by pistons but by a gas turbine – a halfway house between the pure-jet of the future and the tried and trusted piston engines of the past. They called it the Starliner. Douglas adopted a simpler and cheaper solution, stretching the wing-span of the DC–7 to give bigger fuel tanks for conventional piston engines.

Lockheed's design was soon in trouble. There were delays in the development of the Pratt and Whitney PT–2F–1 engines, and Lockheed met political opposition to its tentative proposal to buy British (the Rolls-Royce RB–109 or the Bristol BE–25, neither of which had yet been test flown). When the new Starliner was finally rolled out in September 1956, Douglas's competitor, the DC–7C, had won the race by more than a year and mopped up the overseas market. Against DC–7C sales of 121 models the Starliner could muster only ten (reduced from an initial order of twelve) to Air France, four to Lufthansa, four to LAI of Italy (which went out of business, merging with Alitalia, before they could be delivered) and a mere sprinkling for domestic airlines, mostly TWA. Again Lockheed found itself with badly burnt fingers.

Nor was that all. In 1955 the Lockheed design team laid out plans for an entirely new airliner for the 1960s, the turbo-prop Elektra 188. After an expensive research and development programme the prototype was flying before the end of 1957 and after a further year of 'ironing out the bugs' the Elektra began service with American Airlines early in 1959. But within weeks Lockheed's hopes of a quick climb back to the top of the commercial airline league table were dashed. On February 3, one of American's first Elektra flights crashed on landing at New York, killing 65 people. Eight months later a Braniff-owned Elektra crashed at Buffalo, Texas, killing 34; and early the following year a third Elektra, flown by Northwest, came down near Cannelton, Indiana, with 63 dead. In two of the crashes, engines were found to have broken away in flight. Lockheed called in all 165 remaining models for radical restructuring of wings and engine mountings, which grounded them for up to a year. The company bore the enormous costs of LEAP (Lockheed Elektra Action Program) and were complimented by American Airlines' president Marion Sadler for providing the business world with 'a shining example of responsible business conduct'. But despite the compliment, Sadler purchased no more Elektras, and nor did the overseas market. The Elektra was a financial disaster, and its awful memory kept Lockheed out of the commercial airline business for a decade. That all but final chapter in the story of Lockheed's decline in the civil field still lay ahead and unguessed as the Gross brothers planned their Starfighter sales campaign. But the expensive failure to develop a pure-jet airliner and the débâcle of the Starliner were fresh in the corporate memory. Lockheed, like Douglas, was in the aircraft business to make money. On their civil operations they were losing it. There was one way only to restore confidence and financial stability to Lockheed: through that multi-million dollar Starfighter contract with Germany.

So Lockheed went a-wooing the one man in Germany who held the key to their corporate future, a bellicose, beer-swilling Bavarian politician named Franz Josef Strauss.

2

By the end of 1958 the Grand Hotel in Bonn was so full of Lockheed's salesmen and lobbyists that it was known to German air ministry officials as the 'Lockheedshof'. Looking back on this hectic time sixteen years later, Bill Gunston wrote in *Early Supersonic Fighters of the West*:

> I hope someone has time to tell the full story one day, because the inside tale of this kind of selling uncovers fascinating insights into aggressive big business, the psychology of contrasting people (engineers, pilots, top brass, cabinet ministers and lots of much less obvious participants) ... and countless splendid anecdotes which even now seem to be mostly unprintable.

Clearly the Starfighter campaign was very different from anything that had preceded it. From the 1930s on, Lockheed and most of its competitors had reached the overseas sales market through independent agents who generally worked, like door-to-door brush salesmen, on a straight commission basis. But by the 1950s the stakes had grown immeasurably. A vast European market both for commercial and military planes beckoned Lockheed and the dozen or so other giants of what was now called the aerospace industry. The emergence of a steady stream of newly independent nations multiplied the number of buyers. So too did the cold war, and the one that was hotting up in the Middle East. There was a lot of business to be won, and Lockheed had to scramble for it. Brush salesman techniques had sufficed for the 1930s, but a far more sophisticated strategy was needed in a more ruthlessly competitive world.

Given the rising importance of the European market it was fitting that Lockheed's new strategy should be built around a well-connected European, a shrewd multilingual Dutchman named Frederick C. Meuser. There were few hints in Meuser's early career of the special qualities which would soon make him Lockheed's top international string-puller. He had studied engineering at the Swiss Federal Institute of Technology in Zürich, graduating in 1932 just as, across the Atlantic, the Gross brothers were reviving a moribund Lockheed. Meuser, like them, was an aviation enthusiast and he joined KLM, first as an engineer and then as a pilot. Here he made his first contact with Lockheed's products and the men behind them.

When war came and the Netherlands were overrun by the Nazis, Meuser was among the first of the *Engelandvaarders*, the name given to the young heroes who slipped through Hitler's net to make their way to England and offer their services to the RAF or the Dutch government in exile. In London Meuser was taken to meet the exiled Queen Wilhelmina and her son-in-law, Prince Bernhard. It was the start of a long, close friendship between the two men, a friendship that would eventually end in public disgrace for the prince.

Meuser joined the RAF and twice narrowly escaped being shot down while flying sorties over his own country. After the liberation of the Netherlands he returned briefly to KLM before deciding to make his home in the United States, where he was hired by Lockheed and took American citizenship. His expertise as an engineer and a flier, combined with a sharp flair for finance, brought him rapid advance in the company. Not the least of his assets were his continuing close links with influential friends in Europe, including the prince who had been his comrade in exile and who, in the changed conditions following victory, had become one of the most influential men in Western Europe.

In 1954, with the title of director for Europe, Africa and the Middle East, Meuser was sent back to Europe to begin the new sales offensive. Significantly, he chose to make his base not in his native Netherlands but in Switzerland, whose secrecy laws would play a central part in Lockheed's strategy. Switzerland was also the home of Meuser's close friend Hubert Weisbrod, a lawyer with whom he had shared rooms back in their student days. Weisbrod was soon signed up by Meuser as a Lockheed 'consultant'. Literally millions of dollars — it is impossible to determine the precise total — would flow through his various accounts over the next few hectic years. Weisbrod's work for Lockheed remained for years one of the company's most closely guarded secrets. But in 1974 Fred Meuser wrote a private letter to Tom Jones of Northrop which, when it was made public by the Church Committee, stripped away much of the mystery.

Whenever I had a problem as a student, Hubert was my trusted adviser and he always resolved it in a professional manner. Later, when my career in KLM and wartime service in the RAF took me around the globe, Hubert made a distinguished international legal career from his base in Zürich. He travelled extensively, he made and maintained the highest level contacts but always remained a solid Swiss citizen.

During all these long years Hubert was at my side whenever I needed advice on matters European. Especially since 1954 ... Hubert was my close adviser on the European scene, he indicated channels to follow, whom to contact and how to go about it and how to spread the name of Lockheed as a base for business in the future in the nations of Europe.

But Weisbrod's role was clearly not confined to merely advising Meuser and recommending contacts.

Much of the success I could book to Lockheed in the following years in the field of sales of commercial and military aircraft and particularly of the unique and highly profitable export program of the F–104 Starfighter, was in no small measure due to his expert counselling and behind the scenes pulling of strings. Hardly ever did Hubert appear in the open for the support of Lockheed's interests; practically all his constructive work was done discreetly indirectly.

Meuser's meaning is unmistakable. Weisbrod 'indicated channels to follow, whom to contact and how to go about it'. His work involved 'behind the scenes pulling of strings' and 'discreet, indirect' activity which was 'hardly ever ... in the open'. As we shall see, part of the 'commission' paid ostensibly to Weisbrod was intended by Lockheed for Prince Bernhard. How many other high-placed officials and politicians benefited or were intended to benefit in the same way is still not entirely clear.

Meuser's letter does, however, raise the question of how a hitherto obscure, provincial lawyer, whose sole claim to public distinction was that he had once been a skiing champion and had served a term as president of the Swiss Automobile Club, had come to have so many top-level influential contacts. The answer is to be found in the nature of what the Church Committee later labelled 'the Meuser–Weisbrod connection'. Meuser clearly was the man with the contacts, the real string-puller. Weisbrod's utility evidently lay in the fact that, first, unlike Meuser, he was not a direct employee of Lockheed; and second, he was, in Meuser's words, 'a solid Swiss citizen'. Swiss lawyers, like bankers, enjoy an astonishing degree of protection from investigation or audit. Hubert Weisbrod, trusted old friend of Fred Meuser who in turn was the trusted comrade-in-arms of Prince Bernhard and his highly influential circle of political and business friends, was ideally placed to act as conduit for Lockheed's payments and guardian of the numbered Swiss bank accounts through which the money passed.

By the mid-1950s, then, Lockheed had a European sales organisation more sophisticated than that of any of its competitors. In the open were the salaried salesmen and lobbyists who made good business for the 'Lockheedshof', and behind them the hidden forces of the Meuser–Weisbrod connection. This was the mechanism Lockheed released on Europe: a grease machine designed to smooth the way to a billion-dollar contract.

The machine chalked up its first success with Super-Constellation sales to Meuser's old firm in the Netherlands, KLM, and more spectacularly to Germany's infant airline, Luft AG, the forerunner of Lufthansa. The Luft AG board at first voted against a proposed purchase of 12 Super-Constellations, but was soon persuaded by Lockheed lobbyists to reverse the decision. Inevitably there were rumours of bribery and corruption. When these were eventually investigated in 1977 by a Bonn government commission, the airline was described as a 'victim' of Lockheed's 'influencing tactics', and Lockheed was said to have 'interfered in the management of Lufthansa, and later in the military department and the political field'. The commission's report, never officially made public but leaked to the Munich newspaper *Süddeutsche Zeitung* and published in summary on May 9, 1978, concluded that, whatever form Lockheed's influence may have taken, there was 'no tangible evidence of bribery' in the Super-Constellation deal. But it was in the 'military and political' departments that the Lockheed machine was most active. And the big prize was the Starfighter contract.

3

On March 18, 1959, the defence minister of the German Federal Republic, Franz Josef Strauss, announced that 'after evaluating nearly two dozen of the world's top fighter aircraft', he had signed a contract committing the German air force to the purchase of ninety-six Starfighters.

It was a deal which greatly puzzled informed observers. The contract was signed before any firm agreement had been worked out on delivery dates, offset arrangements (whereby most of the planes would be made in Europe under licence) or even price. Moreover, the Luftwaffe had let it be known that, like its counterpart in Japan, it preferred the Grumman competitor, the Super Tiger.

Perhaps most puzzling of all, the Starfighter was already regarded by German experts as a dangerous buy. Lockheed, despite the evidence of its own trials, pooh-poohed these warnings as the invention of jealous rivals. But it was clear to all that Germany was buying blind, committing most of its air defences for at least a decade to a version of the Starfighter (the F–104G) which had not yet flown, and was the subject of intense controversy.

The kind of plane the Germans (like the Japanese) wanted was an all-weather, multi-mission fighter-bomber, one in which flexibility of role was much more important than the Korean war pilots' obsession with high-flying at Mach 2. So what Lockheed did was to pack into the redesigned model all the heavy, sophisticated avionics they had designed the original F–104 to do without: a powerful radar system to be used in conjunction with an optional fire-control computer for launching bombs and nuclear missiles, infra-red for night sighting, a new auto-pilot and inertial navigational system, a new UHF radio and communications system, a position and homing indicator, an air-data computer, provision for a reconnaissance pod under the fuselage, a more powerful engine fitted with anti-icing inlets, bigger tyres, a heavier braking and anti-skid system and scores of relatively minor modifications. But the one thing that didn't change was the tiny wing area designed for a far lighter plane. Small wonder, then, that expert doubts were raised as to the F–104G's safety under stress.

For Lockheed, however, the controversial contract meant a double windfall, for even the redesigned plane was subject to hundreds of ECPs (equipment change proposals) suggested by

Lockheed, agreed to by the customer and carried out by Lockheed or its licensees. It was these ECPs, above all else, which were first to bring the whole deal into open controversy.

The man who later claimed that the ECP contracts were riddled with bribery and corruption was a former Lockheed official, Ernest F. Hauser, the American son of an Austrian father who emigrated to Massachusetts after the First World War. As a young man of twenty-four in 1945 Hauser led a US military intelligence unit in occupied Germany. Here, according to his own story,[1] he met and befriended the then slim and unknown Franz Josef Strauss who was working as a translator with the occupying forces. Hauser claims he used his influence with the local military governor to get Strauss appointed as deputy to the ageing county commissioner, 'Landrat' Bauer. It was Strauss's first step into public life, consolidated when he hired Bauer's daughter Ermelinde as his confidential secretary.

The friendship between Strauss and Hauser prospered. Strauss co-operated unreservedly with the occupiers and Hauser rewarded him by inviting him to share the pleasures of US army camp life, which contrasted starkly with the drab, depressed conditions of less privileged natives. In 1948 when Hauser married a local girl after divorcing a wife in America, Strauss was his best man. Years later, after Hauser had married a third time, Strauss agreed to be godfather to a son who was given the middle names Franz Josef in honour of the now famous family friend.

Hauser was transferred back to the US in 1950 but the two men maintained regular contact, Strauss signing his letters affectionately, 'your old friend Franz Josef'. After a short spell in Korea, Hauser remained in California, still with military intelligence. Strauss moved from local to national government, rising to the top of the Bavarian-based party, the Christian Social Union (CSU). Strauss's politics were decidedly right-wing (though anti-Nazi) and the CSU at first looked set to split the conservative vote in Bavaria, thereby threatening to deprive Adenauer's Christian Democrats of a parliamentary majority. Strauss skilfully exploited his strategic position and nego-tiated a pact by which the CDU was persuaded not to put up candi-dates in Bavaria in return for CSU support in parliament. So the ground was prepared for successive CDU–CSU coalitions and Strauss was transformed from provincial boss of a provincial party to

---

1 Told in interviews with the author and also in an unpublished manuscript, 'The Lockheed European Caper', by Ernest Hauser.

national politician with his own autonomous power base. He wanted the defence ministry and that is what he got.

Back in California, Major Hauser, now forty, left the army in 1959 and took a job with Aerojet General Corporation, a private firm engaged mainly in subcontracted work for the aerospace giants. In his regular Christmas letter he told Strauss about his 'change of life'. The following summer Strauss wrote suggesting a get-together. He had something in mind, he said, which he wanted to discuss.

Hauser understood that Strauss seemed to be inviting him to Bonn, but Bonn was on the other side of the world and the German defence minister had not offered to pay his expenses. The reunion had to wait a year until Strauss made an official visit to the US. Hauser received a summons to meet his old friend at Hamilton Air Force Base near San Francisco, and they talked privately for an hour. According to Hauser, Strauss came straight to the point and offered him a plum job with Lockheed.

If Hauser was puzzled as to why a German defence minister should have jobs with an American corporation in his gift, Strauss quickly explained. Lockheed was handling the Starfighter deal through its office in Koblenz. NATO had its own Starfighter office in the same town largely manned by Germans. There were 'liaison' problems. Strauss explained that he had already written to Lockheed chief Robert Gross suggesting that his friend Ernest Hauser of Aerojet was the man to sort things out. Strauss wanted a man in Lockheed he could trust. 'I was to be his confidential go-between, his eyes and his ears in the Starfighter office', explained Hauser retrospectively.

Strauss flew back to Germany, touching down at New York on the way. There he received a message from Robert Gross agreeing to his suggestion. Before continuing his journey he scribbled a note to Hauser: 'Lockheed will take you on permanently and will send you after instruction to Koblenz. Looking forward to seeing you again in Bonn.' Three months later, when Hauser landed at Frankfurt, he was presented with a huge bouquet of roses, attached to which was a card reading 'Welcome! FJS'.

Hauser's title at Lockheed's Koblenz office was assistant customer relations manager. He performed an assortment of political and public relations duties, arranging press trips to Lockheed facilities, lobbying in the German parliament, looking after visiting executives and officials from the US and sometimes helping run Lockheed's hospitality apartment in Bonn. But his first responsibility, he claims, was direct liaison with Strauss.

What the liaison entailed is a matter of dispute. There is no agreed record. In the summer of 1976 it was discovered that the entire set of files covering the F–104G purchase had gone missing from defence ministry headquarters in Bonn. Lockheed claim to have no record in Burbank of their Koblenz office's dealings. And Hauser's immediate superiors at Koblenz, Archibald Folden and Russell Cook, told the Church Committee they couldn't remember the details. So what follows is Hauser's uncorroborated version of events, much of which is emphatically denied by Strauss.

When the Starfighter contract was signed in 1959, says Hauser, Lockheed chairman and chief executive Robert Gross made a secret 'gentlemen's agreement' with Strauss whereby a percentage of the sale price of each plane would be paid into the funds of the CSU as 'commission'. To keep the books straight at Burbank, it was arranged that the payments would be deducted from the commission due to Lockheed's official sales agent in Germany, Günther Frank-Fahle. The problem was that Frank-Fahle resisted this arrangement and the dispute was still unresolved when Gross died in September 1961. No one else at Lockheed would admit to any knowledge of the gentlemen's agreement, but Strauss was adamant that it be honoured. What's more, he claimed that the CSU's commission was due not only on sales but on the whole vast continuing ECP programme. Frank-Fahle stood to lose around a million dollars if Strauss's view prevailed.

Hauser's job — according to his version of the story — was to sort out the snarl-up and get payments moving again. That was why Strauss wanted a trusted friend in Lockheed's Koblenz office.

How Hauser set about this delicate task is recorded in a diary he says he kept at the time. His notes were cryptic, often technical, and interspersed with scathing references to colleagues and business acquaintances. 'What a bunch of Pranks', he writes, after a meeting of Lockheed executives. A colleague's assistant is 'an overbearing ass', a London reporter is 'a little English wire-service dwarf, asking some very funny questions in the club regarding Strauss', a rival sales rep. has 'a rather vulgar looking wife' whom he is 'launching' at the German buyers, and so on. The diary records disputes over ECPs, PR problems, Lockheed's embarrassment at being unable to get a Starfighter ready for the 1962 Hanover air show, and the catastrophe of two fatal crashes in June and July which Hauser, as a loyal Lockheed employee, attributed not to the product but to its incompetent German users.

On October 8, 1961, the diary records, Hauser had lunch with Frank-Fahle, who made plain his opposition to the CSU commission payments on follow-on contracts, where Germany would set up its own production lines to build the Starfighter under licence. Nine days later Hauser visited Strauss with Lockheed's Koblenz office boss Archi Folden. The meeting was 'very pleasant' but Strauss 'expressed concern' at the number and cost of Lockheed's proposed ECPs. Only a fortnight earlier Hauser had noted with satisfaction that Major Klapper of the German Starfighter office was 'rubber-stamping all ECPs'.

On December 12 an angry Frank-Fahle called Hauser – 'out of his mind' says the diary. Lockheed headquarters at Burbank had caved in to Strauss and deducted the CSU's share of commission from Frank-Fahle's dues, putting the payment through a CSU account at the Merck Finck Bank, Munich. Hauser later claimed[1] that Strauss himself had nominated this account, writing the number on a sheet of paper and handing it personally to Hauser, but Strauss emphatically denies this and there is no independent evidence. After Frank-Fahle's angry phone-call, Hauser called CSU general secretary Friedrich Zimmermann and suggested he telephone Frank-Fahle to 'explain party policy'. That done, Hauser called Strauss to tell him of Frank-Fahle's rage. The diary records Strauss's response: 'He just laughed, said served the old Nazi right.'

Meanwhile Hauser was having trouble with other pay-offs, referred to euphemistically as 'Xmas gratuities'. Repenning – a German procurement official – was said to have a 'shopping list', and Hauser commented, 'He is a real glutton'. General Schmuckle, Strauss's PR chief, 'when approached on Xmas arrangements [said] that anything he received he would turn over to charity'. Hauser's comment: 'It's a pity he is a real loner in these feelings.' A little later, 'the question of money for everyone gets to be more and more problematic'. Hauser noted that Fred Meuser, who visited Bonn in March 1962, was 'unhappy about arrangements that he was to dispense funds to other than Netherlands', and Hauser didn't like it either: 'I am reluctant to constantly have to rely on the Dutch Mafia but on the other hand we cannot very well channel these sums through normal bank channels. I really should have stayed at Aerojet.'

Frank-Fahle continued to challenge the deduction of the CSU's rake-off from his own commission and on January 3, 1962, a further

1 Interview with the author for Granada Television.

meeting was held 'to attempt to straighten out Frank-Fahle Fr. J. Str dispute'. But the diary records, 'No progress. LCC (Lockheed California Company, the division responsible for the Starfighter) will have to be firm and make decision.'

A week later, according to the diary, Strauss came up with his own solution.

> January 9. FJS wants [his former secretary] Ermelinde's husband Schaffler to oversee financial transfers to CSU. This presents problems. Schaffler is German gov. employee and LAC [Lockheed Aircraft Corporation] unwilling to show exact figures. Also FF has expressed concern re German tax liability. Lockheed stupidly agreed to circumvent German taxes. Official status is that they DO NOT have an office [i.e. a sales office] in Germany as Lockheed Koblenz office is ostensibly only for liaison purposes. All non-US personnel such as secretaries etc are paid through FF office in Frankfurt. Russell Cook handles our end and Frank-Fahle's people are getting rake-off on even simplest typists salaries. Deutsche Bank Koblenz leases 3rd floor to FF office not Lockheed.
>
> I have expressed my fears on such an arrangement. F. J. Str. also very apprehensive since BRD tax laws flagrantly being circumvented. What a mess.

The proposed switch to Schaffler was never made and the dispute rumbled on into the summer when Hauser noted:

> June 4. Folden getting lots of static from F-Fahle. They feel if LCC or LAC want to pay CSU then this should be in addition to contracting commission [i.e. over and above Frank-Fahle's dues]. Only weapon we have is FRG [Federal Republic of Germany] income tax scare to FF. If he wants US deposit then he must agree to cut. Archi [Folden] will get this message to Burbank and the friends of FF there, such as White, Stevenson etc. Whoever started this deal must have been nuts. Talked to Phil Colman [Executive assistant to the president, Lockheed-California] yesterday. He also agrees that things just got out of hand. You just cannot weigh a contract for 800+ fighters the same as 15+ lousy Constellations.

Aside from this last intriguing hint that the Starfighter sale wasn't the first to involve concealed pay-offs, the 'tax scare' weapon seems to have worked wonders. There is no further record of any complaint from Frank-Fahle and only three weeks later Hauser noted that

'FJS ... has calmed considerably since the CSU payments are running smoothly'.

That entry, for June 26, is the last diary reference to the 'secret deal'. Little more than two months later, on September 3, Hauser noted: 'There is political trouble coming, lots of it. The *Spiegel* is going after FJS and I believe we will have to help in a PR probe.' The radical weekly *Der Spiegel* had long led the attack on Strauss's competence as defence minister, singling out the Starfighter contracts for special criticism. A recent issue had carried accounts of a NATO exercise, following which the writers and editor had been arrested on a secrets charge. Strauss strenuously denied intervening against them but was widely disbelieved. The bitter acrimony that resulted forced his resignation from the government, at which point Hauser stopped keeping his diary. His last entry, on December 8, read:

In a few days they will have the torchlite parade for Strauss. Adenauer has really behaved like a weak sister, but I suppose since the CDU did not participate in the deals.

Hauser insisted later that the payments he claims Lockheed made to the CSU, though questionable, were not illegal. (It is indeed permissible for German political parties to accept funds from business corporations so long as they are not intended as bribes.) Asked in a Granada TV interview with the author if these 'commission' payments were not in fact concealed bribes, Hauser responded enigmatically: 'No, not bribes, just an agreement that you buy our planes, we pay you this money.' Why, then, Strauss's and Lockheed's concern that the payments be secret? 'Because if the other parties had known,' said Hauser, 'they might have started screaming for their cut.'

Hauser estimated the total paid to the CSU at 'around $10 million', calculated on his belief that the party was promised 'a little over $5000 for every F-104 aircraft produced by Lockheed or a licensee, regardless of where it was sold'. But denials followed thick, fast and emphatic. Strauss has said that he personally never received a cent from Lockheed (a charge Hauser never made), that he knows of no payment to the CSU or any 'gentlemen's agreement' with Robert Gross, that he never suggested his former secretary's husband as a channel for any Lockheed money and that he never handed Hauser a piece of paper nominating a Merck Finck & Co. bank account. The CSU has also denied receiving any improper payments. Lockheed's vice-president for public relations, William Perreault, has said there is 'no credible basis' for believing Hauser's statements, but refuses to issue a formal denial, commenting that 'a blanket denial is a very stupid thing to make on anything'. Merck Finck maintain the traditional bankers' silence. Günther Frank-Fahle, ill in a Swiss nursing home, has made no statement on the affair. And, as we have seen, the German defence ministry's files on the Starfighter deal have mysteriously disappeared. So the credibility of Hauser's story depends on the authenticity of his diary. We shall look more closely at that in our next chapter.

There is one more entry in the diary which must be noted before we move on. It refers both to more ECP pay-offs and to growing worries about Starfighter safety.

> July 22 (1962). FJS meeting bad omen another crash today. It is really hopeless. The German Air Force is really not up to a sophisticated fighter. Some of the pilots may be but the supporting crews are not. Maintenance bad.
>
> The records of other countries are showing better and it will be a blemish on the GAF. It is really surprising how calm Rall[1] and his staff are taking the whole thing. The cold bloodest of all is Lt.-Col. P. He quite obviously is getting paid off, although Dale Daniels denies this. The Arbeitsstab F–104 group is unique. They approve everything and only give token resistance to new LCC [Lockheed-California] proposals.

The F–104G's safety record was indeed a cumulative disaster. In 1961, when the Luftwaffe first put them into service, the loss rate was 80 per 100,000 hours flown. In 1962 it rose to 139. In 1963, though the loss-rate-per-hour dropped because many more hours were flown, the number of accidents actually rose. By 1965 there was a Starfighter write-off every ten days. By the end of 1975 there had been no fewer than 174 crashes and the Starfighter was known as the 'Flying Coffin' or 'Widowmaker'. Sick jokes abounded. The Luftwaffe's definition of an optimist was 'a Starfighter pilot who gave up smoking because he was afraid of dying of lung cancer'. By the end of 1962 some pilots would only fly after heavily and dangerously sedating themselves, and some refused to fly the plane at all. (One

---

1 Col. Günther Rall, head of the Starfighter planning staff in the German air force. Hauser told the *Wall Street Journal* on December 4, 1975, that he had delivered an envelope containing cash to Col. Rall. Rall denied the story. In September 1975 Col. Rall was forced to resign from the air force after accepting gratuities in an unrelated incident.

was court-martialled and sued Strauss's successor as defence minister, Kai-Uwe von Hassel, for wrongful dismissal. Von Hassel defended the Starfighter as strenuously as Strauss. In 1970 he tragically lost his own son in a Starfighter crash.)

Controversy raged over who was responsible for this carnage, the plane's makers or its fliers. Lockheed took the view indicated in Hauser's diary: the fault lay with inexperienced pilots and 'bad maintenance'. As the years went by, some support for this judgment was adduced from the fact that only in Japan (whose air force, like Germany's, had had to start again from scratch) was the accident rate comparably high.[1] Elsewhere it came within tolerable margins. But by the 1970s it was widely accepted that the immense modification programme which turned the fine-weather-only F–104A into the multi-role F–104G and F–104J, topped by the ECPs endlessly proposed by Lockheed, made of the Starfighter an unforgiving plane that responded disastrously to the least pilot-error. Not until the end of 1975 did Lockheed in effect admit some of the blame when the corporation's insurance companies finally agreed to distribute $1·2 million among thirty-one widows of German Starfighter pilots.

The explosive implications of Hauser's diary note of July 1962, that Lockheed secured German agreement to profitable ECPs by bribery and that these ECPs contributed to the plane's disastrous crash record, have yet to be fully explored in Germany. How far the Bonn commission, hampered by the disappearance of the Starfighter files, was able to investigate the allegations is not clear. Its report remains secret. The summary leaked to and published by the *Süddeutsche Zeitung* on May 9, 1978, indicated that no solid evidence had been found to support Hauser's stories of bribery. Indeed, at one point the stories are apparently dismissed by the commission as 'demonstrably false'. But the same report goes on to paint a devastating picture of Lockheed's 'penetration' of the military, the civil service and the political parties, acknowledging that defence ministry officials and high-ranking officers had supplied Lockheed over the years with confidential and even secret military information, enabling the company to influence vital parliamentary decisions on aircraft purchases. By the early 1970s, Lockheed had 'no fundamental misgivings about making payments to West German political parties' – the Social Democrats as well as the right-wing parties. As Hauser

---

1 By 1975 Japan had lost 54 of the 230 Starfighters she had bought or made under licence.

had acknowledged, such payments may not necessarily constitute bribery in German law. But Lockheed are unlikely to have bothered over-much about the semantics of the operation. They knew what they were doing, and it worked.

4

As Lockheed confidently expected, Germany's first Starfighter order in March 1959 opened the floodgates. The Netherlands followed just over a year later on April 20, 1960, Belgium on June 20, 1960, and Italy on March 2, 1961. Outside Europe, Canada ordered 310 (110 for re-export to 'needy' friendly nations under the US mutual aid programme) and Japan, as we have seen, 230. Of the Europeans, the Netherlands ordered 144, Italy 155 and Belgium 100.

But more remarkable than mere numbers was the unprecedented complexity of the multinational manufacturing programme, for the vast majority of Europe's Starfighters were built under licence on European assembly lines. Work Group South near Munich comprised Messerschmitt, Heinkel, Dornier and Siebel; Work Group North at Schipol, Amsterdam, comprised Hamburger, Weser, Focke-Wulf, Focker and Aviolanda; West Group, at Gasselies, Belgium, was made up of Avions Fairey and SABCA; and the Italian Group at Turin-Caselle comprised Fiat, Aerter, Macchi, SIAI-Marchetti, Piaggio and SACA. To co-ordinate the programme (which was already under way in 1959, even before the Netherlands, Belgium or Italy had formally signed contracts) the NATO Starfighter management office (NASMO) was established in Koblenz, across the road from the Lockheed office where Hauser was stationed.

It wasn't long after his arrival, as his diary indicates, that Hauser began to understand that the complexities of the Starfighter deal did not stop at the Strauss–Frank–Fahle dispute. There were similar problems in the Netherlands and Belgium, and at one stage it seemed that the entire programme might be set back by a revolt of Dutch officials against the latest set of Lockheed ECPs. How Lockheed moved to neutralise that resistance is a recurring sub-plot of the Hauser diary. If Hauser is correct, in Germany Lockheed bought a party, and in the Netherlands they bought a prince.

5

The Netherlands:
A Royal Connection

Quite apart from the economic difficulties of our [European] countries, we princes have financial problems of our own. Like many people these days, most of us have trouble making ends meet. Some people think that kings and queens are still as rich as fabled Midas. It isn't so.

Prince Bernhard of the Netherlands,
Collier's Magazine, 1953

1

Bernhard Leopold Frederic Everhard Julius Coert Karel Godfried Pieter, Prins der Nederlanden, was born Bernhard Leopold Friedrich Eberhard Julius Kurt Karl Gottfried Peter, Prinz zur Lippe-Biesterfeld, a minor principality covering 471 square miles of forested hills and farmland in the Westphalia region of Germany. His family had ruled the Lippe princedom for 700 years, ever since Bernhard the First threw his less than decisive weight behind the Holy Roman Emperor Lotharius in the twelfth century. Lippe had been absorbed into the new German Empire in 1871 but its ruling house retained a royal title and many of its ancient privileges.

Bernhard was born in 1911, three years before the outbreak of the world war which abruptly ended the long rule of Germany's provincial princes and aristocrats. But the Lippe family were more fortunate than most of the German nobility. Though they lost most of their power, they managed to hold on to a comfortable fortune, retaining a castle at Detmold and a stately home at Reckenwalde. The tale that later captivated the world of the pauper-prince who exchanged his rags for the riches of the House of Orange was a romantic legend.

At fourteen he was confirmed in the Lutheran Church. His American biographer, Alden Hatch, records the words of the prince's father on that occasion: 'Beware of vanity, haughtiness and self-conceit; be honest, respect women; meet everybody openly and honestly, and show even the least of people a friendly face. Before all, exercise self-discipline, for only this makes a man a true Christian.'[1] Hatch, writing in 1961, innocent of what the future would hold, adds: 'Prince Bernhard always remembered his father's words, and has tried hard to live by them.'

Bernhard's adolescence and young manhood coincided exactly

[1] Alden Hatch, *H.R.H. Prince Bernhard of the Netherlands* (Harrap, London, 1962).

with the rise to power of Adolf Hitler. He saw the Stormtroopers in action on the streets of Munich, birthplace of Nazism. He was twenty-one when Hitler took power. Bernhard was to claim later that he always loathed and opposed the Nazis – an aristocrat's distaste, perhaps, for the populist politics of a jumped-up corporal – and that he even thought of applying for British citizenship in the 1930s. The fact is that in 1934 he joined the Nazi-sponsored Air Sports League in which the party trained future war pilots. He enrolled under the swastika, he insisted later, only because he wanted to learn to fly and there was no other way. In any case, his membership was short-lived. He was expelled after a few weeks for crash-landing one of the planes in a lake.

He became a law student and while still at university joined Heinrich Himmler's black-shirted SS, this time, according to his later explanations, because he saw no other way of passing examinations which he claimed were made doubly difficult for non-Nazis. 'The extent of my services included the weekly rallies and standing guard occasionally, because if you did that you could have a free garage', he explained. 'We had a lot of fuss and no trouble.' In 1935, his exams duly passed, he resigned. His youthful opportunistic flirtation with Nazism was over.

Bernhard took a job in the Paris office of the German chemical combine I.G. Farben, later famed for its notorious co-operation with Nazi intelligence. (Frank-Fahle, Lockheed's German agent, was also a former Farben man.) A lawyer by training, Bernhard was also a business tycoon by natural instinct. Farben put him through the various departments but it was in sales that he found his *métier*. He was given responsibility for negotiating several barter deals with French Indo-China and took part in other major selling campaigns. 'It gave him a chance', says Hatch, 'to use all his talents – financial acuteness, ability to think fast, persuasiveness, and that God-given charm of which he was completely aware.'

Hatch's hagiographic description of the adult prince's attributes seems now heavy with irony, the more so given the fact that Bernhard himself approved the text. He is credited with 'a reverence for truth' and a rare ability to keep his integrity intact. He 'always wanted to be a businessman', says Hatch, but 'obviously the profit motive which drives most of us to accomplishment is totally lacking'.

Bernhard would perhaps have made the board of Farben had he not taken time off to visit the 1935–6 Winter Olympics in Bavaria. Also holidaying there were Queen Wilhelmina of the Netherlands and her daughter and heir Princess Juliana. Though his title meant little in the Third Reich, Bernhard decided that on such an occasion it was the duty of minor royalty to pay a courtesy visit to major royalty. He charmed Juliana and romance blossomed swiftly. By September 1936 they were engaged. Four months later they were married. Thus did the nominal prince of an obscure German fiefdom enter a new inheritance, one which would give him a powerful voice in the inner councils of Europe.

2

The House of Orange embodies the identity of the Dutch as an independent nation in a way no other royal house can match. William, Prince of Orange had won the independence of the Netherlands by driving out the Spanish in the sixteenth century. Pressed by powerful neighbours, the disparate peoples of Holland, Zealand and Utrecht had struggled hard to hold their nation together. The unifying force was the House of Orange, whose only weakness was an embarrassing infecundity. For a hundred years, succession crisis followed succession crisis. Queen Wilhelmina herself, married to a German duke in 1900, had three miscarriages in ten years before Juliana arrived and survived. But Juliana was the last of the line. And in 1936 she was twenty-six and unattached.

Thus Bernhard was fortunate that the relief of the Dutch people at seeing Juliana safely married overcame whatever misgivings were felt about her husband being a German and an ex-SS man—if only an opportunistic one. And most of what residual doubt remained evaporated when Bernhard did his duty by fathering the next heir, Princess Beatrix, within twelve months.

With the new title Prince of the Netherlands and his rank raised from Serene to Royal Highness, Bernhard settled down to fashion himself into a model Dutchman. He had boldly set two conditions to his marriage. One was that he be allowed to 'build up a sphere of interest outside the constitutional limits of my role', and the other was financial independence. The House of Orange would later have cause to regret its failure to think through the consequences of its too-ready concessions to modernity.

Meanwhile, Bernhard set about learning Dutch (he had courted Juliana in English and German: he still speaks Dutch with a German accent) and picking up the threads of a business career. He had left

Farben for the Nederlandse Handel-Mastschappij, which regulated the economy of the Dutch East Indies, and here he had an opportunity to study the Dutch colonial system and banking. He determined to be a modern, independent, go-getting prince, not just a decorative consort. Commissioned into all three services by the Queen, he wore the uniforms of a Senior Lieutenant in the navy and a Captain both in the Royal Netherlands army and the army of the Dutch colony of Indonesia.

Then came war. As Austria, Czechoslovakia and Poland were engulfed the Dutch reaffirmed their neutrality, and reaffirmed it again when England and France entered the war. Bernhard had better reasons than most for wanting to avoid hostilities since his family was still in Germany, loyal to the Führer. But the Dutch forces were put on alert to defend themselves against a violation of their neutrality by either Germany or England, and Queen Wilhelmina gave her son-in-law the job of personally inspecting all military and naval installations and reporting on their preparedness. Bernhard's inspection tours lasted nearly eight months, at the end of which he was still refusing to entertain the notion of a German invasion. As he put it later, 'In May 1940 I was stupid enough to believe that they would not attack us. Since we did not have very good liaison with the French we foolishly believed that the Maginot line had been extended to the sea. We thought it impregnable. So why should the Nazis attack Holland?'

On the morning of May 10 German armoured columns crossed the Dutch frontier and a squadron of Stuka bombers began bombing The Hague. Bernhard tells how, 'shocked to the core and filled with black rage', he seized a Lewis gun and took up position in the wide treeless court in front of the Noordeinde Palace where he fired burst after unavailing burst at his German kinsmen. It was an emphatic demonstration, perhaps as much to himself as to others, of unflinching faithfulness to his adopted country. But it was clear that Holland could not hope to hold out for more than a few days and the royal family fled to safety in England.

The prince-in-exile became an honorary Air Commodore in the RAF, where he resumed the flying lessons he had begun a few years earlier in Hitler's Air Sports League. 'Has excellent technical ability but must be watched for over-confidence' reported his instructor when he qualified. To his annoyance, his mother-in-law strictly forbade him to fly combat missions, but he later managed to sneak in three flights over France and Italy with the United States Air

Corps, providing himself with false papers and a false name—Wing Commander Gibbs.

Queen Wilhelmina planned a less flamboyant and far more responsible role for the prince. In November 1940 he was appointed Dutch forces head of liaison with the British. In this role he was to meet all the principal *Engelandvaarders*, the growing army of Dutchmen who were slipping through Nazi lines and hitching their way across the North Sea to offer their services in Britain. Some, like the future Lockheed paymaster Frederick Meuser, remained close friends and business partners of the prince for the rest of their lives.

US intelligence noted the prince's success in carving out for himself a clear leadership role in the war effort. An OSS report voiced reservations which would come to seem unusually far-sighted thirty years later:

> Since the beginning of the war Prince Bernhard has shown no reluctance to embark on a year of public service. On the contrary, the greatest danger at the present time is that his personal ambition may lead him to misinterpret the enthusiasm with which he has been received as an evidence of his own personal popularity rather than as a reflection of the esteem in which the royal family is generally held ...
>
> Should the Prince, encouraged by his appraisal of popular sentiment, influence the Queen to overstep the bounds of constitutional propriety, he might endanger not only his position but that of the monarchy as well.

The same report also delved back into Bernhard's work for Farben in Paris, concluding:

> Little is known of this period in his career except that he apparently took the opportunity to enjoy the lighter side of French life and was not too much preoccupied with German politics.

But the secret reservations of the OSS did not prevent the enthusiastic endorsement of Bernhard's leadership by Supreme Allied Commander Eisenhower. As resistance grew in Holland the prince was given charge of the Dutch underground, the so-called Forces of the Interior, and here he really came into his own. The underground was disorganised and divided, protestants quarrelling with catholics, communists with ultra-monarchists. Despite his exceedingly tenuous communication with them—often limited to public radio broadcasts—Bernhard succeeded in unifying and rallying the whole vast, amorphous body of 'free Dutchmen'. Again, some of the resistance leaders became the prince's personal friends for life. One of them was Hans Teengs Gerritsen, who was destined to become Lockheed's agent in the Netherlands after the war.

The heroism of the resistance and the resourcefulness of its royal leader remained a potent legend long after the liberation of the Netherlands. Many local resistance leaders were eventually to become prominent as local mayors and provincial or national politicians. But some were quickly disillusioned when the Utopian dreams which had sustained them in their fight with the Nazis failed to take shape in a grey and hungry post-war world. Late in 1945, in one of the most curious and little-dwelt-upon episodes of recent Dutch history, a group of resistance leaders claiming to be backed by 200,000 followers offered to put Bernhard at the head of a resistance junta. The prince declined to front their proposed coup against his mother-in-law's government but many of the plotters went on to play prominent parts in Dutch life and remained in the prince's powerful inner circle of friends.

Bernhard himself was by now quite simply the most powerful man in the post-war Netherlands. Later in 1945 Queen Wilhelmina appointed him inspector-general of the army and chairman of the chiefs of staff of army, navy and fledgeling air corps. He used his position to force through an expansion of the air corps into an independent, modern, well-equipped air force. Bernhard was never to lose the interest and expertise he acquired at that time in aircraft procurement.

He also resumed his interest in business and finance at a time when the Dutch economy had to be rebuilt virtually from scratch. He joined the boards of the Bank of National Recovery, the State-run steel and coal industries, Fokker Aircraft and the State airline, KLM, where he was one of the most active members of the inner executive which ran the organisation. KLM's president van der Beugel was to say of the prince, in the 1960s:

> P.B's function on the Board is not confined to one subject; he takes an interest in all phases of the business and moves in all of them. As the only expert on aircraft on the Board he is very valuable to us in the selection of aircraft. For example he advised us on the purchase of Douglas DC8 jets, having flown them in America. He also plays a very important part in policy making.[1]

1 Quoted in Alden Hatch, op. cit.

Nor did the unorthodox role of tycoon-prince come to an end when Juliana became Queen on Wilhelmina's abdication in 1948. Bernhard went on to collect no fewer than 300 directorships over a cross-section of Dutch industry. He was dubbed 'the flying Dutchman' and 'the Princely Promoter' when he travelled the world drumming up orders for Dutch industry. In 1951 his personal intervention secured an $80 million order for railway equipment from President Peron of Argentina. The following year the prince was test-flying new Lockheed aircraft in California. While wheeling and dealing as the businessman he had always wanted to be, he also launched the World Wildlife Fund, for which he collected $10 million by forming the '1001 Club' among friends from big business, international politics and royalty, each of whom had to contribute an entry fee of $10,000. He also sponsored the secretive Bilderberg conferences of politicians who shared his own fiercely anti-Communist views. He did all this, and more, on a State allowance of roughly $300,000 a year.

By force of personality as well as by his overlapping offices, Prince Bernhard was strategically placed to influence decisions and guide policy. Complacently, the Dutch saw no dangers: it was inconceivable to them that the Queen's husband could abuse his powers. Prime minister H. E. de Quay spoke for the nation when he told the prince's biographer: 'He uses his influence well. He gets things done without ever going too far.'

3

Bernhard's first encounter with Lockheed nearly cost him his life. Early in the war he flew a Lockheed–12 from the United States to the Dutch West Indies, landing at Curaçao. But he was two hours ahead of his expected arrival time and Dutch and American troops opened fire as he approached the airstrip. The Model 12 wasn't made for dodging shells and Bernhard had no choice but to fly doggedly through the flak and hope he would be recognised before he was hit. He was lucky to survive what he later described wryly as 'a 21-gun salute with live ammunition'.

After the war Bernhard met Robert Gross on one of his world tours and throughout the 1950s the two men maintained regular contact. The Dutch proved good customers for Lockheed. But the prince's contacts with other US aircraft companies – Douglas on the civil side and Northrop on the military—were no less friendly or fruitful. The prince was by no means a one-company man: he foraged wherever there looked to be some advantage for KLM and the Royal Netherlands air force.

In the early stages of the competition for the new NATO multi-role fighter-bomber, Bernhard did not back the Starfighter. His preference was for the Northrop N–156F, prototype of the hugely successful F–5, and he rooted hard for it. Throughout 1958 he conducted a lengthy correspondence with US secretary for the air force Donald Quarles urging the Americans to throw their weight behind a plan to standardise the air forces of European NATO countries, implying that US assistance would result in the choice of a US plane. At the same time, presumably in liaison with the prince, Dutch defence minister C. Staf wrote to NATO secretary-general Paul Henri Spaak putting similar arguments for standardisation with the Northrop fighter.

Spaak, however, declared himself sceptical of any far-reaching scheme of standardisation. The British and French, he thought (rightly), would support their own industries' products, and the West Germans were already set on the Lockheed Starfighter. So Bernhard reluctantly concentrated his efforts on securing RNAF support for the Northrop plane. He again wrote to Quarles, among others in the US administration, asking him to use his best endeavours to get the defense department to keep the Netherlands supplied with all the latest information on the N–156F. He was clearly looking for ammunition with which to wage war on Northrop's opponents in the Netherlands.

In March 1959 the formal choice by Strauss of the Starfighter, though entirely expected, weakened the Bernhard–Northrop camp, and two months later a change of government in the Netherlands removed the pro-Northrop defence minister Staf and replaced him with the less committed S. H. Visser. Bernhard kept closely in touch with Northrop president T. V. Jones and the company's European representatives, even going so far as to advise them on how they should approach the new Dutch government. The prince's perseverance on Northrop's behalf was striking, given that it now directly contradicted his declared belief in European co-operation on aircraft procurement. Even after the decisive rejection of the N–156F in September, the prince arranged for the company's European chief, Geoffrey Parsons, to meet Visser for a last-ditch attempt to have the decision overturned. The attempt failed.

Bernhard was never to lose his strong attachment to the Northrop fighter and six years later he was finally successful in playing midwife to an RNAF order for F–5s (see chapter 8). But the elimination of Northrop in September 1959, along with the Republic F–105 and the Convair F–106, which were judged too heavy and expensive, left only the Starfighter and the Dassault Mirage III in the field. Bernhard shifted his support to Lockheed, whose bandwaggon was already on the roll. Lockheed delegations headed by Fred Meuser had been pressing the RNAF; and Strauss, anxious to enrol the Netherlands and Belgium in multinational production, was applying diplomatic pressure. But the decisive influence belonged not to Meuser, Strauss or Prince Bernhard but to the US defense department, which agreed to give the Netherlands (and Belgium) twenty-five planes from the military aid budget. Dassault could not compete with what they bitterly called 'Yankee bribery', and Lockheed were awarded the contract.[1]

4

Prince Bernhard's apparent lack of decisive influence on the Starfighter sale renders all the more intriguing the circumstances in which Lockheed decided or agreed in 1960 to reward him with one of the biggest single pay-offs in commercial history.

The trail of events which led up to it began in the last quarter of 1959. The Dutch government had still to choose between the Starfighter and the Mirage when Lockheed's executive vice-president, Dan Haughton, got wind of a strange proposal from Fred Meuser to Robert Gross. The proposal was that Lockheed should make a gift to Prince Bernhard of one of the company's new executive aircraft, the Jetstar, then considered the last word in private flying comfort and performance.

Some time around the middle of November, Haughton and another rising star of the corporation, his newly appointed group vice-president, Carl Kotchian, met with the Gross brothers, Robert and Courtlandt, in Robert's Burbank office expressly to discuss

1 The Netherlands actually hoped for 100 free planes under the US support programme, to which they proposed to add 100 by direct purchase. When the US refused to budge beyond twenty-five and made even this lesser offer conditional on Italy being included in the Starfighter consortium, the Netherlands reduced their purchase order from 100 to 95.

Meuser's proposal. There is no record of what was said but it is clear that Robert Gross was in favour while Haughton was against. Meuser had argued that for the much-travelled prince to be seen in a Jetstar would be valuable publicity for Lockheed. Haughton apparently argued on the other hand that Bernhard's usefulness to the company would be diminished if his connection were indiscreetly over-advertised. Kotchian tossed in a practical problem: the difficulty of transferring title of the plane without a commercial transaction going through the books. Gross's wishes nevertheless prevailed, as they always did at Lockheed, and Kotchian was saddled with the job of devising the means. He was still working on the problem early in 1960 when Meuser indicated from Geneva that the prince, who had just been presented with a Fokker Friendship, was no longer interested in a Jetstar but would not be averse to an alternative earnest of goodwill.

The alternative agreed on was $1 million — roughly the value of a Jetstar and, as it happened, the equivalent of the total commission payable on all Lockheed products to be supplied to the Netherlands in the next three years.

On September 2 Robert Gross met the prince secretly in Rome to discuss discreet and secure channels of payment. Both parties must have known that any kind of leak would lead to a hugely damaging scandal. Back in Burbank three weeks later, Gross sent the prince a telegram arranging for Bernhard to meet Lockheed's legal counsel, Roger Bixby Smith. The meeting duly took place at the royal palace of Soestdijk, the 'White House', on September 30.

Meanwhile, Meuser was tapping a tried and trusted channel, his old friend Hubert Weisbrod. He arranged a new 'consultancy' contract between Lockheed and Weisbrod, whereby the $1 million intended for the prince would be accounted for as 'commission paid in advance' to Weisbrod. The novel feature of the contract was its stipulation that the money would be paid not directly to Weisbrod himself, the nominal beneficiary, but into a numbered account, particulars of which would be notified to him. Gross evidently approved these arrangements.

So too did Prince Bernhard, at least according to Bixby Smith as cited in the findings of the Dutch 'Commissie van Drie' which later investigated these events. Smith reported to Robert Gross that 'he was told by HRH during the conversation at Soestdijk which took place on 30 September 1960 that the money should be paid through Weisbrod'. The prince also indicated the next move. Smith was to present himself at the Hotel Dolder in Zürich on October 3, 1960, where he would be contacted by a Mr Pantchoulidzew who — again according to Smith's account and the commission's findings — would 'give instructions about the bank account into which the sums of money transferred through Mr. Weisbrod were to be paid'.

Colonel A. E. Pantchoulidzew turned out to be a more bizarre emissary than Bixby Smith can ever have expected. A White Russian émigré, he had been part of the Bernhard household ever since, before the war, he had moved in as 'house-friend' to Bernhard's mother, whom he was rumoured to have secretly married. Whether or not the elderly refugee from Moscow was actually the prince's stepfather, he was evidently a loyal friend. He presented himself at the agreed time and place and handed Smith a slip of paper bearing his own name and the number of a bank account. These details were passed on by Smith to Weisbrod. Thus the conduit for the $1 million agreed between all parties was Lockheed–Weisbrod–Pantchoulidzew — and finally, of course, so far as Lockheed's intentions were concerned, Bernhard.

The first stage payment of $300,000 was duly paid out in October 1960 over the signature of Robert Gross himself. A further $300,000 followed in 1961, authorised by Courtlandt Gross who had become company chairman on Robert's death. The remaining $400,000 was paid out the following year in three instalments over the signatures of Dudley Brown, senior vice-president for finance, and Frank L. Frain, the company treasurer. 'On the basis of these facts,' the Dutch commission concluded, 'it could and indeed had to be assumed by Lockheed that the money intended for the prince had indeed reached him.'

The Dutch investigations followed in the wake of the Church Committee and SEC hearings of 1975–6. Haughton and Kotchian told the Congressional and SEC investigators that the payments were not meant as a reward for services rendered or to be rendered but were intended 'to create a favourable climate' for Lockheed's products in the Netherlands. According to Kotchian, the payments were made 'from a general goodwill and helpfulness on various programmes that were going on in that area'.[1] It was 'something we could give him [Bernhard] in the spirit of friendship and goodwill and that type of thing'.[2] Kotchian 'assumed' that the prince had

1 Church Committee hearings, February 6, 1976.
2 Church Committee secret session, February 5, 1976.

influence in the purchasing process[1] and conceded that 'hopefully we would make sales'. This led to the following exchange:

Senator Church: Wouldn't you call that a bribe?

Mr Kotchian: I think, sir, that as my understanding of a bribe is a *quid pro quo* for a specific item in return; and I would categorise this more as a gift. But I don't want to quibble with you, sir.

Senator Church: All right, we won't quibble on that. You gave the money because you expected a certain favourable condition?

Mr Kotchian: Yes sir.

Senator Church: In connection with the possible sale of Lockheed aircraft to the Dutch Government?

Mr Kotchian: Yes sir.[2]

The question remains: precisely what was it Lockheed hoped to buy? The obvious assumption that the million-dollar payment was an inducement to the prince to switch his support to the Starfighter doesn't stand up, since it was clear to all, by the time the Jetstar idea was mooted, that the Netherlands would choose the Starfighter with or without princely intervention; and indeed the contract was securely signed by the time it was decided to convert the Jetstar gift into cash. It is possible that the long personal relationship between Gross and Bernhard, extending over a period in which KLM had bought Constellations and Elektras, and the Royal Netherlands navy a fleet of P–2V Neptune antisubmarine patrol planes, had resulted in a cumulative obligation towards the prince, in which case the million dollars might be seen as a thank-you gift, an acknowledgment of a variety of services rendered. But although some support for this view may be adduced from Kotchian's vague recollection that the payments had been entered in Lockheed's books as commission on Neptune sales, the most likely explanation of the payment is that Lockheed wanted to buy the prince's support in future commercial and military sales campaigns.

There is another possible explanation which would probably have seemed beyond the bounds of credibility to US Congressional investigators or to later Dutch investigators but cannot be wholly dismissed in the light of subsequent revelations about secret CIA subventions

1 SEC hearings, April 8, 1976.
2 Church Committee hearings, February 6, 1976.

to foreign heads of state and major politicians. Could the $1 million have been a part of the Agency's world-wide largesse in the 1950s and 1960s? Was Lockheed the conduit for CIA payments to the prince, as it has been suggested other corporations have been?[1] Bernhard's biographer reminds us that CIA chief Bedell Smith was 'one of the prince's closest friends' (as was his successor Allen Dulles) and a backer of the Bilderberg conferences. The notion is tantalising. Lockheed would make an ideal conduit for the CIA, apparently independent and above reproach. The subvention would be well disguised as sales commission. And Lockheed (or perhaps Gross alone, without the knowledge or agreement of his company colleagues) would be glad to help out in a plan where national and corporate interest so neatly coincided – for it was clearly of incalculable advantage to Lockheed to have the prince on the payroll, obligated to the company for ever after ... But speculation is no substitute for evidence, and of that there is none.

More intriguing is why the prince may have wanted the money. Why would the consort of one of the richest heads of state in the world[2] be prepared to risk his position so recklessly? Part of the answer may lie in his determination to be financially independent, and another in the heavy commitments he had undertaken in connection with the World Wildlife Fund, the Bilderberg conferences and other such grandiose schemes. Hints of private commitments of a quite different kind appeared in the Dutch press, linking the royal taste for the 'wild life' with his much gossiped-about friendship with Helen 'Pussy' Grinda, glamorous jet-setting sister of an international tennis star. It was even rumoured that, as a result of a liaison with a 'Paris popette', the prince had a secret illegitimate family to support.

But most intriguing of all is the fact that, even after Lockheed had been forced by Church and the SEC to name the 'high Dutch Government official' on their payroll, Bernhard continued to deny the facts and proclaim his innocence. His story, as told to the 'Commissie van Drie', was that he had turned down the unsolicited offer of a Jetstar and received not a penny of the million dollars. He claimed that the money – all of it – had always been intended not for himself but for Fred Meuser in settlement of a commission dispute.

1 See for instance *Wall Street Journal*, March 1, 1977, on Boeing.

2 Unlike, for instance, the British royal family, whose 'property' belongs largely to the State, the House of Orange has immense private resources estimated to run into billions of dollars.

The prince claimed he had interceded for Meuser with Lockheed, and therefore felt able to suggest to Meuser that 'a small number of people, mostly mutual friends who were in difficulties', should share in the 'windfall'. In support of the prince's story, Meuser claimed he had spent $100,000 on anonymous gifts. He has not been prepared to name the recipients.

Again, the prince claimed he could remember nothing of Pantchoulidzew's being involved and contended that this was 'incomprehensible' and 'a complete surprise' to him. Meuser's story was that he had hired Pantchoulidzew, unknown to the prince, at the behest of Robert Gross who wanted another intermediary to be involved, allegedly (and obscurely) as a means of keeping the whole transaction secret from the Lockheed board. Understandably, the 'Commissie van Drie' found this 'completely unbelievable' and 'difficult to take seriously'. It noted that Meuser had declined to open his books to full inspection, pleading the complications of Swiss banking and secrecy law—a consideration which was hardly accidental.

And where did the money—the $900,000 remaining after Meuser's anonymous charitable dispensations—end up? None of it has been traced beyond the secret account opened in Pantchoulidzew's name but unless one is to suppose that the prince was simply bent on rewarding his elderly retainer by making him a very rich man, it must be assumed that the account was controlled, in the last resort, by Bernhard himself. That, clearly, was Lockheed's intention: they were buying a prince, not one of his courtiers. But the slender fiction of establishing the account in Pantchoulidzew's name imbued the scheme with 'deniability' and enabled the prince to disclaim that he had ever received a penny of Lockheed money.

What the good servant Pantchoulidzew thought of it all we shall never know. He died in modest circumstances in 1965, wholly loyal and altogether silent.

5

During the three years 1960–2 over which the million dollars intended for Bernhard was paid out, the ties between Lockheed and the prince were subtly strengthened by organisational changes within the corporation's sales structure. These began in 1961 when Meuser proposed a new sales agent for the Netherlands. His name was

Teengs Gerritsen and he was something of a national hero: a former Olympic swimming champion, international soccer player, and during the war a much-decorated resistance leader who was captured by the Germans and allegedly used in medical experiments which permanently affected his health. In 1961 he was leader of an organisation of ex-resistance fighters – and one of Prince Bernhard's closest friends.[1]

At first Lockheed resisted Gerritsen's appointment. A memo from Burbank to Meuser dated May 15, 1961, put it, revealingly, like this:

> We do not believe that [Gerritsen] should be moved into the status of an agent since our major sales relationships for everything in the Netherlands are handled between Mr Robert Gross and Prince Bernard when this sort of handling can be most effective.

But Robert Gross's death in September was to change that very quickly. By October Gerritsen was installed as Lockheed's official agent in the Netherlands. And by one account at least it was only a matter of days before he was entrusted with a delicate and highly secret mission.

The story comes from Ernest Hauser, Strauss's appointee in Lockheed's Koblenz office, balefully observing the feverish activity all around him and gleefully recording the more delectable shenanigans in his pocket diary.

Trouble was brewing up, according to Hauser, over Lockheed's Engineering Change Proposals. Because of the complex multinational production arrangements for the Starfighter, with assembly in Germany, Belgium, Holland and Italy, it was necessary to get four-power approval of these ECPs. Germany, as Hauser had noted wonderingly while recording his dealings with Strauss, seemed content to rubber-stamp Lockheed's proposals as they came up. But the Dutch took more convincing. And in October 1961 the head of the NATO Starfighter management office (NASMO) was a Dutch air force officer, Col. H. K. Stockla.

Stockla met worried Lockheed executives in Bonn on October 21 and made his position clear. He was backed by Col. Henry, his opposite number for Belgium. Hauser, who was present, wrote in his diary:

---

1 Alden Hatch acknowledged Gerritsen's assistance in the preparation of Bernhard's official biography.

Stockla RNAF and Henry BAF decline to accept costs ECPs not applicable to their Air Forces. German Air Force must either foot bill all costs or forego ECP.

But the Germans showed little inclination to pay the Dutch and Belgian share of a costly programme running to a total of ninety-three ECPs. Not only did Lockheed stand to lose a substantial bonus on the basic sales contract, but their agents in the field stood to lose their extra commission Hauser describes in his diary entry for October 24 how Lockheed's men moved to break the deadlock by playing their newly acquired ace, Bernhard's friend Teengs Gerritsen. Archi Folden flew to The Hague for a meeting with Gerritsen and the Lockheed man in charge of technical liaison with the Dutch work group, Art Johansen. Folden 'explained Stockla's stand', says Hauser, and Gerritsen was asked to take the matter straight to Bernhard, the one man with sufficient authority to persuade or over-rule Stockla. Gerritsen agreed, according to Hauser, and it was arranged for an unspecified payment to 'B' to be put through Meuser's account at the Schweizerischer Bank Verein, St Moritz. 'B', says Hauser, was shorthand for Bernhard.

Whatever Gerritsen in fact said to the prince (he disputes Hauser's story in its entirety) and the prince to Stockla, the issue was not quickly resolved. It rumbled on for many months. On November 26 an exasperated Hauser wrote:

> To Geneva to meet the Bernhard agency people ... Bernhardt [*sic*] sits right in there like a leech. I do the work and he gets the payoff.

A month later another problem surfaces, complicating an already confused state of affairs. Hauser records a dispute between Gerritsen and Lockheed's agent in Belgium, J. P. Bonsang, over division of commission between themselves and Bernhard. Hauser wearily noted the squabble on December 18 and added graphically: 'Gerritsen has HRH hanging on his ass and he wants all, the bastard.'

Four months later, on April 23, 1962, Hauser wrote again:

> Am seeing Bonsang today. Hope I can convince him to keep cool. If he does he can help a lot. After all there's got to be a C-130 deal coming up in a few years ...

On June 26, after noting with satisfaction that the German CSU payments were at last running smoothly, he added: 'Only pmt. [payment] problem now remains the Netherlands.' And finally, on

July 29: 'The Netherlands/Belgium commission squabble. HRH is really pushing, at least [according to] Meuser.'

And there the story is left hanging. There are no more diary entries on Bernhard or the agents' wrangle, and five months and eight inconsequential entries later the diary itself was discontinued. 'My superiors caught me writing notes and asked, "What the hell are you doing?"' says Hauser. 'That's when I stopped.'

But Hauser filled in the gaps when he testified to the Church Committee – testimony which was given in secret 'executive session'. He had no doubt that the eventual decision of the Dutch (and eventually the Belgians) to accept the ECPs was a direct result of Prince Bernhard's exertions on Lockheed's behalf. The pay-offs, he said, were made by the Meuser – Weisbrod route. In his subsequent interview with the author for Granada TV, Hauser claimed that the prince had received Lockheed pay-offs for sales before the ECP issue ever came up, mentioning KLM's purchases of Constellations and Super-Constellations in the 1940s and 1950s (for which there is no independent corroborative evidence). Hauser claimed that the prince had collected a total of $2 million from Lockheed by 1962. Both Lockheed and Bernhard, he claimed, 'recognised that they were dealing in a grey area which was a little delicate'.

As with his allegations about Strauss and the CSU, Hauser's version of Lockheed's relationship with the prince met with instant and angry denials. Lockheed said Hauser's testimony was 'untrue' and Gerritsen – no longer Lockheed's agent but still under contract as a consultant – said the idea that Bernhard would accept pay-offs was 'ridiculous'.

Meuser said he had never paid Bernhard a penny (no word of the $1 million deal of 1960 had yet surfaced). From the royal palace at The Hague, the prince issued a guarded statement saying, 'No one has found any evidence to support these allegations.'

What, then, should we make of Hauser's uncorroborated story? Clearly it must be assessed on its own merits and tested as to its consistency. The Church Committee did just that, beginning with the diary. When the Committee staff were first given sight of the little black book in September 1975 they suspected a forgery. Two staffmen were despatched to Europe to check out the diary entry by entry so far as was possible after a fourteen-year time-lapse. On their return they reported that they had not been able to find a single inconsistency. If the diary was the hasty concoction in 1975 of a man with a grudge against his former employers, it demonstrated a phenomenal memory and grasp of detail.

Nevertheless, the *Wall Street Journal* decided to have its own tests done on the diary before running Hauser's story. Staff reporter Jerry Landauer sent the diary to documents expert Lyndal L. Shaneyfelt. After testing the paper and the ink, Shaneyfelt concluded: ' ... It is my opinion that the diary was prepared during the normal course of activities for the period indicated for the dated entries and was not fabricated at a recent date.'

So the basic document on which Hauser's account rests would seem to stand. What about the man himself? Lockheed's assessment of their employee during his time with them was wholly enthusiastic. William Perreault, then a divisional director of export sales and later vice-president in charge of public relations, wrote in December 1963 of Hauser's 'intelligence, energy, initiative and enthusiasm' in connection with a company campaign (unsuccessful, as it turned out) to sell C–130s to Germany. But five months later these good relations evidently soured. Hauser's story is that he had a heart attack, and Lockheed, terrified that while under sedation he might let slip some remark that would reveal the pay-off arrangements, tried to transfer him hastily back to the US. He didn't want to go, and a row followed, as a result of which he left Lockheed to set up his own aircraft spare parts business. Lockheed was evidently at pains to reassure Franz Josef Strauss that his friend's departure would not harm relations between the corporation and the head of the CSU. In a letter which seems to suggest that Hauser might still have a liaison role to play, perhaps in transmitting sensitive messages, Lockheed chairman Courtlandt Gross wrote to Strauss in May 1964:

We are phasing out some of the activity of the Koblenz office. Mr Hauser has been offered a job with our California Company but, as stated, cannot accept. I have no doubt that he has some worthwhile and constructive recommendations which could guide us in our future European activities, particularly in Germany, and we would be most happy to receive these observations.

Whatever else the letter may mean, it clearly supports Hauser's claims, central to his whole story, that he occupied a special position between Lockheed and Strauss. Why else would the corporation chairman trouble to write in such terms to the former West German defence minister who, though he had left the ministry, clearly remained a formidable power in the land?

It is when we examine Hauser's career after he left Lockheed that inconsistencies begin to appear. First, his relationship with Strauss evidently deteriorated sharply. There is a chilling note in a diary kept by Strauss's assistant, Marcel Hepp, which records Hauser as threatening suicide and Strauss replying: 'That's the best thing that guy could do.' Then in 1971 Hauser fell foul of the Bonn courts. A firm called Heliparts was unable to meet Hauser's bills, and Hauser illegally arranged for funds due to Heliparts from their customers to be paid directly into his own account. For this he received a twelve months' suspended sentence for fraud and forgery, despite his vigorous assertion that he had done no more than bend the rules to get his own money back.

After that sad and damaging trauma he moved back to the US, relocating his spare parts business in Phoenix, Arizona. Then in the summer of 1975, as the Church Committee began its hearings, Hauser wrote to the *Wall Street Journal* indicating that he had documentary evidence of the kind of improper payments Church was investigating. He also told his story in secret session to the Church Committee and to the SEC. The substance of his testimony to Church, was published in the *Journal* and Hauser was thereupon beseiged by reporters. This meant that he was asked to tell his story several times, further testing his consistency and the accuracy of his memory. It also meant that he was under pressure to come up with new revelations, new evidence, new documents. Everyone wanted a scoop.

How did he meet these tests? There are no significant contradictions in any of his versions of the story, though he did allow himself to elaborate somewhat on his official testimony, putting actual (and improbable) figures to the alleged pay-offs ($10 million, he said, to the CSU, and 'about $2 million' to Bernhard). For the Granada TV interview which was to carry his detailed allegations round the world he received no fee. His veracity remained unchallenged—until the strange affair of the Aalbertsberg memorandum.

In 1976 the German magazine *Der Stern* published a Lockheed document which seemed to provide vital corroboration from within the corporation of Hauser's allegations against Bernhard. Dated May 23, 1962, the typewritten memo 'to A. M. Folden from C. H. Roha' read:

Subj: Verification Meuser payment—Netherlands. Have received telefone confirmation Art Johansen LCC Schipol, that he witnessed transfer by F. Meuser of $873,327 to G. Aalbertsberg for

Bernhard. This covered 143 each model 68.10.19 to include serial D–8834.

The memo was said to have been given to *Der Stern* by Ernest Hauser, which raised a host of questions. Why had he not produced it earlier, notably in his testimony before the Church Committee and the SEC? How had it come to be in his possession? Aalbertsberg turned out to have been public relations chief for Fokker from 1959 to 1961 (but not in 1963, the date of the memo). Why should Meuser use him as a conduit for payments intended for Bernhard when, on the evidence of Hauser's own story, Meuser had a direct line to Bernhard's bank account? Why, anyway, transfer so large a sum in such a way, choosing a public airport like Schipol as venue for the deed?

There were other discrepancies. The typeface used did not match up with any other known memo issuing from the Koblenz office. The initials LCC, for Lockheed California Company, seemed anachronistic since the division was known in 1963 as CALAC. The Netherlands had bought 138 Starfighters (including two-seater trainers), not 143, and the serial number D–8834 matched neither the planes produced on licence in the Netherlands (D–8013 to D–8350) nor those provided by Lockheed (D–6650 to D–6700).

The Dutch 'Commissie van Drie', in its own limited investigation, concluded bluntly that the Aalbertsberg memorandum was 'a forgery put in circulation by Mr Hauser', and from that proceeded to the view that 'the authenticity of Mr Hauser's diary, in the sense that all of it was indeed written on or about the dates stated, is doubted'. Of Hauser's allegations in general, the commission reported: 'Like the documents on which he claims they are based, they prove largely to be incorrect and to be based on false premises.' There was 'no indication at all that any irregularities took place' in the 'relatively small' number of ECPs in the Starfighter programme, and 'no sign of pressure from any quarter'. Hauser's estimate that the ECP programme was worth 'a hundred million dollars and more' was a considerable exaggeration, and there was 'no indication at all that Mr. H. J. Teengs Gerritsen played any part in decision-making on the ECPs'.

The commission's widely publicised strictures all but discredited Hauser, who complains with some justice that he had difficulty in getting his own robust responses published. He says:

During my meeting with them they asked me about this memorandum and I told them that I considered it probably a forgery and that I had never seen it. To ascribe this to me is utter gall. After the Committee's report was published I sent a telegram to their Washington attorneys but was told that the Committee had been disbanded and other than noting my observation, nothing in the matter of correction could be done. A very amazing way of dealing with the truth![1]

That the Aalbertsberg memo is a forgery is certain. That Hauser was involved is unproven. That he emerges as less than a star witness against Bernhard is undeniable, but through the confusion this much remains clear: Hauser *did* have a special relationship with Strauss, as his appointee within Lockheed; this special relationship was never explained satisfactorily by Strauss, the CSU or the West German defence ministry; and without Hauser's charges against Bernhard, gilded as the lily may have been, it is unlikely that Lockheed's secret relationship with the prince would ever have come to the attention of the Church Committee, the SEC or the 'Commissie van Drie'. The importance of Hauser's testimony lay, ultimately, not in its disputed detail but in the simple historic fact that it began the process by which the prince was investigated and ultimately disgraced.

6

By the end of 1962 Prince Bernhard, according to Haughton and Kotchian, had received at least $1 million from Lockheed, excluding Hauser's ECP payments, or considerably more including them. The corporation had good reason to suppose that when it called on the prince's assistance again it would not call in vain. It did call six years later, and more money changed hands. Once again the pay-off was preceded by a long and complex but fascinating run-up.

The Starfighter programme was not the only multinational manufacturing arrangement to emerge from the rush of enthusiasm for a joint European aircraft production plan in the late 1950s. On February 20, 1959, the Dutch, German and French governments agreed to set up joint production facilities between Fokker, Dornier and Breguet respectively for the manufacture of a new naval patrol aircraft, the Breguet-designed Atlantique. Belgium also joined the consortium, the management of which was entrusted to a NATO

1 Hauser, letter to the author, May 13, 1977.

maritime patrol aircraft steering committee on which the US was also represented.

But in one vital respect the arrangement was very different from the Starfighter programme. With the Starfighter, the countries in the consortium committed themselves to purchase the plane their factories were making under Lockheed's licence. But with the Atlantique, the consortium was building more or less speculatively. There was no commitment by the participating countries to purchase a single Atlantique for their own navies.

The arrangement was all the odder in that the NATO steering committee managing production was also responsible for negotiating sales. The intriguing result was that French procurement officials, when they decided they did want to buy, found themselves face to face across the table with a sales team which included officials from their own country. Similarly, German defence ministry officials found themselves negotiating with other officials from their own ministry on secondment to the steering committee.

To complicate matters further, the Dutch let it be known that they themselves did not expect to be buying any naval patrol planes, and if they did they would shop around for them, possibly buying in the US. This announcement caused angry consternation within the steering committee. How could they be expected to make a successful sales pitch for a plane which was publicly spurned by one of the members of the manufacturing consortium? For the Netherlands' representatives on the steering committee, of course, and for Fokker, who were making the Atlantique on Dutch soil, their government's attitude was doubly embarrassing.

Intense diplomatic pressure eventually persuaded the Dutch to modify their position and in June 1961 they told their French, German and Belgian colleagues that, although they were not prepared to place an immediate order, they would buy the Atlantique 'in due course', as and when replacement of their current naval patrol planes—mainly Lockheed P-2V Neptunes—became both necessary and financially possible. Four years later, in February 1965, when a firm order seemed as far away as ever, the Dutch were persuaded by their increasingly agitated partners to repeat the promise.

Two more years passed and the long life of the Neptunes began to draw to a close. The projected withdrawal of the Royal Netherlands navy aircraft carrier HMS *Karel Doorman* in 1968 also necessitated a modernisation of the fleet's air arm. On July 4, 1967, the ministry of defence announced its intention to purchase a new generation of naval patrol aircraft. But in spite of the promises of 1961 and 1965 it now declared itself bound to put the contract out to competitive tender. Accordingly, it invited offers not only from the NATO steering committee for the Atlantique but also from Lockheed for its own successor to the Neptune, the P–3 Orion.

This naturally caused more consternation in the steering committee, whose Dutch members lost no time in mounting a powerful campaign, backed by the labour movement (mindful of Fokker's interest and its effect on employment) in favour of the Atlantique. But Lockheed countered with an offer of their own. They would build only a proportion of the Orions the Dutch needed and the Dutch aircraft industry could build the rest on licence.

A flurry of correspondence and activity followed. Teengs Gerritsen was active on Lockheed's behalf. In October there were technical demonstrations of both the Atlantique and the Orion. Then, at the end of the month, Lockheed picked up a rumour that the decision would be made as early as December 22. This was bad news, since it left them insufficient time to work out the complex finances of their promised offset programme. To put in a competitive tender for December 22 meant that they must guess and gamble, with several million dollars at stake.

There was another alternative. On December 16, just six days before the rumoured deadline, three Lockheed executives, including the corporation's vice-president for legal affairs, Roger Bixby Smith, met Prince Bernhard secretly in Paris. Smith, it will be remembered, had played an important part in arranging the transfer of the million dollars in 1960. This time Bernhard was asked to intervene with the Dutch ministry of defence on Lockheed's behalf (and, incidentally, against the interests of Fokker, of which he was a director). Specifically he was asked to secure a postponement of the day of decision.

Bernhard told them no decision would be made before the new year. It now seems certain that it never had been the Dutch government's intention to conclude matters by December 22, and that Lockheed's intelligence was faulty. But, whether or not it was his deliberate intention to do so, Prince Bernhard left Lockheed with the firm impression that his own royal intervention was behind the invaluable postponement.

The delay gave Lockheed good time to get their complex calculations right. The problem was that any arrangement which allowed the Dutch to build a proportion of Orions on licence was less profitable than a simple, direct sale from the US. The Dutch wanted to maximise the home-built proportion, Lockheed to minimise it. By the spring of 1968 it became clear that the sums wouldn't come right: Lockheed couldn't satisfy Dutch demands, *and* underbid the Atlantique, *and* come in with a profit. At least, not without help.

Lockheed turned for help to the US government, and got it. The US liked Europe to buy American. The Dutch were told that the US was prepared to place 25 per cent of the price of the order as offset procurement in the Netherlands if an order for the P–3B Orion were forthcoming before the end of 1968.

In May, after a detailed evaluation of both planes, top navy officers recorded in a secret report their slight preference for the Lockheed Orion over the Breguet Atlantique, in respect both of flight properties and logistics. At the end of the month Prince Bernhard is said to have written a letter to Lockheed saying that the Orion's chances looked good.[1] He is said also to have suggested that they would look better still if Lockheed used its influence to extend KLM's landing rights in the US. But Lockheed could hardly help on that one: they supplied, and hoped to continue to supply, KLM's competitors.

Nevertheless, despite all this activity—the public intervention of the US government, the private preference of the Dutch navy and the behind-the-scenes influence of the prince—the Dutch council of ministers resolved towards the end of June to put political considerations first and honour their promises of 1961 and 1965 to buy the Atlantique. To have bought American in preference to the French-designed plane would have enraged de Gaulle and plunged the delicate mechanisms of European co-operation into chaos. So, after a last round of negotiations with the NATO steering committee, the government announced its decision on July 5.

But that wasn't the end of the matter, particularly for Prince Bernhard. Immediately after his government's decision he wrote to Lockheed pointing out that it required ratification by a parliamentary majority. He would do his best, he promised, to try to point out to members of the Dutch parliament that the government's choice was mistaken.

Carl Kotchian, by then Lockheed president and number two to Dan Haughton,[2] seems to have read Bernhard's letter as a hint that

1 The letter is referred to by the 'Commissie van Drie', but it is not quoted verbatim, nor is it clear to whom it was sent.
2 Haughton succeeded Courtlandt Gross as chairman of the board in 1967 and Kotchian thereupon succeeded Haughton as president.

Lockheed might help him find the means of changing MPs' minds. He immediately despatched Roger Bixby Smith and Edwinston Robbins, deputy sales director for Europe, to Annecy, where the prince was staying. There, apparently in accordance with Kotchian's instructions, Prince Bernhard was offered $500,000 to get the Dutch decision reversed. To the surprise and bewilderment of Smith and Robbins, the prince refused. He had now taken soundings and concluded that parliamentary approval for the Atlantique was inevitable. The decision could not now be altered.

What followed was one of the most bizarre episodes in the entire Lockheed story. The prince had refused a half-million-dollar bribe because he could not deliver the required *quid pro quo*. But Kotchian was so impressed with his refusal that, 'to show his appreciation of the prince's honesty', he offered $100,000 just the same. Smith and Robbins were again despatched to Europe where they met Bernhard over a round of golf on the 'De Pan' links near Utrecht on September 7. A letter of thanks from Kotchian was handed to the prince, to which he replied on September 13. Neither letter of course referred to the $100,000. The offer was made verbally during the course of the game. Smith and Robbins noted that the prince did not decline it, from which they concluded he would accept.

It remained to find a secure means of transferring the money, one that would not show in Lockheed's books or Bernhard's. Weisbrod could no longer be used: he had by now left Lockheed for Northrop (where we shall renew acquaintance with him in due course). An alternative route had to be worked out. The task was once again allotted to legal affairs vice-president Roger Bixby Smith. Smith contacted an American lawyer, Charles Torem, who was working as a partner in the Paris office of the international law firm Coudert Frères. Torem agreed to open a Swiss bank account with Crédit Suisse in Geneva in the name of 'Victor Baarn', described as 'a Swiss lawyer'.

'Victor Baarn' was a fictitious name. In October 1968 Donald M. Wilder, vice-president marine sales, Lockheed-California (and from 1964 to 1968 Ernest Hauser's successor as customer-relations manager on the Starfighter programme) authorised the issue of a cashier's cheque for $100,000 in 'Victor Baarn's' name. On the basis of this authorisation, instructions were given to Crédit Suisse to write a bearer cheque and deposit it in an office in Geneva. This was done, and the cheque was duly cashed.

Bernhard told the 'Commissie van Drie' that he 'couldn't remember' being offered or receiving this sum, and the commission allowed the possibility that, despite the telling sequence of events and the clear intention of Lockheed, the $100,000 collected from Geneva by 'Victor Baarn' somehow failed to find its way to the royal pocket. Given the prince's continuing and vociferous denials that he has ever taken Lockheed's money, the commission perhaps had little diplomatic choice but to leave open the possibility that the cash had suffered a hijack on its last lap. But disinterested observers would probably consider the possibility a thin one.

As for the so-called Coudert Frères account, it continued to play an intriguing part in Lockheed's overseas sales and intelligence-gathering programme. For Roger Bixby Smith, Lockheed's legal counsel, architect of the Coudert conduit and mastermind of the corporation's secret communications line with Bernhard, the 'off-the-books' arrangement coincided with an important change in his role. In 1968 he left Lockheed's salaried employment to take up residence in Paris, and in 1972 joined Coudert Frères as a partner, only to make a dramatic re-entry into our story in 1974 when Lockheed and Bernhard did business again, and for the last time.

But that was all in the future. Lockheed largesse found other outlets in the 1960s, and it is to that crowded decade that we must return.

6

Indonesia: The Widows' and Orphans' Fund

Widows are always rich.

Old English proverb (1678)

1

On the afternoon of June 6, 1965, Lockheed's man in Djakarta, area sales manager Ned Ridings, stepped from his car outside the offices of the Dasaad Musin Concern on the Indonesian capital's Djalan Tjengkeh Street in the city's business quarter, and moved swiftly towards the doorway to meet his host.

August Dasaad had been Lockheed's agent in Indonesia since 1956. The relationship had been a prickly one, soured from time to time by more than the usual number of wrangles over contracts and commission payments. But the Dasaads, father and sons, were well-connected businessmen, personal friends of President Sukarno and related to Sukarno's right-hand man, General Alamsjah. They could deliver, and that was all Lockheed asked of its agents.

This afternoon's meeting was to discuss the Indonesian government's proposal to add another executive jet to the AURI (Indonesian air force) fleet. AURI already boasted three Lockheed Jetstars and three French Caravelles. Lockheed was keen to see the score rise to 4–3 in the Jetstar's favour. That meant, in the first place, agreeing a sales strategy with the Dasaads. And that was the purpose of Ridings's visit. He faced Dasaad across an immense mahogany desk. On the wall behind the short, greying businessman was a huge idealised portrait of a fatherly Sukarno, just but merciful in the familiar manner of third-world dictators.

Ridings later sent to base in Georgia an account of the odd conversation that followed. What was strange about it was Dasaad's quiet insistence that Lockheed's best chance of securing the favour of the Indonesian air force was to up the price of the Jetstar from a proposed $1,874,000 to $1,974,000.

Ridings didn't need to have it spelled out to him what the additional $100,000 was for. He knew that the basic Jetstar price was only $1,700,000. Dasaad's legitimate commission pushed it up by $74,000. On the last sale a further $100,000 had been added to help

Dasaad meet certain obligations. That $100,000 had been consolidated into the price of the proposed fourth sale, and now, on top of that, Dasaad was proposing yet another $100,000, bringing the total for 'special commitments' to a cool $200,000. And unless Lockheed agreed, Ridings understood Dasaad to imply, AURI's decision was likely to go in favour of the French Caravelle.

The meeting ended indecisively with Ridings indicating that he would have to refer back to Georgia. Early next morning Lockheed-Georgia sales executive Ed Hausman, in Marietta, took Ridings's call. He listened to the details of the Dutch auction with Dasaad, and told Ridings to stall until he had consulted corporate headquarters at Burbank.

Hausman first discussed the problem with his colleague Chuck De Bedts. Chuck recalled that it had all happened before. The Indonesians had threatened to switch to Fokker F-27s unless an earlier contract were suitably padded out. The same thing had happened on a Hercules sale. He agreed that Dasaad's demand for double-the-normal 'extra commission' rate was too sensitive for Georgia to process without reference to Burbank. So together they called the corporate vice-president for marketing, Gifford Myers. A balding, bespectacled man with a thin mouth and the eyes of a Mormon missionary, Giff made an urgent appointment with Dan Haughton for 7.45 the following morning.

Haughton started regularly at 7.30 or earlier. Giff Myers didn't. But this morning he made sure to be there on time. Haughton listened as he outlined the no doubt familiar problem, then asked Myers what action he recommended. 'I say hold at $1,874,000,' said Myers. 'This hanky-panky has gone far enough.'

An air of self-righteousness began to find its way into the meeting. Myers's aide-mémoire detailing his conversation with Haughton and the whole sequence of discussions goes on:

> We discussed the various ethics of it, and agreed that even though it would not be costing the company or the U.S. (ostensibly) any money, it just isn't right, and there is a limit somewhere to going along with this.

One hundred thousand in bribes was all right. Two hundred thousand was wrong. The meeting lasted barely ten minutes. Haughton told Myers to check with Kotchian. If he shared their high ethical view, Myers would send a no-deal message back down the line to Ridings.

Myers caught Kotchian as he was arriving in his office on the dot of eight. But the president showed himself to be made of spongier stuff than his chairman. As Myers memorialised it,

I spoke with Carl. He did not feel strongly on it—could go either way, and would be willing to go to the $1,974,000 price if necessary. We agreed I would call Georgia and tell them we preferred $1,874,000 and tell them to make another try at that number.

At 8.30 Myers called Hausman and De Bedts. He found them somewhat exasperated at Burbank's reluctance to return a firm answer. Georgia wanted to deal at $1,974,000. They were 'doubtful they could negotiate further, but said they would discuss and call back'. They called back three and a half hours later, at noon.

Chuck and Ed reported no room to argue further. Need to take firm position one price or another. Gelac (Lockheed-Georgia) will abide by our decision.

So Myers passed the buck back to Haughton and Kotchian. He met them at 4.45 p.m. next day. Kotchian was still ambivalent but 'Dan indicated he wanted to stay firm on $1,874,000'. Myers told Hausman the verdict and Hausman relayed it to Ridings in Djakarta. Ridings told Dasaad and the Indonesian air force promptly placed an order for a Caravelle.

The dénouement, however, was yet to come. One month after this uncharacteristic show of corporate squeamishness, Jack Clutter, executive officer of the Los Angeles subsidiary Lockheed Aircraft International, received a revealing letter from Marion Vandiver, one of his travelling agents. Vandiver had just returned to Rome after lobbying an Indonesian trade delegation visiting Paris. The delegation was led by President Sukarno himself, fresh from summit meetings with Nasser and Chou En-Lai. Prominent in Sukarno's entourage was August Dasaad.

Vandiver reported that Sukarno was angry at the sudden postponement of an impending conference of non-aligned nations in Algiers. He had 'planned to blast the capitalists, imperialists and neo-colonialists in his speech ... To everyone's benefit, especially ours, this did not materialise due to the postponement.' Then came Vandiver's bombshell (my italics):

The purpose of President Sukarno's visit to Paris ... was to promote more French credits. French industry, as well as the French government, is doing its best to expedite more business with

Indonesia in the form of heavy engineering and aircraft. *Our representatives Dasaad Musin Concern are representing French industries including Sud-Aviation.*

Small wonder, then, that Dasaad had seemed so unperturbed at the prospect of the Jetstar losing to the Caravelle. He represented both. Why accept one commission opportunity when two were available?

Double representation of this kind was, according to Clutter, in clear violation of Dasaad's contractual agreements with Lockheed. Clutter passed the news to Giff Myers and the two men pondered what action to take. In the end, they decided to take none. As Clutter put it to Myers on August 11 in an aide-mémoire on their discussions,

> To be realistic we both agreed nothing should be done about it since Dasaad does occupy a unique position in dealing with the Indonesian Government and with Sukarno himself. As long as Dasaad can be equally effective in the sale of Lockheed products whenever we can sell to Indonesia, we seem to have no alternative but to continue to work with him.

In this, Myers and Clutter reflected Vandiver's own conclusions. Vandiver was up to his ears in direct negotiations with Dasaad and Sukarno himself on a quite different problem. There was a long-running dispute about cracks which had appeared in the wings of the ageing Elektras Lockheed had sold to the Indonesian national airline, Garuda. 'The cracks ... are probably similar to the alarm over the Australian Elektras', wrote Vandiver, 'and perhaps Garuda has not received the necessary bulletins, inspection notices, or has failed to carry them out.' On top of that, there was a row about an acute shortage of Elektra parts, privately blamed by Lockheed on 'the lack of initiative on the part of Garuda, and presumably our agent's efforts, to extend the letter of credits for the purchase'. Both problems suggested careful diplomacy which tended to argue against an immediate show-down with Dasaad. And so too did another current hassle: a complex negotiation on AURI's Hercules C–130s.

AURI had bought the Hercules in the late 1950s. It was Dasaad's first big coup for Lockheed. But now the larger part of the fleet was grounded, again owing to a shortage of spare parts. Lockheed blamed the US government's reluctance to sanction more military exports to so militantly non-aligned a state as Sukarno's. But, as Vandiver reported ruefully, AURI found these excuses puzzling in the light of Washington's evident willingness to let Lockheed sell them Jetstars. Vandiver had even tried blaming the situation on Britain, arguing that the British were pressurising the Americans not to send the Hercules parts in case the revitalised fleet was used against Malaysia, which Britain was backing in the Indonesian–Malaysia confrontation. But the Indonesians didn't buy this one either. Why, they asked, should the British take so hard a line when they were allowing the export of Rolls-Royce Dart engine parts for AURI's Fokker F–27s?

As it happened, although AURI found it convenient to blame Lockheed, responsibility for the Hercules spare parts famine did lie squarely with the US state department and its selective policy of embargoes. Other arms exporters got round the problem by selling to Norway, which obligingly resold to Indonesia. But Lockheed devised a simpler plan dreamed up by Bob Mitchell, a rising star in the Georgia office whose creativity would soon be rewarded by promotion to the rank of vice-president, international operations. Mitchell's plan was that Lockheed would sell one Hercules plane, not to AURI but to the civilian line Garuda. A sale to a civil airline could hardly be interpreted as an arms deal, he pointed out, and once in possession of one plane, Garuda could order unlimited spares, which, of course, they could then pass on to the AURI fleet. Vandiver put this plan to Sukarno himself during the Paris talks, selling it frankly as 'ways and means to get round Washington's embargo'.

With so many sensitive matters in the air, including a deliberate corporate policy-decision to deceive and outwit the American government and its embargo policy, it would have been unsubtle to choose that particular time to pick a quarrel with a man as close to Sukarno as Dasaad. 'I recommend that we follow through with what is necessary to keep Lockheed's name in the forefront in Indonesia', wrote Vandiver forthrightly to Clutter. 'I will continue to maintain close personal relationship with the responsible parties of the Indonesian government.'

If Lockheed dared not face Dasaad with his own double representation, knowledge of it nevertheless seems to have encouraged a flurry of activity in the corporation's legal offices where all Dasaad's contracts with the various Lockheed subsidiaries were subjected to thorough review. There turned out to be a string of them, going back to August 22, 1956, and the lawyers found them a jumble—loose, ambiguous and sometimes overlapping. If Dasaad wanted to play games, they realised in some alarm, he could have a field day, possibly invoking two or more contracts, for instance, to claim two or more commissions on a single deal. Myers and assistant chief counsel Bob Canan began to look for ways of rationalising the agreements without alerting Dasaad's suspicion: a delicate task since, of course, the contracts could hardly be revised unilaterally.

As it happened, Dasaad gave them the opening they needed. He indicated that he would like to find a way of dividing his commissions between two of his companies, the old Dasaad Musin Concern and a new company, P.T. Indesco Raya. In particular, Dasaad wanted the 'special payment' of $100,000 which had been added to the price of the third Jetstar to be paid to Raya, not Dasaad Musin. Lockheed's men supposed Old Das was reorganising his affairs for tax reasons, perhaps running one company for the agency fees he would keep for himself and the other for commissions he would use as bribes. No matter, Dasaad's need was Lockheed's opportunity. A radical revision of contracts followed, acceptable to both parties. It left Dasaad Musin Concern the beneficiary of 'normal' commissions, and Indesco Raya the recipient of 'certain special compensations which are in addition to those payable by the normal terms', set at 3 per cent of the value of all Lockheed's Indonesian contracts. Since the corporation had contracted to assist in setting up a brand-new Hercules base at Bandung, undertake emergency corrosion repairs on eight C–130s and general repairs on two more, train AURI personnel and keep supplies of materials and spare parts flowing, Dasaad wasn't exactly going to lose out. But for Lockheed, it was not the *level* of the payments which mattered so much as being sure that the relationship was properly defined and the contracts clear. Even after the rewritten contracts were signed and exchanged, Bob Canan continued to express in interdepartmental memos a nagging worry that Dasaad might one day catch them out — by claiming on an old Dasaad Musin contract, for instance, after payments had been made to Indesco Raya. The suspicion, as we shall see, was mutual.

In the short term, however, Lockheed soon had good reason to be glad that the relationship had been rationalised. In 1964, under the old, loose contracts, the corporation had paid Dasaad a total of $152,000. Instead of being paid in Indonesia, two-thirds of this sum was paid into a Dasaad account at the Wells Fargo Bank in San Francisco. The payment inevitably came to the attention of the Internal Revenue Service during an audit in 1966 and an IRS agent began asking questions. Accountant D. D. Stone reported that the agent was 'apparently mainly concerned with ... what Dasaad did with the money, apparently feeling that if there were a pay-off in the United States such a thing would contravene public interest and thereby create a situation where he should disallow these payments as a business expense.' Stone gave the agent the party line: 'We paid Dasaad this $152,000 as a commission on a sale to the Government of Indonesia. We paid him this commission as and where directed by him to fulfil our legal obligation. We have no knowledge or concern with what he did with his commission after he received it.' The IRS demanded to see certified copies of the cheques and other relevant papers and for several weeks Lockheed men in the know were biting their finger-nails. But Stone was right. Seemingly the IRS's only concern was whether there was evidence of pay-offs *in the United States*. There wasn't, so they lost interest, unwittingly missing a golden opportunity to unravel Lockheed's briberies eight years in advance of Congress.

2

Dasaad's usefulness to Lockheed derived from his closeness to Sukarno. Barely six weeks after Jack Clutter agreed with Giff Myers that 'we seem to have no alternative but to continue to work with' Dasaad, an event occurred which would soon reopen the question in an even sharper form. On September 30, 1965, the leftist commander of Sukarno's presidential guards attempted a coup against rightists in the government but was foiled by the Indonesian army. Sukarno himself was accused by the right of complicity in the coup. The event led to his downfall.

For several years throughout the 1960s, Sukarno had authorised a colossal level of defence spending amounting to no less than 75 per cent of the nation's budget. The obvious effect of this was to strengthen the military at the expense of the civil administration. Most of Sukarno's army officers had little sympathy with his neutralist sentiments and increasing reliance on the Indonesian Communist party, dominated as it was by a Chinese minority suspected of greater devotion to communist China than nationalist Indonesia. By the summer of 1965 the animosity between Sukarno's leftist supporters and the right-wing military was intense. The abortive coup of September 30, whether planned by Sukarno, as some believe, to quash the military by military means, or used by the generals to discredit the President, proved to be the prelude to one of the bloodiest massacres in history. Throughout Indonesia the army sought out communists and their sympathisers – to be Chinese was itself regarded as proof of communist sympathies – and butchered them. The rivers of Indonesia were literally choked with bodies. At least 200,000, and some authorities say more than two million, died. For a while Sukarno was kept under virtual house arrest, President now in name only. Finally, in March 1966, he was forced to hand over power to his army minister, General Suharto.

Lockheed watched all this with anxious interest, the more so since the Georgia company was preparing a lucrative proposal for the 'rehabilitation' of the entire AURI fleet of C–130s. Dasaad's Indesco Raya company was, as per contract, the nominated agent. The question was, given the new political circumstances, would Dasaad's involvement be a help or hindrance? Was he acceptable to the new regime? Did he still have useful contacts? Could he deliver?

The question began to take on some urgency in September 1966 when Lockheed's export sales department was contacted by Bob Hasan, a Washington businessman well connected with the new Indonesian regime. Hasan told Lockheed that the new President, Suharto, wanted to buy an executive jet. Lockheed understood Hasan would expect a commission, but they were bound by their agreement with Indesco Raya. So Ned Ridings called Hasan to suggest that, on his return to Djakarta, he should 'work with our agent and advise us the total fee necessary', meaning that Hasan could expect to be paid out of a suitably inflated 'commission' payment to Dasaad. But Hasan said this was unacceptable. Dasaad was a known Sukarno man, he (Hasan) was 'connected with the present regime', and there was no way they could work together. Ridings said he was sorry but a contract was a contract. And there, for a time, the matter seemed to rest. In a long, detailed memo to his boss Dan Cederberg (August 8, 1967), recounting this and subsequent problems reflecting doubts about Dasaad's good standing, Ridings added: 'Nothing more has ever been heard from Bob Hasan, nor has the Indonesian Government bought an executive jet for Suharto.'

Lockheed had no certain way of knowing whether Hasan's negative view of Dasaad's influence was true or merely reflected a wish to arrange the commission for himself. But it so happened that on September 24, the day after Hasan's call, Lockheed's man in charge of the Washington office, Bob McCune, had a golf date with two members of the Indonesian UN delegation, Air Marshal Rusmin and

Colonel Wisnu. Hearing of Hasan's Jetstar proposal, McCune invited him to join them. During the game, in the presence and presumably within the hearing of Air Marshal Rusmin, Hasan told McCune bluntly that AURI did not want to do any more business with Lockheed if it involved Dasaad as agent. But Rusmin himself stayed enigmatically silent.

McCune assumed that Hasan was probably acting as authorised spokesman for the Indonesians, but decided to put his hunch to the test. Six days later Rusmin and Wisnu were invited to the plant at Georgia where they were extravagantly wined and dined in an attempt to loosen their tongues. But neither volunteered a word on Dasaad nor mentioned an alternative agency, despite the fact that, as D. D. Stone put it, they were 'given every opportunity and virtually led into a position' to come clean.

So Lockheed were no nearer knowing whether their agent was an asset or a liability; and time was running out. The proposed par mod programme[1] to rehabilitate all AURI's C–130s was due to be presented to the Indonesians by December 1. On September 30 Ridings left Marietta for Djakarta to check things out on the ground.

His first call was on Dasaad, who was bluntly confronted with Hasan's negative view of his usefulness. Unperturbed, Dasaad told Ridings 'not to worry': he was 'well in' with Suharto and was 'being used as something of a bridge between the new regime and Sukarno'. Not entirely satisfied, Ridings called on Col. Freddie Slade, USAF air attaché in the American embassy, who might be expected to know what was going on. Slade was emphatic that Dasaad had 'made the transition from Sukarno to Suharto in good shape'. He had been assigned several important missions for the regime, reported the colonel, being the first businessman to be permitted to travel abroad. Suharto had sent him to Tokyo to reassure the Japanese about the safety of their oil interests in Indonesia. Lockheed, said Slade, should 'be careful and give a lot of thought' before changing its representative.

Slade also casually offered the services of the embassy's CIA personnel to do an undercover check. Ridings accepted. A day or two later the CIA turned in its preliminary report: Dasaad was 'in'. A week later a fuller report followed, confirming that 'Dasaad was definitely well connected with the Suharto regime'.

That seemed to clinch it. Ridings prepared to leave Djakarta on

1 i.e. a follow-on programme of modifications.

October 5, but his last day was occupied with what was planned as a routine technical review at AURI headquarters. Towards the end of the meeting Air Marshal Rusmin suddenly asked if Dasaad was still Lockheed's agent and would be paid a commission on the repairs contract. Ridings told him yes, Dasaad was Lockheed's agent, but no, he wouldn't be getting any commission because commission was never paid on par mod or rehabilitation contracts.

This was not entirely true. Commission was paid on some items, such as spare parts. Rusmin, who clearly knew more than he let on, replied that he had been instructed by his superiors that 'AURI was not to contract with any company where a commission would be paid to an individual Indonesian'. Instead, AURI had set up its own company, headquartered at 25 Djalan Garuda, which would require a 3 per cent commission on the value of the $5·3 million contract: a total of $159,000. The company was run by AURI officers and was soon to become known coyly in Lockheed circles as the Widows' and Orphans' Fund.

Ridings just had time to fill in Dasaad on this development before flying home. Dasaad, shaken, said he didn't understand. He would ask his son Ike to 'find out what was wrong and straighten it out'.

Ridings felt thoroughly confused as he flew back to Marietta. The USAF air attaché had said Dasaad was in, the CIA had twice said he was in — but the AURI chiefs themselves had said he was out. The confusion wasn't helped when, a few days after his return, Ridings received a 'restricted' communication from the Djakarta embassy. It was the CIA's final report and, in flat contradiction to its earlier two, it stated baldly that Dasaad was 'out' with the Suharto regime. 'These contradicting reports', wrote Ridings with acid understatement, 'create doubts as to the US Embassy's ability to really evaluate the question.'

What was Lockheed to do? D. D. Stone minuted the company's ingenious solution:

> Indesco Raya ... will be paid commission on the spare parts. However, Gelac is covering itself from a price standpoint by including sufficient funds in the price to also pay government-sponsored firm in case we are forced to do so.

Prepared, then, to pay commissions to both sides, Ridings and Ed Hausman began negotiations in Djakarta on the draft contract for the par mod programme. On February 18, 1967, it was signed by AURI officials without so much as a mention of the Widows' and

Orphans' Fund or Dasaad. The Lockheed men were wary. They took care to ask Air Marshal Rusmin if he was sure that all subjects had been satisfactorily covered, or if there was anything else he wanted to raise? No, said Rusmin, everything had been covered. The demands of the widows and orphans, it seemed, had been dropped.

Three months later Ned Ridings was again in Djakarta. He found Dasaad 'in his usually good spirits' and noted: 'One change in the decor of Das's office was that a big picture of General Suharto now occupies the place where Sukarno's picture used to be.' Ned concluded that Dasaad was riding high: so high, he thought, that he had probably been responsible, by top-level string-pulling, for quashing the mysterious Widows' and Orphans' Fund. No doubt Dasaad himself encouraged this view. But it proved hopelessly over-optimistic.

It was soon apparent that the Dasaad company really was in political trouble. Paul McKusker, the Djakarta embassy's economic counsellor, told Lockheed's W. J. Broderick that Dasaad senior was splitting the business between his two sons, Ike and Abe. According to McKusker, 'Ike was okay and apparently in good graces with the present government. The government however seems to be ignoring Abe and sort of treating him like he is in limbo.'[1] A little later D. D. Stone was writing to Giff Myers: 'Information indicated that the Dasaads are completely without influence ... It is Gelac's opinion that although the Dasaads are not standing in line to be liquidated, their usefulness is at an end.'[2] Stone bluntly suggested the corporation's contracts with Dasaad be terminated forthwith.

There was another reason why it seemed politic to break with Old Das. As Stone put it to Myers:

Suharto is determined to economise to the greatest possible extent and looks with extreme disfavour on inclusion of commissions in any future procurements. Gelac has been forced to confirm to General Rasmussen, present Air Force Chief of Staff, that we are *not* paying commissions to *anybody* on the present Gelac C–130 Par Mod Program. For these reasons, Gelac feels the present Indesco Raya agreement can become an increasingly embarrassing document as time goes by.

It could indeed, since the clause promising a 3 per cent commission on spare parts sales gave the lie to Gelac's bland assurances.

1 Reported by Broderick to D. D. Stone, memo, April 1968.
2 Memo, May 7, 1968.

The final break with Dasaad was discussed at Kotchian's presidential staff meeting on April 14 and Myers scribbled at the foot of Stone's memo, 'OK with all attending'. But the decision was opposed by one influential figure who was not there. The long arm of Fred Meuser reached out from Switzerland to defend Dasaad. He wrote to point out Dasaad's relationship to General Alamsjah, who, despite his former intimacy with the disgraced Sukarno, remained in Meuser's view 'the second important man after the President'. In particular, said Meuser, Alamsjah was in charge of a proposed Djakarta airport project where Lockheed Aircraft International was bidding for the refuelling contract. Lockheed's interest 'might conceivably be pushed by Dassaad [*sic*] at the office of Alamsjah', argued Meuser.

But for once Meuser's advice was ignored. On August 30 Lockheed's Ben Methvin delivered the necessary notices terminating the agreements to Dasaad senior in Djakarta. 'The meetings with Mr. Dasaad were businesslike with no evidence of animosity on his part', reported Methvin on returning home. But 'attempts to contact young Ike were futile since he was at a beach resort in Southern Java and would not or could not answer our calls'.

Lockheed was now in an unexpectedly happy position. The par mod programme had been priced to take account of two potential commission demands, one from Dasaad and one from the Widows' and Orphans' Fund. Dasaad had been cut off and nothing more had been heard from Rusmin. It seemed that, from having to contemplate double commissions, the company could now hope to get away with none at all—a welcome bonus.

But that hope didn't last long. By January 1969 Methvin was reporting by telegram from Djakarta that the atmosphere at AURI was 'charged and clouded' and that renewed demands for a percentage contribution to the 'orphans' welfare fund' were possible. Then, in March, Ike Dasaad suddenly arrived in Los Angeles to 'touch base with Lockheed' and table a cool demand for 5 per cent of $7·5 million, the revised price of the par mod programme. On top of that, Dasaad complained that a succession of AURI generals were pressing him to fulfil promises they claimed had been made to them by Lockheed personnel during the currency of Dasaad's agency agreement. Would Lockheed help him meet these obligations? D. D. Stone at Burbank hurriedly conferred with Charlie Valentine, who had replaced Ed Hausman in Marietta. Valentine was unyielding. The par mod programme on eight C–130s currently being undertaken bore no relation, he claimed, to the identical par mod programme devised before Sukarno's fall—the programme to which the Dasaad contract related. This fiction was too much for some of Valentine's colleagues. Stone confided to his memo-pad a 'personal feeling ... that we will have difficulty convincing a layman judge, if Ike decides to take the matter to court, that the programs are indeed separate and that Ike's efforts in 1964 had no bearing on the 1966 contract'. Stone was in favour of a 'policy settlement' with Dasaad, and 'some kind of arrangement to supply the "golf clubs"[1] which were apparently involved with different Indonesian Air Force people in order to preserve our reputation with the Indonesian Air Force in the light of possible future programs'.[2]

Stone's view eventually prevailed and the 'policy settlement' agreed on was $125,000. But the 'golf clubs' evidently amounted to much more than that. Dasaad was soon reporting that an anonymous air vice-marshal was demanding $210,000, which he, Dasaad, had 'no intention of paying' since the officer in question was 'on his way out'. Dasaad's system of distribution was simple. He told Lockheed that he was only 'taking good care of the higher-ups that mean something for the future'.[3] Whatever promises had been made in the past, 'lame ducks' would get nothing. But the air vice-marshal promptly proved himself no lame duck by initiating the purchase of an additional Hercules and offering a used Jetstar in part exchange. Lockheed accepted and agreed to pay him $150,000 for his 'retirement fund', recording the bribe as 'avionics charges'. Ridings pointedly asked him if he understood that his bribe upped the price of the plane, and reported that he 'laughed and said that he understood it very well'.[4]

But although Lockheed was now almost indiscriminately handing out 'golf clubs' in preparation for *forthcoming* games, Ridings' instructions were to stall on demands arising from *past* contracts, particularly the large par mod programme. When the insatiable air vice-marshal followed up his success on the Hercules buy with a renewed offensive for par mod commissions, the discussion, according to Ridings, 'became somewhat heated'. Ridings told him: 'We regret the lack of communication and understanding that has occurred but do not know of anything that can be done.' The air

1 Bribes promised on the golf course?
2 Stone's 'memo for file', March 27, 1969.
3 Quoted in memo, Cederberg to Crockett, June 5, 1969.
4 Ibid.

vice-marshal's 'parting remark' was: 'I expect to be paid.'[1] Ridings concluded, rightly as it happened, that 'our salvation may be [his] being replaced', and advised against any '"try this on for size" propositions'. He also warned Cederberg, ominously, that cables and letters were frequently censored and that 'some of our Lockheed code words may be compromised'.[2]

The air vice-marshal's retirement, when at last it came, seems to have given Lockheed but brief respite. Eight months later, Ridings reported back to Marietta that he had won agreement for a £300,000 contract for replacing Hercules wing corner fittings. But

> As a necessary part of doing business with the AURI, we had to sign an agreement to repay five per cent of the total amount of Contract GLX–199, or $15,000, to the AURI. Payment is to be made at a time and to the place to be specified by the AURI ...
>
> I want to advise further, that this will be the 'way of life' in any future business dealings with the AURI. We will have to refund five per cent, 'off the top,' of any new programs contracted for by the AURI ... We now have our 'fences pretty well mended' with the AURI and we don't want to disturb this happy state of affairs.[3]

The Widows' and Orphans' Fund was back in business. Indeed, it was beginning to gather a host of rivals as *korupsi* — by no means unknown but never flaunted under Sukarno — gradually became an accepted factor in Suharto's economy. The President's wife, Madame Tien Suharto, opened her own 'charitable' organisation, Yayasan Harapan Kita, 'Our Hope Foundation', big in tobacco and flour milling. Madame Tien was soon known in the American business community as Madame Tien Per Cent, later adjusted to Madame Twenty Per Cent and even Madame Fifty Per Cent. Her son, Sigit, opened a charter airline, Bayu Air, which, although it owned but one ageing Corvair 340 which had been cannibalised for spare parts and thereby permanently grounded, nevertheless successfully demanded a royalty on every charter flight in Indonesian air space. As the London magazine *Airtrade* commented, 'With probably the most corrupt Government in the world, conditions are extremely variable. If the Indonesian consignee is well connected with the Government

---

1 Cable, Ridings to Cederberg, June 2, 1969.
2 Memo, Cederberg to Crockett, June 5, 1969.
3 Memo, Ridings to John P. Johnston Jr, February 18, 1970.

or Army anything goes ... If the consignee is not well connected operating rights are very difficult to obtain.'

Outside Suharto's own immediate circle it was the military which was clearly calling the shots. As the armed forces' own newspaper, *Angatan Bersenjata*, put it: 'To make up for shortages in its routine budget, the Army has been forced to establish limited liability companies outside the Army.' By the mid-1970s rival units were running competing bus companies, and military vehicles, ships and planes were regularly used for commercial freight. The Brawijaya Division in East Java ran much of the steel industry, the crack Siliwangi Division in West Java had interests in engineering, construction, car assembly and real estate, with a controlling interest in most of the hotels in Bandung, and the military police were strong in brothels. A major-general on a salary of less than $400 a month succeeded in having a writer imprisoned for alluding to his savings of $330 million in the Bank Central Asia. The General Telephone and Electronics Corporation, prepared for a 'normal pay-off' of around $4 million on a major contract for supplying communications satellites, reportedly faced a demand for no less than $40 million from Major-General Soehardjono, who had the postal and tele-communications concession. 'Graft goes into orbit', GTE complained.

By these standards the Widows' and Orphans' Fund was still a modest affair in 1970. Even so, some discretion was deemed necessary since Suharto had recently set up an anti-corruption squad, Opstib, which had yet to prove itself virtually toothless. Thus, when Lockheed made its first payment to the fund by cheque, the generals were unable to find a safe way of cashing it, and the corporation's Pacific regional representative, Charlie Murphy, had to fly in and make the pay-off in banknotes. Arrangements were made to pay future contributions into a numbered bank account in Singapore, where safety and secrecy were assured.

Was this bribery or extortion? Certainly the generals put the squeeze on Lockheed once they learned the rules of the game, but if Lockheed showed reluctance to being squeezed it was to the size of the squeeze rather than the principle. And soon after agreeing to the 5 per cent rake-off on all contracts, Lockheed found themselves in a bizarre situation where their own commercial interest and their customers' greed combined not against Lockheed's American and foreign competitors but against the Pentagon itself.

In the late summer of 1970, Lockheed discovered that the Pentagon's military advisory agency in Djakarta, an office known as DLG, was offering a huge assortment of Hercules spares free of charge to the now officially US-approved Suharto government. 'DLG is promising these people the sun and delivering it with extras' complained salesman Tom Kelly to the Hercules field service manager, Earl Rainwater.

> They have given the AURI C–130 program approximately 150,000 dollars worth of spares and equipment so far and recently another 50,000 dollars was made available for the program. It is difficult for the AURI to obtain funds from the [Indonesian] Department of Defense and Security so when DLG comes along and offers everything for nothing, you know what they are going to do. The only way we can fight this competition is to offer a commission or rebate.[1]

What this meant, of course, was that the AURI generals had to be bribed to buy from Lockheed what they could have obtained free from the Pentagon.

It was neither the first nor the last time that Lockheed found itself in competition with free government aid. In the mid-1960s a major sale of C–130s to Brazil had almost come to grief when the Pentagon stepped in to offer a free squadron of used C–119s. Lockheed had finally managed to persuade the Brazilian defence minister to buy the C–130s instead of 'accepting the United States' cast-off junk' (as Lockheed put it), but the memory rankled. Seven years later, when Lockheed's campaign to sell the Philippines two Hercules aircraft was suddenly undermined by a Pentagon free offer of twelve antiquated C–119s, Lockheed pulled out all the stops to persuade the impoverished Philippine government to spend nearly $4 million on two planes instead of accepting twelve which would cost them nothing. Lockheed had hired a Philippine public relations consultant, Buddy Orara, of the American-owned McCann Erickson agency, who had spent three years in the protocol department of the Philippine President's office—a connection which 'could be put to use, at the proper time, to assist our efforts', wrote Lockheed's Stan McKinney to Bill Cowden. Orara was instructed by McKinney, in a letter on October 15, 1971, to organise a press campaign in Manila exposing the Pentagon's free offer as 'a travesty on the Philippine people for several reasons and also on the American taxpayer for

1 Letter, Kelly to Rainwater, September 22, 1970.

economic reasons'. McKinney concluded: 'I feel sure you can find a way to profitably expose the situation. Public knowledge and the resultant indignation could possibly reverse the Pentagon's decision to your country's benefit. In any event, Lockheed's name must, of course be kept completely out of it for obvious reasons.' Orara replied that he had fed the story to a major business publication and was spreading it to other papers, after which he would 'follow up with informal contacts with people concerned in government ... to fuel the issue further and provide counsel on how the government can make hay out of the controversy. From there, things should fall into place automatically, and hopefully reach a level where the authorities will feel pressured to "request" the US Government for a review of the matter.' Orara concluded his disingenuous and revealing sketch of a Lockheed agent at work by raising 'a rather delicate matter': 'As you know, moving around in the local circles for this kind of objective involves financial requirements, whether one is dealing with press people, government people or army officers. In fact, I have already spent a little for this project and now foresee heavier requirements.' It was the old familiar pattern—except that this time Lockheed's competitor was the US government.

That's how it had been in Brazil and the Philippines, and now that was the situation in Indonesia with the Pentagon offering AURI a free spare parts service. Again, the answer was to exploit the simple conflict between the Indonesian government's public interest in obtaining free goods and the AURI generals' private interest in making a 'commission', which they could only do on a sale. So the Widows' and Orphans' Fund, which at first had seemed a necessary evil to Lockheed, became their own indispensable tool in fending off Pentagon competition.

Even so, the strategy was slow to succeed. Lockheed's men were puzzled by the discovery that, though the Pentagon seemed suddenly to run out of customers for its free offers, Lockheed's own order books were not filling up as they should. It dawned on them that a third party was at work, scooping the pool with contributions more generous than their own to the Widows' and Orphans' Fund. The culprit was soon tracked down. It was a company called Aviquipo Inc., which boasted that, with twenty-two branches in seventeen countries, it was 'the world's oldest and largest organization for the export of aviation parts'. Aviquipo, Lockheed discovered, paid AURI commissions of no less than 10 per cent—twice Lockheed's rate. But far more chastening for Lockheed's men was the discovery that Aviquipo was a wholly-owned Lockheed subsidiary. The corporation had taken it over two years earlier, in 1969. Lockheed was competing not only against the Pentagon but against itself. 'It's tough enough doing business nowadays,' wrote an exasperated salesman, D. T. ('Davy') Crockett Jr, 'without having someone in your own house making the job more difficult!'

AURI made it clear that the price of getting back into business was a doubling of Lockheed-Georgia's commission to match Aviquipo's. The generals now wanted 10 per cent on everything: not just spares but new aircraft orders too. And since negotiations were under way for the sale of a full squadron of eight new C–130s worth $40 million, the stakes had become very high indeed. This was no longer a matter of minor backhanders to minor Third World beggars. Lockheed's men decided it was time to refer back to their Marietta base for new instructions. Marietta in turn referred the question to corporate headquarters in Burbank.

So it was that on the morning of May 14, 1971, Bob Mitchell, corporate vice-president, international operations, found on his desk a long memo explaining the history of the Georgia company's dealings in Indonesia, outlining the new demands, summarising what was at stake, and asking for instructions. It began with the Dasaad saga and told how, following the termination of his contract, Gelac (Lockheed-Georgia) had been 'dealing on a direct basis with the Indonesia Air Force without benefit of an agency'.

> Herein lies our problem ... [AURI] are well aware that we paid commissions to our consultants and were very frank in discussing it with our people. They stated that since the consultant is no longer in the picture, they expect commissions to be paid direct to a numbered bank account in Singapore which they say is a 'support fund' for the AURI.

Commissions had started at 5 per cent. Now AURI was demanding 10 per cent.

> It was pointed out that Lockheed does not normally conduct business of this nature on a direct basis. [AURI] was asked to seriously consider a third party through whom we could mutually conduct business, and our people indicated that we were quite willing to welcome an individual of [AURI's] choosing. The advantages to be gained in mutual protection were pointed out; however, [AURI] summarily refused this suggestion on the basis

that a third party would have to be paid, which would only dilute the AURI 'commission'. [They] made it quite clear that if we want to continue doing business with the AURI we will do it their way.

The memo then set out the hazards of complying with these demands:

1. Since we have no agency agreement in Indonesia, we have no legal means of charging off these 'commissions'. Thus, they may not be considered allowable deductions by the Internal Revenue Service.

2. If such payments should some day become public knowledge, the repercussions could be damaging to Lockheed's name and reputation.

If Lockheed refused to comply, however, it risked losing the following business:

1. $300,000 or more per year in spare sales, contract technical service and parts overhaul business.

2. Sales of eight new Hercules and complete support in the 1973–1974 period; amounting to an estimated $40 million.

3. IRAN/Overhaul work at the LAS Singapore facility. Value unknown.

It thus becomes a matter of which alternative to choose.

Mitchell pondered and no doubt consulted. On May 26 he replied to Marietta, 'With reference to your ... memo of May 14, 1971 requesting Corporate policy decisions on this subject [Indonesia], I am quite concerned about two aspects: The AURI resistance to establishing a third party buffer, and the suggested level of the commission.' It was 'simply imperative' that the generals accept a 'buffer', if only for 'the significant protection provided for them as well as for us'. The introduction of a third-party consultant need not change payment arrangements (the Widows' and Orphans' Fund), nor need there be any dilution of commissions 'because we see no requirement for any active participation by the third party'. If the generals wouldn't go along with these sensible precautions, wrote Mitchell, 'we should accept the calculated risk you visualise in refusing "to do business the AURI way"'.

This sounded tough. So did Mitchell's views on AURI's demand for 10 per cent. 'My idea of a *reasonable* scale would be 3 per cent on airplanes and 5 per cent on other sales. We definitely should fight for a *maximum* of 5 per cent on the sale of airplanes and major modification programs, with a ceiling of 10 per cent on smaller spares orders.' And he concluded with a defiant flourish: 'We are still in business for the long term, not for the quick buck, and I feel these guidelines are better for the long pull. As you say, we *could* lose some business but the risk seems acceptably small.'

It was Stan McKinney's job in Djakarta to take this back to AURI. He found the generals unimpressed. A few weeks later, Mitchell himself flew out for a series of discreet meetings with the top brass. But despite his tough talk, he soon found he was forced to concede 10 per cent commissions on everything except aircraft purchases, which remained negotiable. However, he had more success in persuading the generals to accept a third-party buffer. Accordingly, a dummy company called International Traders was established as the recipient of AURI's commissions – a collecting agency, as it were, for the Widows and Orphans. At last, it seemed, everyone was happy. The generals were getting their 10 per cent and Lockheed had a respectable-sounding consultancy firm to which the commissions could be booked to the satisfaction of the corporation's auditors.

But this arrangement, too, turned out to be short-lived. The generals were soon complaining that International Traders had failed to pass on a promised payment of 'back funds'. Mitchell despairingly cancelled the agreement, retrieved the money and had it paid direct to the Widows' and Orphans' Fund through the Lockheed Aircraft International office in Hong Kong. But this was only a one-off arrangement, and the sudden shut-down of International Traders again left Lockheed without its protective buffer and AURI without an established channel for the routine receipt of commissions. McKinney was anxious to prevent the whole Lockheed–AURI relationship from falling apart again. 'However, this is exactly what will happen,' he warned Marietta, 'unless an agreement is drawn which will activate repayment to the AURI automatically, as required, and a channel established through which the money can be paid ... The agreement must be such that it will withstand Internal Revenue Service scrutiny, inasmuch as funds repaid the AURI should be tax deductible.'[1]

Marietta and Burbank took the point and yet another company, Lockheed Aircraft (Asia) Ltd, was registered in Hong Kong, with one of the corporation's own senior executives, Jack Clutter, installed as president. Burbank ruled that '*all* commissions paid into

1 McKinney to G. B. Methvin, January 10, 1972.

Singapore must go through a "sanitizing" process involving Clutter's office'.[1] LAAL proved more durable than its predecessor and, as we shall see, later played a vital role in the transmission of Japanese bribes.

In Indonesia, the transmission chain eventually ran like this: 'commission' was paid into LAAL's account (number 06626–06348) at the Bank of America, 101 West Seventh Street, Los Angeles; transferred from there to LAAL's account in Hong Kong; and paid out, with Clutter's authorisation, to the generals' 'welfare' account in Singapore. No doubt the five-star widows and much-decorated orphans had their own means of repatriating their ill-gotten gains from Singapore to Indonesia.

Mishaps and misunderstandings were still not wholly eliminated. The generals sometimes complained about the three-month time-lapse between the signing of a contract and receipt of the pay-off; on at least one occasion Burbank forgot to trigger Clutter to transfer $20,000 due to the Widows and Orphans on a Jetstar engine deal; and there were problems with a group of air force officers outside the Widows and Orphans set-up who demanded an additional 1½ per cent commission for their own welfare fund. But by and large, the establishment of LAAL as a conduit firmly under Lock-heed's own control brought order to the corporation's troubled history of bribery and extortion in the Indonesian islands. Lockheed had jousted with Dasaad, survived a revolution, mobilised the CIA on a private spying operation, competed with the Pentagon, competed with itself and enriched the strong-arm men who thrived under a corrupt dictatorship. For Lockheed, as for Indonesia's top brass, 'hanky-panky' paid handsome dividends. In less than a decade, the corporation notched up more than $100 million of business in Indonesia. It was business which, added to Hercules sales elsewhere, helped keep the Marietta production line moving. And on that production line, in the harsh economic climate of the 1970s, depended the viability of Lockheed-Georgia and the jobs of 16,000 men.

---

1 Memo, 'Personal and Confidential', Cederberg to B. H. Menke, May 16, 1973.

7

Italy: The Buying of a Republic

The Lockheed affair has revealed for the first time who are the real princes of the Italian republic.

Corriere della Sera, Rome

1

Many of Lockheed's most aggressive sales campaigns were triggered by failure. Such was the case in Italy, where the Lockheed affair served both to reinforce the widespread notion that corruption is endemic in Italian public life and to disprove the equally widely held assumption that it has lost all power to shock.

In 1964 Lockheed suggested to the then defence minister Luigi Andreotti that the Italian air force might care to consider the merits of a long-range transporter and heavy troop-carrier such as, for instance, the Hercules. Lockheed knew it was a long shot: of all the NATO powers, probably none had less strategic need for such a plane. So Burbank cannot have been in the least surprised when Andreotti replied that the air force would continue to give priority to the acquisition of short-range transporters like the old C-119 and the new C-222 which was being developed in Italy by Fiat.

But Lockheed had experience of Italy through the NATO Starfighter consortium. The Italian government, Lockheed decided, was persuadable.

Their next opportunity came in 1968 when the Italians let it be known that they were interested in buying a new generation of anti-submarine reconnaissance planes. Lockheed despatched to Rome a high-powered sales team led by Don Wilder, a chubby, baby-faced but canny salesman who had risen to prominence within the corporation as Archi Folden's successor in Koblenz and was now vice-president, marine sales. It was Wilder's team who had tried unsuccessfully to sell the P-3 Orion to the Netherlands a few weeks before, failing despite Prince Bernhard's advocacy and his $100,000 payment.

Lockheed also sent in Roger Bixby Smith, counsel in the Netherlands payments, to carry out a similar mission in Rome. Once again money passed hands — but once again Lockheed lost out. The Italians, like the Dutch, chose the French Breguet Atlantique in preference to the Orion. With the Netherlands, Lockheed had the consolation of knowing that the Atlantique had won the competition because of Dutch participation with the French in its manufacture, a factor which, from the beginning, left the American entrant something of a rank outsider. But there were no easy excuses in Italy. There were only two possible reasons why the Italian government should prefer the Atlantique to the Orion. Either it was a better buy, or the French bribed more generously. Lockheed's view was clear: the French had out-bribed them.

President Carl Kotchian was prepared to say as much eight years later when, with the cat half out of the bag, he faced the Church Committee.

> *Senator Percy:* Did you lose to the French because of the technical superiority of their plane, or did you lose because they paid more in your judgment?
> *Kotchian:* In my judgment it was the latter because our airplane was much superior.
> *Percy:* In other words, an inferior product was purchased because they were willing to pay more, and those were the circumstances that you faced, then, in your campaign in Italy?
> *Kotchian:* Yes, sir.[1]

It was the old, old story: we have to do it because our competitors do it. But it was an excuse built on a significant admission. To Kotchian, Lockheed's only misjudgment was that their bribes had not been big enough to win the order and that led to a determination that they would not again be so easily out-smarted.

Kotchian also gave the Church Committee a calculated hint at how the Italian bribes had started. 'Our man Mr Wilder', he said, 'was approached by an Italian senator in the Italian Senate and told us we should obtain a consultant in Rome if we wished to sell airplanes.' The implication that the corporation's innocents abroad knew nothing of the unpleasant realities of business life in Italy until they were put in the picture by one of the locals seems audacious, but did have a basis in fact. Wilder did indeed meet 'an Italian senator in the Italian Senate'. His name, not vouchsafed to the Church Committee, was Girolamo Messeri, and his memory of the meeting is somewhat more colourful than Kotchian's account. As he recalls it, he came across the Lockheed team, somewhat drunk and maudlin, in a restaurant. He gathered that their low spirits and high consump-

1 Church Committee hearings, February 6, 1976.

tion reflected their perception that the French were already ahead on points. He suggested that they might save themselves a lot of trouble and begin to see positive results if they hired themselves a good consultant, and, stating the obvious as he saw it, added: 'It would help if you made a contribution to one of the political parties.'

The Lockheed men were not, as it turned out, too drunk to remember his advice and follow it to the letter. With the Italian government's choice of the Atlantique not yet irrevocably confirmed, the consultant they hired was a flamboyant Rome lawyer, Ovidio Lefebvre, a man later described by Carl Kotchian as 'one of the finest gentlemen that I have run into in the world, very conscientious'.[1]

Ovidio and his almost equally colourful brother Antonio were typical 'princes of the Italian republic'. Coming from a well-to-do Neapolitan family, the brothers grew up to flourish in the world of *commis* — fixing, introductions, favours financial and otherwise that turn the wheels of Italian business-politics. Ovidio, head of the family law business, spent most of his time abroad, forming useful and profitable connections in Brazil and Mexico. (His Mexican interests were to stand him in good stead: when his name was linked to the Lockheed scandal in 1976 he sought an extradition-proof refuge there.) Business contacts elsewhere ranged from multi-millionaire American industrialist Bruno Pagliari, best known to the public at large as a one-time husband of Merle Oberon, to assorted royal princes in Saudi Arabia. (He played a major part in organising President Giovanni Leone's state visit to the Saudi capital, and was himself among the presidential retinue.)

Younger brother Antonio was, if anything, still closer to the President, their friendship dating from shared student days at the University of Bari. After the war, fellow-Neapolitan Leone called on his old friend to help him draft Italy's new navigation laws, an experience which Antonio must have found useful when he became heavily involved in the Panamanian flag of convenience business. Leone later became godfather to one of Antonio's sons. So much were the Lefebvre brothers part of the President's circle that Leone himself would eventually be widely touted by sections of the Italian press as implicated in Lockheed's web of bribery, though he was never indicted, let alone convicted.

1 Church Committee hearings, February 6, 1976.

One member of the parliamentary commission which in 1976 investigated the Lefebvres' business activities was moved to describe Antonio as possessing 'the ability of a technician, the presence of a great actor, the arrogance of a man of power'. The same commission member succinctly summed up Antonio's business life: 'Being a consultant is his job, state companies are his pasture.'

Despite his ostentatious wealth – he drove a Rolls and an Alfa 2000 and entertained lavishly at a huge villa on the fashionable Amalfi coast outside Rome, where his guest-list included Princess Margaret – he shared a privilege common among 'princes of the republic': he paid virtually no taxes. His tax bill for 1975, for instance, was a meagre 5 million lire – about £8,000. And his means of accomplishing this miracle of financial ingenuity have a direct bearing on Lockheed's efforts to break into the Italian market.

The basis of the system – presumably a great spur to incentive among Italy's captains of industry – is to make sure that you don't actually own anything. Antonio's Amalfi villa, for instance, was registered in the name of a company called Contrade Vaduz, based outside Italy in Liechtenstein. Where they are not registered in Liechtenstein, Switzerland, the Bahamas or a similar haven, the usual practice is to arrange for such companies to have the title of ownership vested in a very old man (or, latterly, in more progressive times, a very old woman). There are specialists in Rome's legal underworld known to ply a thriving trade in supplying these quavering signatories, who are generally paid about 10,000 lire – enough to keep them in food for a month – for the use of their name. As soon as one such ghost company is deemed to have outlived its usefulness, its assets are passed to another ghost company 'owned' by another old man, and the first is abandoned. It is a system with which the Lockheed accountants, if they did not know of it already, were to become very familiar.

Despite what were no doubt the best efforts of the conscientious Ovidio Lefebvre and his well-connected brother, the Italians confirmed their choice of the Breguet Atlantique rather than the Lockheed P-3. The brothers were paid $40,000 for their efforts and, more important, they were retained to fight another day on another front. For Lockheed, having taken the measure of what was required to sell to Italy, was about to re-persuade the Italian government that what its forces really needed was the long-range Hercules transporter, the very plane Andreotti had spurned almost exactly four years earlier.

The offensive began in 1968, when the deputy head of the air force procurement agency, General Gianbattisto Nicolo, apparently made a casual request, in conversation with Lockheed executives, for information on the Hercules – prices, availability of spares, delivery dates and suchlike. Clarence 'Lefty' Roha, another graduate from the Koblenz office and newly appointed to Paris to oversee Lockheed's European operations, obligingly submitted a detailed offer for the sale of twenty C–130s at $2,700,000 each. When Nicolo let it be known that the Franco-German Transall transporter was also in the running, Roha from Paris and Kotchian from Burbank descended on Rome to plot strategy with the Lefebvres. This time they were determined to do whatever was necessary to persuade the government in Lockheed's favour.

The four men met for dinner at Antonio's fifty-nine-room Amalfi villa. Roha and Kotchian quizzed their consultants on the next move and Ovidio tabled a trump: he suggested Lockheed go straight to the top, to the prime minister himself. The Lefebvres assured their eager but sceptical clients that they would have no difficulty arranging a meeting.

The Lockheed high command can have been under no illusion about the heavy 'compensation' or 'insurance' they would have to pay to win the deal. Neither Kotchian nor Roha had reached their corporate eminence merely by handing out brochures or by showing clients the polished promotional films American arms exporters are so adept at making. As we have seen, on Kotchian's own confused admission eight years later, Lockheed believed the P–3 contract had only been lost because they had failed to bribe as generously as their competitors. Nevertheless, Lockheed's president sought to persuade the Church Committee that he had no idea at the time of the Amalfi meeting that bribes were a central part of the Lefebvres' strategy. According to his story, Ovidio broke the news in a subsequent car journey. As Kotchian recalled it, Ovidio told him: 'I'm embarrassed, and I'm just chagrined, but I'm going to have to recommend to you that you make some payments if you wish to sell airplanes in this country.' Kotchian's phlegmatic response was to put up the price of the planes to pay for the bribes.

The rise of 5 per cent was specifically to 'provide for the probable contributions to Italian political parties'[1] and followed a report from

1 From Lockheed documents supplied to the Italian judicial investigation by the SEC.

Ovidio to Kotchian that the prime minister had agreed to a meeting in March. And there were clearly no illusions as to the purpose of the meeting. As a Lockheed memorandum put it, 'The meeting planned for March between Kotchian and the Italian Prime Minister was to be the effective key in order to specify the demands relative to compensation.'[1]

So far so simple. The necessary bribes would be agreed with the Italians involved in the deal, and would then be paid for by upping the price, so that the cost would ultimately be borne not by Lockheed but by the Italian taxpayers (those who couldn't afford ghost companies). Corporate headquarters at Burbank were anxious to keep this crude scenario — robbing Peter to pay Peter — a secret even from their own consultants, fearing that the conscientious, gentlemanly Lefebvre would use it as leverage to raise his own fees to Lockheed. 'Please don't discuss how the price was established or what it may include,' ran an anxious message from Burbank to Roha in Paris on February 5, 'given that any discussion on contributions should be discussed with discretion during later conversations through our legal channel as before.' A week later, presumably after a thorough review of their likely obligations, Lockheed again raised the price of the Hercules to $2,995,000 per plane, which now included, as sales executive William Cowden explained in another memo, 'six per cent for eventual contributions to political parties and consultants'.[2]

Meanwhile the planemakers were keen that nothing should go wrong with what they regarded as the crucial meeting with the prime minister. In February Roha was anxiously cabling Ovidio from Paris, asking whether an interpreter would be required and who should accompany Kotchian. On March 25 Kotchian arrived in Rome, and next day Ovidio conducted him and Roha to the ornate Palazzo where the prime minister had his private office. There, after the ritual exchange of courtesies, Lockheed's men began to discuss the details of Contract GLX–19B with the Lefebvres' friend and prime minister of three months, Mariano Rumor.

1 Ibid.
2 Ibid.

2

Rumor was wont to boast that at university he had studied under the celebrated philosopher Benedetto Croce. He was less inclined to boast about what Croce had written in the margin of his graduation thesis: 'Author seems obtuse in understanding problems of beauty and art, and the moral ideals of beauty.' Not that the young Rumor was a complete philistine. He claimed to enjoy Beethoven – an unusually Germanic taste for an Italian – and, more conventionally, Vivaldi. In literature, no one doubted his self-proclaimed intimacy with Machiavelli. But the moral ideals of beauty and art are not the stuff of which the Italian Christian Democrat party is made, and Rumor has been part of the Christian Democrat machine since 1948. He hails from the Veneto, the rich hinterland of merchantmen's Venice, rock-solid Christian Democrat territory despite Euro-communist encroachment in Venice itself. His family were not rich, but not so poor they couldn't afford shoes. He began in politics as a protégé of Amintore Fanfani, who helped make the Christian Democrats not so much a party of government as the government itself. Under Fanfani, State and party bureaucracy became almost inseparably intertwined: the only way government could function was through the party machine. The Italian citizen came to rely on the party and its officers to get things done for him, and in return the party expected a bloc vote from the beneficiary of the fix and from his whole family. This, since 1948, and probably earlier, has been Italy's version of the social contract.

By 1959 Rumor had a strong power-base of his own in the party. In 1960 he helped set up the so-called 'Corrente Dorotea', named after a convent outside Rome where its members met. The 'Corrente' was a faction of Christian Democrat politicians who advocated a 'centre-left' alliance with socialists in order to isolate both the powerful Communist party and the extreme right. The alliance was to dominate Italian politics for the next fifteen years until, para-doxically, it foundered in 1976 on the rocks of the Lockheed affair.

Backed by his faction following, Rumor joined the cabinet, first as minister of agriculture and then as minister of the interior. In December 1968, after a seven-month crisis in which the socialists refused to join a formal coalition, Rumor persuaded them to back him and assumed the premiership, an office he was to hold five times in the next six years. For a man so much in the limelight, however, he remained something of an enigma to the Italian public. He chose to distance himself from Rome society by living outside the capital in the futuristic satellite town of Eur. Unmarried, he shares his house with one of his sisters. He is a non-smoker and an assertive teetotaller.

This, then, was the man Lockheed's president met on the afternoon of March 26, 1969. There is no record of what was said: nobody took minutes. But next day Kotchian summoned Roger Bixby Smith to his suite in the expensive but unflamboyant Grand Hotel in Rome. Smith now had the status of an independent consultant, based in Paris. Although no longer a direct employee of Lockheed, he was still entrusted with 'sensitive' matters such as those in hand. Kotchian gave him the job of smoothing the way in Italy.

The day after his meeting with Kotchian, during which he was extensively briefed on the all-important conversation with Rumor, Smith wrote an astonishing but illuminating letter to Charles Valentine, director of contracts for Lockheed-Georgia in Marietta. It explained in graphic terms what the state of play was on the Hercules campaign. The letter was written on sheets torn from a note-pad in what Smith apologetically called his own 'execrable' hand-writing, but, as he explained, 'I am in no position to disclose to third parties the contents hereof.' The letter was too sensitive even to entrust to a typist.

It began routinely enough with an account of negotiations with Ovidio Lefebvre on the size of his 'legal fee' and the stages by which it should be paid. Lefebvre wanted a substantial down-payment immediately, followed by a further instalment when the Italian government signed a letter of intent to buy the Hercules. Lockheed wanted to delay the major part of the payment till the sale was con-firmed by registration of contract. Smith recommended that Lock-heed do it Lefebvre's way.

They [the Lefebvre brothers] point out that they are not really commission salesmen [though that, of course, is precisely how Lockheed listed them for audit and tax purposes] and that this is a one-shot deal in which, by the very nature of the assignment, their work will be completed, theoretically without follow-up or surveillance or continuing customer contact when the definitive contract is executed and delivered.

The Lefebvres are not trying to pressure you—perhaps I am ... Incidentally the Lefebvres never submitted an incidental expense statement respecting the P–3 matter, and they do not propose to do so respecting the C–130 matter for expenses incurred prior to this date.

What these 'expenses' were Smith did not explain. Presumably Valentine knew or could guess. Emphasising his recommendation that Lockheed accept the brothers' 'legal fee' of $210,000, Smith added:

> They do not come cheap, but I believe that but for what they have done and will do, Gelac [Lockheed-Georgia] could very well get kissed off, and, further, I am convinced that but for them ACK [Kotchian] and other sales gents from several areas – and I think that they would agree – could have been and would be beating their heads against a stone wall of Italian indifference, to put it most mildly.

But still more revealing was the middle section of the letter, helpfully headed 'Compensation to Third Persons':

> Please hold on to your seat, as what follows may be a shocker to you. (I am somewhat inured, due to the P–3 exercise.) To get you in the proper state of mind, you should know that Ovidio Lefebvre (this is strictly his department) states that Gelac, if it wishes the maximum run for success, must be prepared to go as high as $120,000 *per airplane* for the cumshaw pot. He hopes it will be less and will try to keep it less (and I believe him to be sincere in this) but he says that such is a nasty part of life in the arena in which we are trying to offset the same type tactics by a combination (this time) of both the French and the Germans. (In the last go-around the French beat us single-handedly!)
>
> I cannot talk poor-mouth to Ovidio because someone else (as he informed me) has disclosed to him the 6% increase in price which, to him, appears to produce some $150,000 per airplane additional over normal profit unless that sum is expended for purposes not connected with the manufacture and assembly of the aircraft. Furthermore, he said that, unlike in the P–3 matter, there will not again be a face to face negotiation between a representative of the 'party' and Lockheed representatives but that he will be told, probably by the Antelope Cobbler (get out your little black book – mine is dated October 15, 1965), just how much the 'party' demands.
>
> Further there will be the Cobbler himself and Pun and various others of lesser but highly placed personnel.

In this connection he insists that he will only give names and figures to one person in Lockheed. He says he wishes it to be me (probably because I am the only survivor around of the P–3 exercise). If you want it to be someone else, then it must be someone who will be able to be here in person when needed, since he will not put any of the information in the mails. If I get the information, I would propose to seal it up and deliver it, so sealed, to our Paris lawyer for safe keeping, with instructions to deliver it to the President of Lockheed in the event of my death, disability or disappearance. Actually, he said he wanted it to be me, of those he has been dealing with, because I am a lawyer. (Doesn't that just make *you* available as a repository for guilty knowledge??) If you wish me to bow out of this phase of the matter please let me know, but at the same time nominate someone else as soon as possible to be in personal contact with Ovidio.

I really should not be putting even the foregoing in writing but I have no choice.

When you communicate with me as to the form of the legal retainer letter agreement please also include either (a) the statement 'maximum outside expenses approved' (which I will interpret to mean that Gelac is willing to go as high as $120,000 per airplane for cumshaw if such becomes necessary) or (b) the statement 'outside expenses of $XXX approved' (which I will interpret to mean that the figure you put in where I put the three XXXs above will be the maximum *per airplane* which Gelac is willing to commit, win lose or draw, to the cumshaw pot). I will pass the word along (orally).

I recognise what the payment will be and I can only say (a) we are not negotiating with Ovidio but merely establishing parameters within which he can negotiate for us, (b) our first commitment may be the only commitment we may have an opportunity to make, i.e., events may stop us from being able later to increase the ante, (c) those who will be making the decision might well bear in mind the old adage about penny wise and pound foolish and (d), and finally, I entertain the impression that the winning of the C–130 sale to Italy is of tremendously greater significance to Lockheed the corporation than the bare sale of x number of airplanes, at least in this point of time. Please advise.

The letter concluded:

I apologise for the length of this. I hope you keep this letter on a *very* strict need-to-know basis with respect to your compatriots. As for the compensation to Third Persons past we are dealing with dynamite that could blow Lockheed right out of Italy with terrible repercussions. Best regards, Roger.

Smith's uneasiness at putting such revealing and incriminating material on paper was justified by events. Ever since February 1976, when the letter was included in documents released by the Church Committee, he must have been wishing he had saved his reflections on cumshaw for a personal chat with Charlie Valentine. So too must Charlie Valentine, not to mention Kotchian, Haughton, 'Antelope Cobbler' and 'Pun'. Lockheed has consistently refused to reveal the identities of the men referred to by these codewords (selected at random by computer), and Italy had to await the enterprise of the Rome weekly magazine, *Panorama*, which obtained and published the 'little black book', before cynics who guessed they meant 'prime minister' and 'head of the air force' respectively had their hunches confirmed. For a while there was confusion as to which prime minister was referred to. As we have seen, Leone himself (prime minister before he became President) was suspected by those who knew of his close friendship with the Lefebvres. Andreotti, premier when the scandal broke, was another suspect until documents which seemed to nail him were shown to be politically motivated forgeries. Now that Smith's letter can be read in the light of Kotchian's meeting with prime minister Rumor only two days earlier, the identity of the 'cobbler' seems clear enough – which, of course, is not to say that Rumor asked for or received payments for himself. (He is not among the politicians who were subsequently prosecuted.)

'Cumshaw' presents no difficulty. The context makes it clear enough in any case, and the *Concise Oxford Dictionary* informs us helpfully that it is a dialect form of the Chinese *kan hsieh*, meaning 'grateful thanks'. It would be hard to better Carl Kotchian's own definition to the Church Committee hearings:

> *Senator Percy:* Now, what is a cumshaw pot? ... How do you, as an executive, understand the implications of it?
> *Mr Kotchian:* Like, cumshaw is something you give to get something done.[1]

Given the little black book's translation of 'Pun' as the air force chief, his identification, too, becomes a straightforward matter.

---

1 Church Committee hearings, February 6, 1976.

General Diulio Fanali, who occupied the post under Rumor's first premiership, was a ubiquitous figure in the politics of the period. In Italy the military tend to play a more open role in politics than would be thought seemly in, say, Britain or the United States—so much so that in the chaotic late 1960s many Italians talked openly of a 'Greek solution' to the problems of democracy. Fanali's name lumbers endlessly through contemporary accounts of fascist and extreme-right intrigues, anti-fascist counter-attacks, NATO politics —and bribery.

A wartime fighter pilot for Mussolini, Fanali was part of the key group selected by the Americans to rebuild the Italian armed forces after the war—a group from which Lockheed seem to have recruited again and again, in Japan, West Germany and the Netherlands as well as Italy. When the top air force job became vacant, American pressure is said to have swung the appointment of Fanali even against a 'moderate' Christian Democrat nominee. No doubt his virulent anti-communism was an asset. Anyway, his sponsors seemed little concerned by his already established links with the fascist MSI party (which later wanted him as one of its parliamentary candidates in the 1972 election) or his connection with the fascist General Borghese, who was soon to attempt a comic-opera coup using as his shock-troops the uniformed but otherwise apparently harmless gendarmerie of the Italian forestry service. Fanali was held for questioning along with Borghese when the forest rangers proved no match for more orthodox state forces and the coup ended in ignominy. It was Fanali's last brush with the law before his Lockheed connection became public.

Lockheed's consultants believed, back in 1969, that Fanali could be convinced of the merits of the Hercules. Cynical Italians profess to see the proof of his convictions about sixty miles outside Rome: a sumptuous villa overlooking the sea near the village of Sassolini. Fanali, who denies taking Lockheed money, attributes his good fortune to the wisdom of his wife in selling her family jewels. But the magistrates who began investigating the affair in 1976 saw an alternative explanation when they came to examine the bank statements of Fanali's friend and colleague, Camillo Crociani—yet another of Lockheed's secret special agents.

3

When police raided Crociani's huge but empty apartment in the Porioli district of Rome after he had fled, one jump ahead of the prosecutors, to Mexico, they found four guns—unlicensed. This was strange: as one of the most powerful and influential men in the country, Crociani would have had no trouble in acquiring licences for an entire armoury. But the investigating magistrates found even more of interest in the records, carelessly left behind, of one of his bank accounts at the Istituto Bancaro Italiano in the Via del Caro, where Crociani was a good friend of the manager, Carlo Alsisi, later arrested at the Swiss border for illegally exporting Italian currency.

From this one account it was clear that Crociani had distributed huge sums to high-level political contacts, some for Lockheed, some for other interests and some, no doubt, for a general goodwill which would benefit all Crociani's clients indiscriminately. To Franco Evangelisti, Andreotti's under-secretary, 15 million lire; to Ermino Penacchini, under-secretary at the ministry of justice, 6 million lire per year; to Francesco Cosentino, secretary of the chamber of deputies, 70 million lire; to the defence minister's brother, 10 million lire; to Mauro Bubico, a powerful backbench Christian Democrat, 5 million lire; and to the air force chief Diulio Fanali, Lockheed's 'Pun', 15 million lire.

When Crociani finally fled Italy in his private plane he was fifty-six years old and president of Finmeccanica, a company within the huge state industrial holding group IRI, with 90,000 employees and thirty-six subsidiaries, including Aer Italia and Alfa Romeo. Like other Lockheed 'consultants' in Italy, he was not a well-known figure except to the people who counted. And few of them knew how, starting in the war years, he had built up his business and his connections.

One man who did take the trouble to find out was Colonel Bruno Benedettini of the air force branch of the Carabinieri—just one of a bewildering number of Italian police forces. In 1965 Benedettini submitted to the ministry of defence a report on Crociani, according to which he had served in Mussolini's army as a paratrooper and had been seconded to the German SS for training in sabotage. Later he was hired by the German embassy in Rome, a position he turned to his own advantage, according to Benedettini, by selling travel permits for 50,000 lire a time. After the liberation he found it expedient to invent a distinguished career as a partisan in the famous Matteotti brigade, which perhaps helped him find willing sponsors among the American occupying forces, who in turn helped him set up in the military surplus disposal business. By 1948 he was well enough established to register his own company, Industrial Imports. He was already displaying spectacular talent in persuading defence ministry officials to see things his way on procurement. On one occasion, records the incredulous Benedettini, Crociani sold them a batch of equipment for 22 million lire after they had turned it down at 8 million. This was the kind of talent Lockheed was seeking out and buying all over the world.

Col. Benedettini's report went to prime minister Andreotti, who sent it to the defence ministry, who sent it back to the Carabinieri with a request for more details, after which the enquiry became, as the Italians say, *insabatio* — literally 'running into the sand': one of a dozen words the Italian language offers for 'cover-up'.

Undaunted by, and probably ignorant of, these aspersions on his personal history, Crociani continued onwards and upwards. In 1967 he arrived in the rich pastures of state industry and commerce, first running Inapli, the industrial retraining organisation, then Finmare, the state shipping company for whose presidency he was nominated by minister for state holdings Gacinto Bosco, with the support of prime minister Rumor. His private company, Industrial Imports, had grown into the giant Ciset corporation, supplying sophisticated electronics to the air force, with a board of directors bristling with retired military men. Crociani was enjoying the fruits of his success which, according to Italian rumour, even ran to a Mercedes equipped with a lavatory. To cynics who suggested that his private wealth and public office were not entirely unconnected, he would respond that only the rich were incorruptible. 'The Italians', he told a friend, 'would like beggars to be presidents of state industries in order to say they enrich themselves by stealing. But I am already rich, and with rich presidents like me the state's money is safe.'

Finally, in 1974, when Rumor became prime minister for the fifth time, Crociani was appointed president of Finmeccanica. He was at the top of the tree, one of the richest men in Italy, and well protected by powerful friends. Guests were whisked by helicopter to land on the roof of his stately villa at San Felice di Circeo, on the coast near Rome, built around a Saracen tower and set beside a swimming pool equipped with an artificial wave-making machine. (It was owned, no doubt, by a very old man.) But an even more impressive tribute to

Crociani's power than the Mercedes with plumbing and the pool which mimicked the sea was the ease with which he got a church annulment of his first marriage (which produced two children) in order to wed a slender starlet. And as a final demonstration of his qualities as a master salesman and persuader, his discarded wife was smooth-talked into remaining on the board of one of his companies. Just the man for Lockheed.

By March 1969, then, Lockheed had the Lefebvre brothers and Crociani rooting for them, and they in turn had the support of General Nicolo, deputy head of the air force procurement agency; General Fanali, air force chief of staff; and a handful of top politicians, including prime minister Rumor himself. The next stage was to widen the circle of Hercules enthusiasts in the military procurement agencies. Some of the technical staff were proving a little slow in understanding why the C–130 had suddenly become so vital to the defence of Italy and the western alliance, and General Fillipone, head of Costamaero, the air force arms procurement agency, wrote a memo criticising the Hercules as wholly unsuited to Italy's needs. Fortunately for Lockheed and its allies, General Nicolo, Fillipone's deputy and an early Lefebvre recruit, was on hand to add a postscript explaining away his boss's doubts before passing the memo on.

Another problem seemed less easily resolved. Defence minister Luigi Gui was as yet unpersuaded. Even when Fanali suggested that the planes could probably be paid for eventually out of American aid, Gui refused to allocate funds for the Hercules in his defence budget. Lockheed concluded he was playing hard-to-get and resolved to play still harder to get him.

Meanwhile, in the middle of October, the chiefs of staff met to discuss the issue. General Marchesi of the army favoured Fiat's G–222, for which 20 billion lire ($150 million) had already been appropriated. That money, he argued, would buy sixty Italian-made planes of the short-range type suited to Italy's needs, compared with only twenty American-made planes of a type wholly irrelevant to the country's foreseeable military requirements. The navy agreed. Fanali, for the air force, fought back heatedly, denigrating the G–222, extolling the C–130 and even advancing the argument that, as Italy had had to obtain essential strategic supplies during the war from as far afield as Brazil, and therefore might have to do so again, only the long-range Hercules was worth buying. Somehow Fanali carried the day. The army and navy deferred to the air force and Hercules received the military chiefs' stamp of approval. A jubilant

Lefebvre reported the victory to Lockheed on October 16; which is why, two days later, sales executive Maurice Egan addressed a letter to an obscure address in Panama.

The 'Tezorefo Temperate Zone Research Foundation' had its official headquarters in Apartment 7412 in the Estafeta Balboa, Panama City, but it transacted little business from this exotic location. The imposingly-titled foundation's only listed director was John Vassar House, an American sculptor living not in Panama City but Rome. House was a friend of Antonio Lefebvre. He had agreed, as a favour, to be titular head of Tezorefo, which was in reality neither a foundation nor a research organisation but one of more than 200 Lefebvre dummy companies. Tezorefo was the enterprising brothers' designated recipient of Lockheed's bribe money, and Egan solemnly notified the Panamanian post-box that 'we accept your assistance as for the transaction with the Italian Government for the sale of twenty "C–130" or "Hercules" planes ... It is understood that, as a commission and reimbursement of expenses, you will receive US $120,000 for each aircraft which will be sold'.

On the same day Egan wrote an almost identical letter—it even duplicated minor spelling mistakes—to 'S.p.A. COM.EL', an abbreviation for Componenti Elettronici, headquartered on the Via Savoia, Rome. Com.El. had started life in 1964, the creation of Crociani's personal lawyer and chief of staff, Vittorio Antonelli. One of Antonelli's tasks was to supervise the setting up of his master's ghost companies, and Antonelli in turn employed a personnel officer, one Giugliemo Ferretti, to seek out senior citizens qualified by ignorance, hunger or senility to become instant company directors. Before Crociani's deal with Lockheed, Com.El. was in fact run by a middle-aged spinster, Maria Fava, whose connection with 700 such companies (none of which paid tax) would later result in her being dubbed by the Rome press 'La Donna Lockheed'. But with the Lockheed commission secured and a potentially taxable sum on its way through the books, ownership of Com.El. passed rapidly from Maria Fava; first to a dying eighty-year-old, Rocco Mariani, who signed the papers for the price of the last good meal of his life; then, after his death, to eighty-six-year-old Eduardo Lugresso, permanently bedridden, poverty-stricken and the director of twenty-six companies. These were the businessmen to whom Lockheed, in the person of Maurice Egan, wrote on October 18, 1969, promising, in return for Com.El.'s 'irrestricted [*sic*] assistance whenever required and your advise [*sic*] to the best of your knowledge and concience [*sic*] ... ten million lire for each aircraft which will be sold'. October 18 was a good day for the cumshaw pot.

All was now going well, but all was not yet won. There was still the stubborn figure of defence minister Gui to persuade. Gui was a colourless politician: his opponents, both within and without the Christian Democrat party, dismissed him as a hack. He had entered parliament in 1948, risen under Fanfani, switched allegiance to Rumor and become minister of education. His tenure there, though it lasted six years, was undistinguished: he managed to stir even conservative Catholic students to riot. In 1968 he was moved to defence.

The date by which a ministerial choice between the Fiat and Lockheed offering had to be made was January 31, 1970. In mid-December, with time running out, Carl Kotchian paid his second visit to Rome and, with Egan, met Gui privately. One week later, Lockheed transferred $2,020,000 into a Rome bank account, withdrawable only by Maurice Egan.

On January 15 Gui signed a letter of intent to buy fourteen C–130s — six less than the twenty Lockheed had originally hoped for. The corporation overcame its disappointment by successfully negotiating a price increase to $3,345,000 per plane. But then a series of crises followed, each threatening to smash the deal and deprive an ever-growing band of Italian politicians, officials and businessmen of their promised share of cumshaw.

The first complication was a national financial crisis. It transpired that the Italian government did not have the cash in hand to pay for this fleet of unneeded behemoths. The Lefebvres, aghast at seeing the fruits of victory slip from their grasp, suggested that the American government's export-import bank, Ex-Im, might be prepared to lend the purchase price. No go. Egan returned to America: so did the $2,020,000.

Then, in February, Rumor's government collapsed in a tangled controversy over a liberal divorce bill and labour unrest. It was five weeks before a new four-party government could be put together. Rumor survived as prime minister, but Gui disappeared from defence in the new distribution of cabinet seats, to be replaced by a new player for Lockheed, Social Democrat Mario Tanassi.

The Social Democrats, known cynically by their left-wing opponents as the 'Partito Socialista Democratico Americano', had broken with the Socialist party in 1948 in protest against an official Socialist attitude towards communism which seemed altogether too benign both to the American government and to the likes of Mario Tanassi. Despite his right-wing stance and visceral anti-communism, Tanassi was always treated with a certain condescension by his colleagues, as when, in 1959, Social Democrat leader Giuseppe Saragat opposed his attempt to become editor of the party newspaper with the jibe that 'to run a newspaper it helps to be able to read and write'. But Tanassi the populist thrived on the jibes of intellectuals. By 1968 it was unthinkable that a coalition which included the Social Democrats would not find a cabinet place for him. He served first at industry, then, in 1970, at defence. His four-year tenure was remarkable not only for his part in the Lockheed affair but also for his open links with Vito Michele, the sinister head of one of Italy's two rival secret services, the military-controlled SIS. Tanassi appointed Michele to this post, and consequently picked up some of the opprobrium which resulted from Michele's suspected links with neo-fascist terrorists.

The weeks which followed Tanassi's replacement of Gui were an anxious time for Lockheed. But the wheels of the grease machine turned smoothly. Tanassi was soon persuaded of the merits of the Hercules, and on June 2, William Cowden, who had succeeded Maurice Egan as Lockheed's paymaster, deposited $600,000 in the corporation's Rome bank account. Next day Tanassi signed the updated letter of intent on behalf of the new government.

That, according to the arrangements made while Gui was minister, should have triggered payment of the first third of the bribe, routed through Tezorefo but destined, in theory, for Christian Democrat party funds. So far, apart from Bixby Smith's tortured confessional, everyone involved had taken care to dress the bribes in a cloak of antiseptic memoese – 'promotional expenses', 'consultancy agreement', 'commission', etc. But Mario Tanassi was made of cruder stuff. As a Social Democrat he was suspicious of complex arrangements which had been designed to benefit his Christian Democrat predecessor and the Christian Democrat party. He wanted the money in cash. Ovidio Lefebvre passed his demand to Cowden, who had little choice but to draw $575,000 from Lockheed's account, stuff the notes in a suitcase and hand it over to Lefebvre. Summoned a little later to the minister's office, he saw the same blue suitcase sitting in the corner.

One man who wasn't amused by this turn of events was Luigi Gui who had, after all, done his best, and wasn't prepared to see his successor and a rival party scoop the pool. Thus it was that Cowden found himself dealing with yet another ghost company, Ikaria Establissement, registered in Vaduz, Liechtenstein. Lockheed advised Ovidio Lefebvre that Ikaria had 'rendered invaluable assistance' and authorised him to pay the company $78,000. This sum was despatched to Lefebvre on June 3, passed by him to Ikaria and receipted on June 21. A year later, Cowden accounted to his superiors for the transaction in a private memo:

> Early in 1970 Lockheed recognised the need for additional special expenses of $78,000 and this amount was to be paid on receipt of the letter of intent. These expenses actually were to compensate the previous Minister and certain members of his team, who are now in the Ministry and will review the contract.

The position, then, by the end of June, was that Lockheed had paid Lefebvre $575,000 in cash, one-third of the agreed bribe, which Lefebvre had 'booked' to his Tezorefo Temperate Zone Research Foundation before passing it, in a suitcase, to Tanassi. In addition, $78,000 had been paid to Ikaria, again through Lefebvre, intended for Gui and friends. The second instalment of the main bribe would become due when the banks released cash to the Italian government to pay Lockheed, and the remainder would become due on contract registration.

Both deadlines, given the hazards of Italian politics, seemed some way away. The government was hoping to raise the bulk of the cash needed to buy the planes (and incidentally repay Lockheed for the bribes so far advanced) from the state bank, IMI. But IMI was in no hurry to oblige. On June 24, prime minister Rumor's private secretary, Antonio Bisaglia, wrote to the bank's state-appointed directors stating that 'the Prime Minister's office has followed the Lockheed negotiations with great interest' and asked them to *preferanze* the deal.[1] Despite this high-level interest, however, the loan remained in the bank's pending tray.

In July, to the Lockheed men's horror, the government again fell. Rumor was replaced by Colombo, but Tanassi retained his post at defence. Still nothing was heard from IMI. Lockheed's costs were rising fast, and in December they pushed the price of the Hercules up to $3,826,000 per plane, more than a million dollars higher than the original offer. The corporation expected Tanassi to drive a hard

---

1 Bisaglia has since stated that, although the letter carries his signature, he does not remember writing it.

bargain over this inflationary trend and indeed he did so — though in precisely the opposite way to what Lockheed expected. As Cowden reported back to Burbank in a memo three months later:

> We have recently agreed to an additional payment for special compensation to the Minister for his activities in connection with the price increase that was negotiated in December. Originally, this was to amount to more than $200,000, but agreement has been reached on a single payment of $50,000.

Far from resisting the increase, Tanassi had readily agreed it — at a price. Cowden went on in the same memo to complain:

> The continuing delay in completing interim financing loan arrangements ... and the resultant delay in making the second payment of commissions and fees is jeopardising the progress of our Italian C–130 contract. In addition, our consultant reports that the delay, regardless of the circumstances, is damaging our Corporate image with key personnel in the MOD and in other Italian Government circles.

What was happening, according to Cowden, was that Tanassi was blaming Lockheed for not doing all it could to hasten the IMI loan. The memo continued:

> He is also suspicious that perhaps the reason for our lack of action is that we are merely waiting for a government change so no payment to his party will be necessary. Lefebvre has done all he could to combat this feeling, but IMI people have apparently contributed to our problem [by] passing the blame to us ... According to Lefebvre, the Minister's current position is that he will not process the contract further until the second payment is made to him. He feels that this is his last really effective pressure point, and apparently he intends to use it. He also states that Lockheed should not propose any new programs, such as the CL–1200, until the C–130 matter is cleared up. However, positive action by Lockheed will get positive and co-operative results.

Reluctantly, Cowden concluded that Tanassi had them over a barrel:

> We are acutely aware of the Corporate cash problem and know full well that making the second commission payment before obtaining any loan proceeds would only increase that problem.

However, it appears to us that we really don't have a choice if we want our contract to continue the processing cycle – and we do.

With the known instability of the Italian Government we consider it imperative to assure that the contract is firmed up as soon as possible. The last thing we want is a new government and a new set of players at this stage of the game, and this possibility is getting stronger all the time according to Lefebvre ... We therefore request authorisation to make the second payment of $765,000 as soon as possible.

Authorisation was sent. In June Cowden again stuffed his suitcase with cash – $575,000 plus the 'additional payment' of $50,000 for Tanassi, and $140,000 as first instalment of Lefebvre's 'legal fees' – and the log-jam miraculously broke. Tanassi signed the contract and Cowden jubilantly cabled back to base:

ALL DOCUMENTS SIGNED YESTERDAY STOP VISITED MINISTER RE-
VIEWED DOCUMENTS OF THE CONSULTANT AND RECEIVED PROMISE
OF HELP FOR FINAL DETAILS STOP MONEY TRANSFERRED ACCORDING
TO AGREEMENT STOP WE FEEL WE ARE ALMOST AT THE END OF AN
ERA STOP WE LEAVE TODAY FOR LIBYA STOP COWDEN.

But once again the celebratory message (with its interesting postscript) was premature. IMI still sat on the loan, and in August an innocent air force officer named Gianbattisto Collegiovanni complained that the budget office of the defence ministry was spending its entire time working on ways to guarantee the C–130 contract. But their efforts were about to pay off. On November 5, 1971, after IMI's loan approval had finally come through, Carl Kotchian approved the final payment of $600,000, including a further $70,000 in 'legal fees' for Lefebvre. And Cowden was instructed to collect 'global receipts' from Tezorefo and Com.El. 'in order to reach a satisfactory solution from the legal point of view'.

Altogether Lockheed paid out $1,456,000 to Tezorefo (ministers and parties), $224,000 to Com.El. (Crociani and Fanali), $78,000 to the 'former Minister' (Gui), $50,000 in 'special compensation to the Minister [Tanassi]' in connection with the price rise, and $210,000 to the Lefebvre brothers' law firm. Grand total $2,018,000.

Early in January 1972, fourteen immaculate Hercules aircraft landed at Pisa airfield and were ceremonially handed over to the Italian air force. Lockheed breathed a sigh of relief. The affair, it seemed, was over at last.

They couldn't have been more wrong. Four years later, when the Church Committee questioned Lockheed on the Italian contract, Bixby Smith's letter came to light, along with a string of tantalising memos and receipts. No names were named: Lockheed scratched them out before turning them over to the Committee. But an all-party Italian commission of enquiry voted to pursue charges against Gui and Tanassi, Rumor escaping investigation only by the Christian Democrat chairman's casting vote. On March 10, 1977, the combined houses of parliament voted to impeach the two former defence ministers, Gui denying that he had received any money from Lockheed and Tanassi claiming that whatever he had done had been done only for the good of the party. Crociani and Ovidio Lefebvre fled the country but eventually returned to face trial with nine party or government officials and two former ministers. After long delays the trials eventually began in April 1978. The scandal, coinciding when it first broke with revelations of huge oil company pay-offs to politicians, was widely supposed to have helped the communists make their best-ever showing in the 1976 general election, at the expense of the two 'Lockheed parties'. (To the astonishment of their critics, however, both Gui and Tanassi held their seats.)

As for those fourteen C–130s, ostensibly bought to give Italy the capability of rushing its regiments to the furthest corners of the earth whenever called upon (though who would call, and why, remained, as ever, obscure), they remained at Pisa. And for most of the time they stayed firmly on the ground. In six years, no more than four ever took to the air at any one time. The reason: a chronic shortage of spare parts.

Lockheed's contract was vague about spare parts. And Lockheed stuck to the letter of the contract.

8

The Rival Grease Machine

As a matter of fact, I don't know a damn thing about an airplane except the nose and the tail.

Frank De Francis, Northrop consultant

1

In Italy, as in Japan and probably in the Netherlands, an important consideration in Lockheed's decision to bribe was the conviction that its rivals were bribing too. A little palm-greasing was the done thing, the customary way of doing business. How far was Lockheed correct in ascribing its own venal behaviour to others? To what extent are the practices so far described exclusive to the Lockheed Corporation?

Anthony Sampson has charted in *The Arms Bazaar* the century-old tradition of bribery and corruption in international arms sales, starting with archetypal 'merchant of death' Basil Zaharoff whose telegrams to Vickers show him 'greasing the wheels' in Russia in 1900, 'doing the needful' in Portugal in 1906, 'administering doses of Vickers to Spanish friends' in the same year, and generally flitting through Europe's capitals leaving well-stuffed wallets on politicians' desks. Sampson quotes Vickers's historian J. D. Scott on the nineteenth-century arms trade:

> It would be naive to imagine that the standards of the business ethics in the Balkans and in South America in the 'Seventies and 'Eighties were the standards of Whitehall or the Bank of England. Bribery was not accidental or occasional, but essential and systematic in every field of commerce. It would be equally naive, however, to imagine that when Zaharoff paid bribes, the money paid appeared under a ledger entry of 'Bribes' in the books in London ... Zaharoff paid secrecy commissions, or bribes, of sums running from about £100 to possibly several thousand pounds. There is no evidence about whom they were paid to and what they were paid for, but the likeliest thing is that they went to forestall German and other rivals.

No doubt the 'German and other rivals' were similarly engaged in forestalling Vickers and sterling wasn't the only currency crammed into ministers' wallets. Lockheed's super-salesmen of half a century later probably knew nothing of the details of Zaharoff's bogus commission system, Krupp's countervailing corruption or even the celebrated Vickers–Mitsui bribery scandal of 1913 which, with extraordinary pre-echoes of 1976, precipitated the fall of leading Japanese politicians. What they did know was that bribery in their business was not dead history but living reality. 'Other rivals', they believed, were still at it. They were right.

The best-documented (which is not to say necessarily the biggest or most successful) of Lockheed's rival grease machines was that of Northrop. It was Northrop's claim to the Church Committee that their 'questionable' sales practices were based on a 'Lockheed model' which triggered the Lockheed investigation. But Northrop has more substantial claim than that to a prominent place in the Lockheed story. Examination of the Northrop papers, subpoena'd and made public by the Church Committee, helps us determine to what extent the Lockheed practices were unique to the company and to what extent they were common to much of the rest of the aerospace industry. Still more important, they show that in parts of Europe and the Middle East the two rivals not only employed identical methods but actually used the same small group of secret agents: a flourishing, multinational underworld grasping at the coattails of the powerful and well-connected.

Northrop had been linked with Lockheed from the start. Jack Northrop was a co-founder with the Lockheed brothers of the first Lockheed Aircraft Company. (Curiously, just as the brothers had had difficulty in deciding whether to spell their name Loughhead or Lockheed, Northrop was alternatively spelt Northrup until the 1930s, and the discarded form continued to pop up from time to time until the scandals of the 1970s ironically gave the company the kind of instant fame and recognition which banishes misspellings.) Jack Northrop left Lockheed in the 1920s to set up his own firm, but was soon bought out by a holding company, United Aircraft and Transport. On the eve of European war in 1939, Northrop again established a plant of his own to specialise in military planes, and his highly successful Black Widow night fighter quickly put him among the top seven airframe producers on the west coast.

The Northrop firm survived the end of the war but by the 1950s it was in increasing financial difficulties. Jack Northrop was seen by his peers and competitors as a brilliant engineer and designer lacking the shrewd, competitive abilities of Lockheed's Robert Gross. In 1960 his own board ousted him (he was allowed a modest retainer as a 'consultant') and appointed in his place a high-flier recruited in the mid-1950s from the Rand Corporation think-tank, Thomas V. Jones.

Tom Jones, then barely forty, was a man made in the image of Gross: a society charmer with a ranch-style house near Bel Air, friend of movie actors (he married the daughter of *Midsummer Madness* star Conrad Nagel), collector of modern French paintings, wine connoisseur—and ruthless businessman. When I talked to him in the immediate aftermath of the Church Committee hearings he seemed a sad, hesitant, almost broken man—though he was soon to come bouncing back. Sampson describes him uncompromisingly as 'a driven man, single-minded in his pursuit of money and power. Within the company he increasingly dominated every department, concealing his dealings from his board—and with good reason. For he exerted every possible pressure, legal or illegal, in pursuit of his profits.'

Jones's strategy for Northrop, once control of the company was in his hands, was no less single-minded than his pursuit of money and power. His first big decision was to scrap a cash-consuming development programme for a complex Mach 3 fighter and switch production to a much less ambitious, cheaper model, the Tiger, designed to catch the eye of buyers from low-budget but arms-hungry Third World countries. But it was Jones's method of selling his Tigers which displayed his special qualities.

There are two ways of selling military planes. One is the manufacturer-to-customer way, where the buying country will contract directly with the maker. Most makers prefer this: it gives them more control over price and leaves them with a free hand when it comes to commission payments. The other way is by government-to-government sale, where the buying country contracts not with the maker directly but with the US government, the Pentagon. With the Pentagon as middleman the scope for offering commissions or bribes is more limited. Lockheed's sales strategy was based whenever possible on direct manufacturer-to-customer deals. But Tom Jones noted the Pentagon's expanding arms sales programme and declared himself a firm supporter of government-to-government sales. His strategy was designed to ensure for Northrop a greatly expanded share of Pentagon-sponsored export sales. Where Lockheed had put most emphasis on courting the overseas buyer, Northrop courted the middleman who placed the contracts. To Gross's largesse to foreigners, Jones added a similarly motivated generosity towards influential politicians in Washington.

Since 'political commitments' at home were far more sensitive than questionable commission payments to foreigners, which could always be rationalised by reference to other customs and laws, a means had to be found of fulfilling these 'commitments' in the greatest secrecy, which meant finding ways of making available large sums of corporate money without making book entries which would alert auditors and tax investigators to what was going on.

The operation was put in the hands of Jimmy Allen, like Jones himself a former Rand Corporation man, whom Jones had promoted to vice-president and director. Allen was experienced in the mysteries of corporation accountancy: he had served as an aide to William O. Douglas when Douglas was chairman of the companies' watchdog agency, the SEC. Allen was advised by Stanley Simon, a lawyer with a reputation as a 'doctor' of corporations, to adopt what was known as the 'Kennedy plan' because it was said to have been worked out by Joseph Kennedy (company lawyer, ambassador to London and father of J.F.K.). The Kennedy plan was a simple, ingenious and apparently foolproof method of laundering huge sums of money by sending it abroad in the guise of legal sales commissions or marketing fees, and then returning it illegally as untraceable cash for distribution to the lucky recipients.

Simon proposed as chief laundryman a French lawyer named William Savy, a former 'intelligence officer' who was later said by Jones to have been used by the French government in 'various investigations' of the American aerospace industry, having worked for several European companies including Rolls-Royce, and had been generally active, one way or another, in assisting corporations solve their financial problems. Allen met Savy, approved him, and recommended him to Jones who hired him for 'intelligence work' in Paris. He was paid a retainer of $10,000 a year plus variable sums (up to $10,000 a month) for 'special duties'. The payments were entered in Northrop's books as bona fide commissions. Ostensibly, Savy was to provide intelligence reports on the European aerospace market. But in thirteen years, from his hiring in October 1961, Savy never wrote a single intelligence report for Northrop. In that time more than $1,100,000 in commission and fees were booked to three companies Savy ran: Wilco Holding in Luxembourg, Wilco S.A. in Geneva and Euradvice in Basel. Savy's real job was to hold this cash as a secret slush fund and to return it to America on demand.

Shortly after being hired by Northrop, and for the next thirteen years, Savy made regular trips to New York every two months with up to $40,000 in $100 bills divided between his coat pockets. The money was handed over to Allen in regular rendezvous in Savy's hotel room.[1] The cash was then redistributed in accordance with Northrop's commitments, with no record kept of how much was returned (in contravention of both French and American currency laws) or how it was disbursed. 'The confidential relationship between Savy and Northrop became even more so once they got into this funnelling of funds', Allen told Northrop's auditors when they investigated the connection in the wake of the Watergate scandal, adding: 'A decision was made early to keep *no* records as to what was changing hands.' Jones too admitted that Savy's 'political commitment work' was specifically set up with the intent that records would not be kept.[2]

Precisely which politicians and officials benefited most from the secret Savy fund is not clear. The glimpses that we are given in the Northrop papers clearly show us no more than the tip of the iceberg. Thus, between 1960 and 1969 Jones collected $8,000 from the fund for cash contributions to a variety of both Republican and Democrat campaigns—$1,000 for the 1964 Johnson for President Committee; $1,000 for the Johnson–Humphrey campaign treasurer, Brian P. Leeb; $1,000 for the United Republican Finance Committee in 1968 and another $1,500 in 1969, plus sums varying from $250 to $2,000 for the campaign committees of Senators Kuchel, Mansfield, Russell and Murphy.[3] Similar payments totalling $7,000 continued after 1970. In addition, we have glimpses of larger and more mysterious contributions: $20,000 to Republican Fund-raiser Holmes Tuttle, an unknown sum to Tuttle's Democrat counterpart Gene Wyman, and two payments of $3,000 each to the 1968 Nixon Campaign.[4] Later came the huge contributions to buy the silence of the Watergate conspirators which finally exposed the Savy conduit.[5] That there were other payments is clear first from the fact that these fall well short of the almost certainly underestimated total of $400,000[6] which Allen recollected having received from Savy at those New York hotel meetings, and second from the evidence of the lobbying activities of

1 Allen to Ernst and Ernst, Northrop's auditors, June 27, 1974.
2 Jones to Ernst and Ernst, June 26, 1974.
3 Jones to Ernst and Ernst, August 20, 1974.
4 Jones to Ernst and Ernst, June 26, 1974, and Church Committee hearings, June 9 and 10, 1975.
5 See chapter 11.
6 Northrop's auditors estimated the amount returned at about $476,000.

Northrop consultant Frank De Francis, which we shall look at later. Suffice it for the present to note that the demands on Savy were highest in election years and at those times when Congressional support was needed for Northrop — to finance the company's retooling programme, for example.

Much less integrated into the military-industrial complex, then, than its bigger rival, Northrop differed from Lockheed in deciding that, when it comes to the distribution of slush, charity begins at home. But this is not to say that Northrop resisted bribery and extortion overseas. Of the $1,100,000 credited to Savy's three accounts, barely half is accounted for by the unbooked cash returned to Allen and Savy's $10,000-a-year retainer. Of the use to which the rest was put we can but speculate: Savy has refused to be interviewed by investigators and no doubt has good reason to congratulate himself on his foresight in banking in the sanctuaries of Switzerland and Luxembourg. The only scrap of information we have to help our speculation is Jones's reference, when questioned by his auditors in 1974, to Savy's 'commitments'. 'The thrust of the implication', noted auditor E. Raymond Crim, 'is that he uses others to which he has to make payments.' Jones confirmed that the 'commitments' were indeed 'Savy's various agents or others which he in fact did use to further his own career' and which Northrop recognised as 'part of Savy's cost of doing business'.[1]

So Savy's grease was spread both at home and abroad. But melodramatic as it was — bundles of bills smuggled across the Atlantic, secret meetings in hotel rooms and yet more secret drops in Washington — the Savy fund was only one of many hidden weapons in Tom Jones's diverse armoury.

2

By 1964 Northrop was poised for one of the most successful military plane export programmes in aviation industry. In the F–5 Tiger it had a small, cheap, adaptable product, destined to contribute $2 billion to the US balance of payments. The Tiger's success — by 1975 it had been sold to twenty-two countries — rested on three factors: the genuine excellence of the product; Northrop's evident ability to win financial and political support among influential Washington

1 Jones to Ernst and Ernst, June 26, 1974.

politicians and Pentagon officials; and the development of a secret overseas sales network which came to be modelled directly on the Lockheed pattern.

The first important sales consultant to be hired by Tom Jones was Kermit Roosevelt, grandson of President Theodore Roosevelt and for many years a senior CIA operative specialising in covert activities in the Middle East and Latin America. Jones had won his first foreign order from the Shah of Iran in 1962 when the Shah had visited California and seen the Tiger in production. Jones's plan was to harness the Shah's enthusiasm for the plane to trigger more Middle East sales, and it was in furtherance of this idea that he hired Roosevelt early in 1965, just as Iran's first orders were being delivered.

Roosevelt was a shrewd choice. Back in 1953 when the Shah was suddenly removed from his throne by nationalist prime minister Mossadeq, Roosevelt had organised the CIA and British secret service counter-coup which in turn ousted Mossadeq and restored the Shah. At a stroke, Jones added to his payroll the one man to whom the increasingly influential and arms-hungry monarch literally owed his throne. Roosevelt was paid what Jones curiously called 'compensation' of '$15,000 minimum' a year, raised to $45,000 in 1968, $60,000 in 1971 and $75,000 in 1973. This did not include 'expenses incurred on behalf of Northrop' which were reimbursed on presentation of accounts. Roosevelt's job, according to Jones, was 'to monitor all activities in the Middle East and inform Northrop of important events and trends; also to actively participate in establishing and maintaining the contacts of Northrop with the highest levels of government in the Middle East'. Jones later credited him with being the 'key figure' in establishing Northrop's 'very high level of activity ... in the Middle East, with contract values in this area ... running close to a billion dollars'.[1]

This included not only Tiger sales but electronics hardware and services both for the Iranian air force and SAVAK, the Shah's notorious torture squad. Roosevelt was also instrumental in setting up

---

[1] Jones to Ernst and Ernst, August 23, 1974. Interestingly, one of Roosevelt's associates in the covert operation which put the Shah back on his throne was an Anglo-Indian named Shapoor Reporter, a political adviser to the US embassy in Teheran and a British secret service agent. Sir Shapoor — he was knighted in the 1973 New Year's Honours List — became a consultant for several British companies selling in Iran and collected £1 million on a £100 million sale of Chieftain tanks.

Iranian Aircraft Industries, in which Northrop had a 49 per cent holding, and in establishing a huge Northrop presence across the Gulf in Saudi Arabia, where he had a hand in selecting as the company's agent the soon-to-be-notorious Adnan Khashoggi.

What Kim Roosevelt was not, was a crude Lockheed-style influence peddler. There is no suggestion that he was involved in Northrop's more questionable actions in Iran which included a substantial bribe to a tax official, 'commission' payments (possibly from the Savy fund) to a number of officials and businessmen who formed themselves into an agency consortium not unlike the 'widows and orphans' of Indonesia, and improper payments totalling at least $1,016,000 by a Northrop subsidiary, Page-Europa.[1] Roosevelt operated on a more exalted level, even to the extent of trying to turn the Shah himself into a royal super-salesman for the corporation. Thus in September 1968 we find Tom Jones suggesting to him ways by which the Shah might be persuaded to mention his enthusiasm for the P–530 Cobra during a forthcoming meeting with the German Chancellor, Kurt Kiesinger, whose government was known to be divided between the merits of the Cobra and those of the multinational MRCA Tornado. The episode gives us a rare insight into high politics in the arms trade. Jones wrote:

> It is terribly important that we take advantage of this opportunity to have His Majesty mention to the Chancellor his concern about the equipment problems of the future and his feelings about Northrop and the 530 solution. It is important that he tell the Chancellor of his conversation with the President, stating that he felt that the US — in the interest of those countries that look to us for certain types of help or leadership in the military area — that the US should put some earnest money behind the Northrop 530.

Sections of the German cabinet were bound to be pro-MRCA, Jones wrote, but a good word for the Cobra from the Shah could swing the Chancellor.

> He must contend, as I have said, with the views of his Defense Minister and Chief of Staff, and he has a hard time getting into the loop properly. But if His Majesty tells him that the initiative on it came from him, His Majesty, it will help the Chancellor keep his discussion at home on a policy level. The main purpose of His Majesty's stating this simply, not expecting an answer, is to help

1 Disclosed by Northrop to the SEC on April 14, 1977.

establish the fact that the 530 project was viewed as of world-wide importance to those nations that have common objectives with respect to freedom ... The important thing is not to sell the Chancellor at all but to communicate to him at this high policy level that the initiative has been taken by the Shah himself and that it was this that led the US to support the 530. We want the Chancellor to be able to say that the 530 project does not represent a narrow sales effort on the part of a contractor who is trying to compete with German and British industry—and you can be sure that this is the way it will be twisted in a competitive situation like this.[1]

Whether or not the Shah obliged with his endorsement, the Germans eventually opted for the MRCA (despite further attempts by Northrop consultant Frank De Francis to sabotage the decision). But if Roosevelt wasn't always successful, it wasn't for lack of long reach. In South America too (where, hard on the heels of his Iran coup, he had won the respect and gratitude of every right-wing politician on the continent by organising a similar CIA putsch against the short-lived leftist government in Guatemala) his top-level contacts, and probably his old CIA comrades, were enrolled to give Northrop an enviable intelligence of procurement politics. Thus, correspondence in mid 1965 between Roosevelt and General Patrick Timberlake, USAF (Ret.), a newly-recruited executive of Northrop International, shows that they not only knew what was going on in the procurement ministries in Venezuela, Argentina and Chile, where Northrop hoped to sell the Tiger, but also had a full file on the opposition. 'We have evidence that Hawker of the Hawker-Siddeley Group of England has offered the Venezuelan Government fifteen Hawker Hunters for $13·5m. The British Embassy in Caracas, lending full support to this sale, has stationed a Commercial Attaché Specialist named Raymond Smith at the Embassy.'[2] A run-down of Smith's track record followed. Detailed information of this kind was invaluable to those entrusted with the delicate task of lobbying department of defense officials to put political muscle behind Northrop's sales pitches.

But Roosevelt's influence was not quite world-wide. He had never toppled an unfriendly government in Europe, and Jones had to look elsewhere for his inside information there and in the counsels of NATO. The man he chose to be his European eyes and ears had

1 Jones to Roosevelt, September 3, 1968.
2 Timberlake to Roosevelt, May 11, 1965, and subsequent correspondence.

equally impeccable qualifications. General Paul-Marie Victor Stehlin boasted an outstanding career in France as both air force officer and diplomat. He had been air attaché to Germany before the war and to Britain and the United States since, rising to become chief of the French tactical air command and finally air force chief of staff.

But, unusual for a French official and particularly a high-placed military man, Stehlin was a passionate Atlanticist even under the ultra-chauvinist regime of de Gaulle. As outward expressions of his pro-American feelings, he had married an American wife, lectured at Harvard and briefly represented the Hughes Aircraft Corporation. He made no secret of his faith in NATO and his contempt for Gaullist isolationism, which made him many enemies in his own country. But it also made a friend of Tom Jones, who in April 1964 signed him up as Northrop's Paris consultant at the modest fee of $5,000 a year. His responsibilities, as somewhat vaguely described by Jones, were 'analyses of all political, economic and military situations in Europe', with 'emphasis on defense-related programs' and 'the alerting of Northrop to business opportunities in the defense-related areas as they arise'.

There was no impropriety whatever about Northrop's relationship with the stubbornly individualistic general – except that Stehlin kept it secret and actually lied about it. In 1968 he was elected to the French National Assembly (Jones upped his fee by $1,000 a year), but although he made many speeches about the importance of the American connection he not only never declared his own financial interest but denied it when challenged. In September 1974, after rashly writing to President Giscard d'Estaing that France would be better served by buying American than French in the impending 'sale of the century' where Northrop's Cobra and Dassault's Mirage were leading contenders, and still more rashly circulating the letter among selected officials, he was loudly denounced for his lack of patriotism and honour. *Le Monde* called for his resignation, and soon afterwards he did indeed resign his position as a vice-president of the Assembly, though he remained a deputy (whereupon the sympathetic Jones upped his annual fee again to the still modest figure of $7,500). At the height of the row, Marcel Dassault himself wrote to *Le Figaro* recalling Stehlin's old link with the Hughes corporation and suggesting darkly that Stehlin was backing the Cobra to suit his old employers who were doubtless scheming to persuade Northrop to stuff the Cobra with Hughes's electronics. In fact, of course, Stehlin's interest was more direct than Dassault guessed, but he nevertheless vociferously denied that he had any financial interest whatever in the matter.

The consequences were tragic. On June 6 the following year—ironically the very day it was announced that neither Northrop nor Dassault but General Dynamics, with the F-16, had won victory in the 'sale of the century'—Senator Church's committee in Washington made public the first batch of Northrop papers subpoena'd for its hearings a few days later. Among them was a letter from Stehlin to Jones dated January 23, 1973, in which Stehlin disparaged Dassault, advised Jones to mount a press campaign for the Cobra, discussed 'exploitable elements of a good strategy' and promised assistance 'by all means at my disposal'. The papers also included a run-down by Jones of Stehlin's work for Northrop since 1964 (the name Stehlin was gallantly obliterated, but the general's distinctive biographical details were left untouched) and—most damning of all—a schedule of the fees Northrop had paid him.

An agency reporter, reading the newly-released letter, telephoned to question him and the general realised the game was up. It was the early hours of the morning. Stehlin left his wife sleeping in their new apartment at 6 rue du Cirque, near the Élysée Palace, walked to his office near the Opéra, burned his files, left the office and stepped from the pavement in front of a bus. He was knocked down and died ten days later in hospital, leaving an unsolved mystery as to whether his death was suicide or the accidental result of a state of shock. The tough Tom Jones is said to have wept on hearing the news. Marcel Dassault's reaction is unrecorded.

As with Kim Roosevelt, there is not the slightest reason to suppose that General Stehlin was either a recipient or a distributor of bribes. He was an important—but, because of the strength of his convictions, an inexpensive—element of Tom Jones's world-wide intelligence network. When there was really dirty work to be done in Europe, Jones by-passed Stehlin and found others more experienced in the ways of the world of arms sales. Which brings us to the Lockheed connection.

3

Tom Jones began courting Prince Bernhard even before his elevation to the top job at Northrop. The two met at a military aircraft convention in the mid-1950s and Jones, like Robert Gross, quickly appreciated the prince's potential value. Bernhard actively promoted the Tiger prototype in the late 1950s (see chapter 5), and when he later switched his support to the Lockheed Starfighter he did not break his contacts with Northrop – contacts which were greatly strengthened in 1961 when Northrop bought a 20 per cent share in the Dutch Fokker company. Fokker had first offered the partnership to Lockheed, and when they turned it down Jones was quick to fill the breach. It gave him a seat on the Fokker board, alongside Bernhard.

As the Tiger became operational and the big sales drive began, the Netherlands looked the most likely buyer in Europe. The Starfighter had replaced half of the RNAF's ageing Thunderstreaks and by 1965 it was time to seek a replacement for the remaining veterans. Tom Jones was determined that this time the Tiger would come out on top. What more natural course was there than to seek the advice of his top-level contacts in Amsterdam as to how best to push the Tiger's merits?

Jones was later to testify that 'high Dutch Government officials' suggested the man he recruited to head the sales drive: our old friend from Lockheed, Fred Meuser. Given Jones's links with Bernhard and Bernhard's with Meuser, it is only natural to assume that the prince was among the high officials who made the recommendation. Be that as it may, Jones arranged to meet Meuser in a Zurich hotel in March 1965. The two men got on well, and Jones was happy to accept Meuser's suggested formula for a working relationship, a formula which had the advantage of having been tried, tested and proved under Lockheed. For what Meuser proposed was that the consultancy contract be drawn up with his well-placed, well-connected friend Hubert Weisbrod in Zurich. The Meuser–Weisbrod connection which had operated so successfully for Lockheed was now transferred wholesale to Northrop. Weisbrod was appointed the company's European representative for the F–5. How much Northrop paid him in the first three years isn't clear, but by 1968 he was collecting $125,000 a year (compared with Stehlin's $5,000). Given the Lockheed precedent it is unlikely that he kept it all himself.

Soon after, again at the suggestion of 'several of the highest levels in the Dutch Government', Jones completed the team by hiring as an 'independent contractor' Prince Bernhard's old war-time friend Teengs Gerritsen, who was still Lockheed's Dutch sales agent. 'One of those Dutch beyond-reproach types' and 'a completely trusted individual', according to Jones, Gerritsen was supposedly rooting for Lockheed's answer to the Tiger, the prototype Lancer, but neglected to tell them that he had accepted $10,000 a year from the rival Northrop company to back the F–5 and 'to act as a trusted communications channel ... in sensitive areas ... between the highest levels in the Dutch Government and the President of the Northrop Corporation'.[1]

By the middle of 1965, then, Tom Jones had a formidable machine gearing up for Northrop in Europe. There were the secret beneficiaries of the Savy fund. There was secret agent Paul Stehlin. And there was the team that had worked for Lockheed in the Netherlands – Meuser, Weisbrod and Gerritsen.

Thirteen planes or prototypes were under consideration by the Dutch and Belgian air forces, which had agreed to make a joint buy. By the end of 1965 ten contenders (including Lockheed's Lancer) had been rejected as too expensive or unsuitable. The three finalists were the Dassault Mirage V, the McDonnell-Douglas A–4 and the Tiger. None perfectly fitted the Dutch specification: the Mirage was expensive and its two-seater trainer version inadequate, the A–4 was a revamp which would become obsolete before the others, and the Tiger had too short a range and required drastic modifications to the wings and landing gear to bring it up to specification. And because there was no clear-cut choice on technical grounds, political considerations soon became paramount. The two governments were faced with a familiar dilemma: buy French in the interests of European co-operation, or American in the interests of the Atlantic Alliance. The Belgians leaned towards the French, the Dutch towards the Americans.

There was no doubt, of course, where Bernhard stood. He had let the Pentagon know of his interest in the Tiger before the end of 1965, and, more significantly, had insisted on being present – which was not customary – at the two final evaluation meetings which preceded the selection of the Tiger as the Netherlands' choice. Again, in June 1966, when defence minister P. J. S. de Jong wrote to US defense secretary McNamara on the subject of royalties payable on the F–5, Bernhard actually drafted the letter for him.

The Dutch and German defence ministers met on June 28, 1966, and a bizarre power-play began. They agreed on one thing only: to exclude the A–4, leaving a straight choice between Dassault and

1 Jones to Ernst and Ernst, September 1974.

Northrop. The Belgians then secured a postponement of the final decision to October, well aware that Northrop's offer expired in July. The Dutch made hasty attempts to get the Northrop offer extended for six months until December 31 — and there then followed what seems to have been a monumental misunderstanding between the two parties. What happened is that Northrop agreed to an extension if the Dutch and Belgians chose to build the planes themselves on licence, but not if they wished to buy outright. The Dutch, however, missed the distinction and believed the extension was agreed unconditionally.

To complicate matters further, the Dutch Catholic–Labour coalition collapsed on October 15 on the eve of renewed meetings with the Belgians. Ten days later, when the Belgians still refused to buy American, the Dutch ministry of defence decided to go it alone. But time was running out fast. An attempt was made to negotiate a licensing agreement for Fokker to build 105 planes, but Fokker resisted the terms and as the end of December approached it was clear that the deadlock would not be broken in time. On December 30, with one day to go (as they thought), the ministry decided to accept Northrop's offer of a direct sale, only to learn that in Northrop's view the offer had expired on July 31.

The Dutch were now in a position as desperate as it was ludicrous. Any new offer would involve a price far in excess of the budget available for the F–5 procurement. On New Year's Eve, Bernhard received a call from the chief of air force staff. Would he telephone Jones and plead for more time? The prince agreed — but Jones could not be found.

It is hard to believe that Northrop and the prince were unaware of the Dutch confusion. As the Dutch themselves came to realise in retrospect, the company was quietly confident that the Dutch rejection of all alternatives, confirmed by the break with their Belgian partners, left the Netherlands no alternative but to buy Northrop on Northrop's terms. The prince, in private, probably shared the company's confidence. If so, they were both wrong.

There *was* an alternative, and in the closing hours of 1966 the Dutch stumbled across it. Northrop and the Pentagon were not the only suppliers of Tigers. The Canadians were also building them under licence from Northrop. A frantic, last-minute call established Canadian interest in a deal. The Dutch let Northrop's deadline pass and opened rapid negotiations with the Canadians which were successfully concluded within a month. So the Dutch got their

Tigers—105 of them—at a favourable price. And Northrop got nothing.

Where did that leave Prince Bernhard and Dr Weisbrod? It was suggested during the Church Committee's hearings that a sum of $750,000 paid to Weisbrod by Northrop was connected with the F–5 purchase, with the implication that, as in the Lockheed parallel, some of this money was intended for the prince. The 'Commissie van Drie', investigating the bribery charges against the prince, concluded that any 'direct connection' was unlikely. It based this view not only on the fact that the plane was bought from Canada instead of direct from Northrop but also on the date of Weisbrod's contract—April 26, 1968, more than a year *after* the deal had gone through.

On this, however, the Commission seems to have been less than thorough. Weisbrod did indeed have a 1968 contract, but it was not his first. As Tom Jones made clear to Northrop's auditors, Weisbrod was first hired in 1965 when the F–5 campaign was just beginning. And in Weisbrod's own view, at least, that first contract entitled him to commission on all F–5 sales in Europe, whether or not Northrop was the direct supplier. Jones put his own view of the matter in a letter to auditor Raymond Crim in September 1974. The Dutch had purchased the F–5s 'as a result of Northrop's overall efforts', but the Canadian route was 'a complicating factor in paying Dr. Weisbrod under the terms of the agreement'. As a result, Northrop was suing the Canadian government, and 'the actual resolutions of monies due under the Weisbrod contract' could only be resolved when the litigation was over.

Clearly, then, it was at least Northrop's *intention* that Weisbrod should benefit, and presumably, as with Lockheed, not Weisbrod alone. But the ultimate beneficiaries of the connection have had a long wait for their money. Eleven years after the deal with Canada, and three years after Jones's revealing letter to Crim, the complicated litigation is no nearer resolution. But there were clearly no hard feelings between the parties. Weisbrod's rewritten contract of 1968 provided 'advance monies to continue his efforts in Northrop's behalf not only in the F–5 but also in the 530 (Cobra) program'.[1]

Three years later we find the prince closely involved in the selection of yet another Northrop lobbyist in the Netherlands. Geoffrey Parsons, the company's man in Paris, wrote to Tom Jones on September 27, 1971, backing the appointment of H. L. Visser—

1 Jones's letter to Crim, September 1974.

'recommended to us by Maj. Gen. Bosch of the Royal Netherlands Air Force' – and suggesting that Jones discuss the matter with Bernhard and Gerritsen. (Gerritsen had suggested that Visser join his firm and work on the Northrop account while he, Gerritsen, continued to handle Lockheed.) Visser's job, explained Parsons, was 'to get the P–530 programme past the economic and political barriers in the Dutch Parliament'.

How this was to be accomplished was not spelt out, nor is it clear what, if anything, Visser eventually did for Northrop. But what is apparent again and again in the story of Northrop's sales efforts in the Netherlands is the extent of the company's reliance on the prince's friends – Meuser, Weisbrod, Gerritsen, Visser. The evident fact is that Northrop and Lockheed, fierce rivals, were each greasing the same wheels. Lockheed had created the model, Northrop had followed.

4

It was in the as yet unburgled Watergate building on the Potomac waterfront in Washington that Tom Jones found a secret agent so secret that Northrop's board of directors knew nothing of him until scandal broke in 1975.

Frank De Francis, soon to become Jones's most important conduit for the secret slush fund, ran his one-man law office from Suite 812, Watergate (cable address: 'DELAW'). When Jones was introduced to him in 1966, De Francis was just turned forty, a thick-set attorney whose most important client was the German embassy, which he had represented for some twenty years. De Francis had two brothers-in-law working for Northrop, one of whom, Rick Delsasso, was assistant to Jim Holcombe, corporate vice-president and manager of the company's Washington office. It was Delsasso and Holcombe who brought Jones and De Francis together.

Their meeting had a purpose. Northrop had made little headway in its efforts to interest the Germans in the Tiger as a replacement for the first generation of Lockheed Starfighters. The company had a representative in Bonn, General Adolph Galland, a former chief of the Luftwaffe, but as De Francis put it later, 'it was clear that Galland did not get to first base'. Jones set out to discover for himself what was wrong and according to his testimony to the Church

Committee he was visited and put in the picture by two officials of the German defence department, whom he named as F. J. Rath and Richard Fromsdorf, accompanied by a man he believed to be an official of the US state department, Fred Bauer. The visitors told Jones it was a waste of time to rely on open representation. As Jones told Northrop's auditors, 'They were surprised that we were not more knowledgeable than we were in our relationships with the German Government in the procurement area.' Jones took this as a broad hint that Northrop should study Lockheed's methods of doing business in Germany.[1]

So who better to advise them how to change their ways than the German government's own attorney in Washington, with his network of connections in the Bundestag and the Bonn ministries. Early in 1967 Jones and Holcombe paid their first visit to De Francis, who agreed to see what he could do to help. De Francis accordingly flew to Bonn on March 27 to talk to 'two or three top Government officials'[2] and returned to sign a contract with Northrop which in effect named him as undercover replacement for the unfortunate General Galland, who was speedily phased out.

The mutual intention, expressed in the first draft of the 1967 contract, was that De Francis should pick up a 10 per cent commission on F-5 sales to Germany. But this ran into trouble when Jones sent the contract to Northrop chief counsel George Gore who replied bluntly that it was illegal. Gore pointed out that a provision of German law known as the 'Strauss proclamation' specifically forbade commissions to third parties without the approval of the government. Despite a later claim by De Francis that his representation of Northrop alongside that of Germany had been cleared 'orally' not only with the embassy and the defence ministry but even with the Chancellor himself,[3] it was clearly not his intention that his commission arrangement should be publicised – 'Frank has requested that we make every effort not to identify him' explained Jim Hol-

---

1 From Jones's written answer to questions put by the auditors, Ernst and Ernst, August 20, 1974, published by Church. Jones also wrote of his unexpected visitors: 'They informed me that investigations in Germany on their procurement practices had indicated that Northrop was being put at a disadvantage over other American competitors through illegal activities and influences on the part of others.'

2 Holcombe to Northrop executive Glenn Lord, in a letter dated March 8, 1967, and marked 'PERSONAL–PRIVATE–SENSITIVE'.

3 'Memorandum of Discussions with Mr. De Francis' by Northrop auditor Raymond Crim, September 9, 1974.

combe to one of the few Northrop men who were allowed into the secret.[1] As a result, the contract was redrafted to provide for a flat fee of $50,000 a year for two years, plus expenses, which gave De Francis a way to deny that he was a 'salesman' as defined under the 'Strauss proclamation' and thus to claim he was not obliged to declare his interest. The agreement provided that De Francis report only to Jones or to others at Jones's request, and added:

> If you and Mr. Jones agree that in certain circumstances the services rendered by you hereunder were extraordinary and unusual, in terms of activity and effort and value to us, and beyond those contemplated by this agreement, then additional compensation will be paid you for such services, in such amounts as Mr. Jones, in his discretion, may determine to be equitable.

It is not easy to evaluate what De Francis did for Northrop during the period of his first two-year contract. Certainly neither he nor the Weisbrod connection (Weisbrod's contract also covered Germany) managed to sell any Tigers in Bonn. But Jones later credited De Francis with a sale of electronics equipment to the German air force and, more importantly, with initiating a joint venture with the German firm Siemens which produced $200 million of activity for Northrop in Iran. Jones also attributed to De Francis a German expression of interest in an improved version of the Tiger, the F–5E, as a potential alternative to the Anglo-German MRCA project. It was his activities, said Jones, 'centred on the top policy-level in Germany, especially the Foreign Ministry and later the Finance and Economics Ministries', which 'created the German interest which was the stimulus that got the program started ... We were then in a position to interest the US Government in the F–5E as an aircraft to provide to Southeast Asia as part of the withdrawal policy of the government and also as an instrument of foreign sales'. Jones put the contract value to Northrop at 'well over a billion dollars, with expectancies for total sales of well over $2 billion'.[2]

This generous appraisal of De Francis's influence has to be evaluated in its context as a statement to auditors who, by 1974, and in the light of the Watergate prosecutions, were asking why De Francis was paid such generous fees and what he did for the money. The best evidence that Jones had his own good reasons to be satisfied with De

1 Holcombe's letter to Lord, March 8, 1967.
2 Jones to Ernst and Ernst, August 20, 1974.

Francis's work is that in May 1969 he renewed his contract for four years on the same generous terms.

The glimpses we get of De Francis's activities at this time show his involvement in increasingly sensitive lobbying. There were negotiations for a German offset contribution to the Cobra, scuppered eventually by the MRCA (which De Francis attacked 'with every fibre of my being'). There was a $10,000 payment, made under the heading 'Project Italy', to a Lockheed consultant in Rome who was apparently induced to switch his support from the Lockheed Lancer to the Cobra. And there were secret discussions on Cobra co-production between the Germans and the Dutch, apparently arranged and orchestrated by De Francis.

But the egregious lawyer's most intriguing and ingenious contribution to the art of selling military aircraft was still to come. Jones had not hired De Francis primarily to negotiate offset deals or arrange minor backhanders to low-level Italians. His engagement was a direct follow-through to Jones's meeting with the German officials who had attributed the greater success of Northrop's rivals to their greater skill in winning friends and influencing people. De Francis's job was to take the 'Lockheed model' and build a replica for Northrop. The organisation he eventually created to recruit politicians and government officials into a secret network of Northrop agents was called, innocuously enough, the Economic and Development Corporation.

EDC was incorporated in Switzerland 'to work behind the scenes through use of the right people in the right places'.[1] Northrop financed its establishment, but thereafter left it to run its own affairs. As Jones explained later, in carefully chosen words:

> One of the underlying factors and conditions that was a pre-requisite in the organization of the Economic and Development Corporation was that it remain a separate and independent organization. As a consequence, the methods and utilization of personnel on behalf of the corporation are so structured that it is able to advance the cause of Northrop in the sale of the International Fighter (F–5E) not only on the basis of confidentiality, but also uniquely independent of any Northrop connection. This principle provides a wide degree of flexibility in procuring the best people for the particular assignment at hand and, in many in-

---

1 Report, 'Special Investigation of Northrop Corporation and Subsidiaries', by Ernst and Ernst (auditors), 1974.

stances, enables the securing of persons who otherwise could not be directly involved for variant reasons with Northrop as such.[1]

De Francis made the same point rather more directly:

> EDC, as a Lockheed concept, is a non-subsidiary organization and is not directed by Northrop ... Various people may own shares under the stock distribution arrangement ... I don't know if they are ministers of other countries or otherwise ... The theory of the Lockheed or EDC type arrangement is that it lets people in each country work for themselves. In effect, enough money is put into the company to cover each person's out-of-pocket expenses. Each person recruited by the EDC is promised his expenses and in addition a share of the stock in EDC, so that he is in effect working for himself and the benefits he achieves accrue to him through his stock ownership ... It is not necessary that they know a lot about the technical aspects of the airplane they are selling. As a matter of fact, I don't know a damn thing about an airplane except the nose and the tail. This theme would apply to the EDC people.[2]

De Francis supported his claim that the EDC originated with Lockheed by producing for Northrop's auditors a Lockheed contract – 'a weak xeroxed copy with pencil changes to reflect Northrop instead of Lockheed as one of the participants'.[3] 'I simply inserted Northrop for Lockheed and De Francis for Weisbrod', explained De Francis. 'If it looks unusual, remember it's the Lockheed contract.' Lockheed later denied that they had ever funded an organisation like the EDC, and it may well be that De Francis exaggerated the precision with which his scheme followed theirs. But what the arrangement certainly owed to Lockheed was the secret agent concept deployed so effectively on their behalf through Weisbrod before he joined Northrop.

Northrop provided $200,000 to set up EDC in Zürich and contracted to pay commissions of $\frac{1}{2}$ to $1\frac{1}{2}$ per cent on all direct sales of the F–5E anywhere in the world, and on indirect sales at their discretion. De Francis was paid $50,000 (over and above his $50,000-a-year retainer) for his 'legal work' in establishing the company. He wanted to participate on a percentage commission basis and the first draft contract was written with De Francis as an EDC principal. But that was considered inappropriate by Jones, who feared that 'it

1 Jones to Ernst and Ernst, August 20, 1974.
2 Auditors' notes of interview with De Francis, September 9, 1974.
3 Ibid.

could be questioned within the US Government'.[1] So a new contract was drawn up, vesting ownership and control of EDC in Swiss principals, previously unconnected with Northrop.

De Francis later described how he 'went to extreme measures to insure [sic] that EDC's corporate head would be a man of impeccable reputation and international accumen [sic]'.[2] He 'passed over the names of many outstanding international figures', including 'the world-renowned Dr. Fabian von Schlabrendorff, the principal subject of General Donovan's book *The Man Who Almost Killed Hitler*'. Eventually he settled on a man he had never met, chosen on the basis of 'numerous recommendations obtained in Italy and Switzerland, as well as from my own bank'.[3] The successful candidate was one Andreas Froriep, senior partner in a Zürich law firm, Froriep and Reuggli. Jones clearly cared little whom De Francis found to do the job. When Northrop counsel George Gore sent him the contract for approval Jones noted at the bottom against Froriep's name: 'George — I trust this is in order. I can't recognize the signature but I guess it's one of those European lawyers who is president.'[4]

Swiss law required that EDC should have at least two more registered shareholders, but De Francis and Jones left Froriep to look after that. Questioned later by his outside directors when the existence of the under-cover sales organisation eventually came to light, Jones described Froriep's co-shareholders vaguely as 'businessmen and bankers of broad and trusted ability'. In fact they were neither, and their abilities were obscure. One, Ida Isler, was reportedly a lady friend of Froriep and the other, Rudolph Kleiner, was said to be his chauffeur. Froriep owned 498 shares and Ms Isler and Kleiner one apiece.

After several false starts, EDC was incorporated in September 1971 and the search began for the shadowy figures whose lobbying and influence-peddling would do for Northrop what Weisbrod's contacts had done for Lockheed. There is no way of knowing who was recruited, or at how high a level: the records are in Froriep's safe and the vaults of his Swiss bank. But we get a tantalising glimpse in an incautious letter from De Francis to Jones on August 9, 1974:

1 Jones, letter to Northrop's outside directors, quoted in auditors' report.
2 De Francis to Jones, letter, August 9, 1974.
3 De Francis, interview with Raymond Crim, September 9, 1974.
4 EDC contract, September 1971.

In reviewing most thoroughly with Dr. Froriep the basic principles of organization and implementation of your [sic] marketing concepts, I emphasised that the personnel he would subsequently engage should be in keeping with the high standards that characterize his personal and professional career. As I previously reported to you, an illustration of the type [of] individual we discussed was Dr. Franz Bach who at one time was Chancellor Adenauer's key political and foreign advisor, held Ambassador or counsellor posts in Iran, Saudi Arabia and Hong Kong, was a former member of the Bundestag and is the Middle East consultant and advisor to one of the world's largest electrical companies, Siemens A.G.

Bach did indeed join EDC, though he resigned after the Church Committee made De Francis's letter public and Jones confirmed his connection.

It wasn't long before the EDC arrangement began to go badly wrong for Northrop, and its weaknesses, ironically, resulted from the unexpected success of the F–5E. Jones was to admit candidly, later, that at the time he and De Francis set up EDC and promised it commission on 'all direct sales throughout the world', Northrop had actually abandoned hope of making any significant *direct* sales anywhere. Their sights were really set on *indirect* government-to-government sales, where commission to EDC was entirely within Northrop's discretion and was payable only where EDC activity was believed to have swung the sale. But in 1972 the Pentagon chose the F–5E for the South Vietnamese air force, and that triggered a sudden flood of orders, both direct and indirect, around the world. Chile placed a $41·2 million order, and Brazil, Nationalist China, Saudi Arabia, Malaysia and Iran followed. Suddenly Dr Froriep and friends were due for a huge windfall, despite the evident fact that none of these sales was in any way connected with EDC activity, and they didn't wait long before knocking on Jones's door and demanding their dues.

Jones was now in a predicament. The commission payments were far too high to hide from colleagues or auditors, and questions were bound to be asked about the identity of the shadowy men behind the EDC and what they could possibly have done to secure orders in far-away South America and the Middle East. Jones did not know who they were or what they had or had not done. De Francis claimed he didn't know either. That was of course the whole basis of the arrangement. And the astute Dr Froriep understood it very well. When De Francis, at Jones's instigation, questioned him about the specific involvement of EDC in these sales efforts, Froriep reminded him that it was fundamental to the arrangement that EDC was not answerable to Northrop. Thus Jones was neatly hoist with his own petard, and Northrop had no option but to pay out the $1·2 million due on direct sales. Jones had to explain to his incredulous board that he didn't know what EDC had done for the money and had no means of knowing where it would end up. He couldn't even be sure that the secret network of agents really existed outside the intimate clique of the Zürich lawyer, the lady-friend, the chauffeur and Dr Bach.

As if all this were not irony enough, it is clear that the very success of the F–5E which turned the EDC arrangement into such an embarrassment was itself, at least in part, due to the behind-the-scenes activities of Frank De Francis. A crucial element of Northrop's strategy, as we have seen, was assiduous cultivation of the Pentagon and of Congress—the prime task of the company's Washington office. Much of this cultivation took the form of lavish hospitality in Washington or at Northrop's secluded duck-hunting lodge on the wild shores of Chesapeake Bay. (Washington call-girls were said to regard the 'hunting-lodge circuit' as second only to that of Congress itself.) But there were more insidious forms of cultivation, including the Savy Fund, and at one point in 1972 we find De Francis collecting $40,000 in cash from the fund, ostensibly for paying Franz Bach and another official in Germany, Dr Eddy Hess, but using at least part of it for honouring 'commitments' nearer home. De Francis carried the money in four $10,000 packets, two in the inside and two in the outside pockets of his coat. 'Some people don't want to be identified with Northrop', he told the auditors, 'thus the need for making cash payments. I served simply as a conduit for movement of the funds from Northrop to these individuals.'[1]

De Francis was also involved in Northrop's drive to secure Pentagon and Congressional backing for the Tiger retooling programme. Early in 1972 he called on Congressman Mendel Rivers, chairman of the House Armed Services Committee, to solicit his support. Rivers and his chief counsel, Russ Blandford, succeeded in persuading the House–Senate Conference Committee to allocate $28 million

1 De Francis interview with Raymond Crim of Ernst and Ernst, September 9, 1974.

to the programme, which not only placed the F–5E development on a sound financial base but gave Congress and the Pentagon the keenest of incentives to sell the plane around the world. Northrop was duly grateful. When Blandford retired from the Armed Services Committee in 1972 he was hired as a $1,000-a-month consultant to an air charter company, United Governmental Services, of which De Francis was sole owner. Blandford, the Northrop board's investigation reported later, agreed that 'a fair interpretation of his employment by UGS might be that he was retained to provide some services to Northrop'.

Certainly De Francis wasn't slow in claiming credit both for the Pentagon adoption of the F–5E as the 'International Fighter' and for its subsequent world-wide success. By the end of 1971, barely half-way through his second four-year consultancy contract, he was pressing for a substantial increase in his $50,000-a-year fee, which led to a number of 'hassles' (his word) with Tom Jones. He particularly regretted having accepted a fee rather than the 10 per cent commission originally envisaged. 'I was not Santa Claus', he told the auditors. 'At the time I did not recognize the eventual success and sales results of the F–5E program; in retrospect, I can say it probably was one of my biggest mistakes in my life to give up that contract – if I had known all this in advance I would have hung on to it.'[1] Jones seems to have agreed. In 1973 he gave De Francis an unprecedented fifteen-year contract at no less than $100,000 a year. Thus the man who boasted he didn't know a plane's nose from its tail stood to collect a colossal $1,850,000 from Northrop – not including expenses and monies intended for third parties.

First with the Weisbrod connection and then with De Francis and EDC, Northrop followed where Lockheed led. But their cunningly constructed replica achieved little on the overseas markets except pour small fortunes into the pockets of a handful of Europeans who were lucky enough to be acquainted with the right lawyer. At home, Northrop's own distinctive mode of corruption proved more successful – at least until Jones dipped into the Savy fund to help buy the silence of Nixon's Watergate burglars. But Northrop never made the Lockheed league, never matched its much larger rival either in the scale or the sophistication of its organised graft. There was always more than one hand on the grease machine – but the tightest grip remained Lockheed's.

1 Northrop Special Report.

9

Saudi Arabia: The Pirate

I would say anything done to get a favour is morally wrong.
Adnan Khashoggi, Granada TV interview, 1976

1

Of all the persuaders, visible and invisible, who contrived to defy the biblical injunction against serving two masters by working simultaneously for both Lockheed and Northrop, the undisputed crown prince is the fleshly figure of a Syrian doctor's son, Adnan Khashoggi, the paradigm New Arab of the 1960s and 1970s.

Khashoggi's friendship with Richard Nixon and Nixon's soulmates Bebe Rebozo and Robert Vesco had already attracted the attention of the gossip columnists and cartoonists when the precise nature of his work for the aerospace giants was still a well-kept secret. The dazzling opulence of his life-style—luxury homes scattered throughout the world, and his own private jumbo equipped with all mod cons from bathroom, and bedroom, to a casino—combined with ever-expanding business interests including banks in California, cattle ranches in Arizona, insurance in Britain, a fashion house in Paris, meat packaging in Brazil, shipping in Indonesia, huge land holdings in the Seychelles and a company formed to sell Egypt's Sadat a full-size gold-plated pyramid—all this combined to make him a legend and superstar when dazed onlookers could only speculate as to the source of such fabulous wealth. Robert Gross's proudest boast was that he had made the front cover of *Time* magazine. Khashoggi, while in his twenties, did better still, sharing with Howard Hughes the ultimate accolade of having a Harold Robbins novel—*The Pirate*—based on his career.

Anthony Sampson has a good description of Khashoggi as he was in his mid-twenties, when Lockheed signed him up:

> an electric personality [with] all the mobility of a man of two worlds. Cool and immaculate, he talked quickly and incisively, changing from explosive Arabic to smooth American English. His genial style and wide laugh concealed the watchfulness in his dark eyes. His hands moved constantly, squeezing, punching, spreading

over his heart, slicing the air, weaving his own world around him in eloquent mime. He epitomised the vigour of a young Arab generation determined to leave its mark on the West, to rival the international power of the Jews.

And of the gap between not only different continents but different centuries which Khashoggi spanned, Sampson comments: 'It is as if men in grey flannel suits walked into the middle of a Shakespeare play'.[1]

Saudi Arabia's emergence from the middle ages, the historic backdrop to Khashoggi's success story, can scarcely be said to have begun before the 1920s. Until then the immense deserts of the Arabian peninsula were the homeland of warrior-tribesmen almost wholly unacquainted with the outside world. The most powerful of these tribal kings was Abdul Aziz Ibn Saud who in the 1920s subdued his rivals and established the dual kingdoms of Hejaz and Najd under the ferocious Islamic code of the Wahhabi brotherhood, puritanical and fanatically xenophobic. In 1932 he united his territories as the Kingdom of Saudi Arabia and to the disgust of his Wahhabi divines began to make cautious contact with the modern world.

When the global depression of the 1930s hit his only source of foreign exchange revenue, the annual pilgrimages to Mecca, Ibn Saud was forced to listen to the growing number of pilgrims of a very different kind who came to his desert capital Riyadh on behalf of American oil companies. The king eventually succumbed and sold a concession to Standard Oil for the modest sum of £50,000. Though none knew it at the time, a new world power was conceived in that transaction.

By the outbreak of the Second World War the United States and Britain were supplying and training the Saudi armed forces. The British concentrated on the so-called 'White Army' of the Bedouins, later renamed the National Guard and used by Ibn Saud to crush internal dissent. The Americans helped the king build up a force to resist external attack, and in 1945, with Hitler dead and Germany's unconditional surrender only hours away, Saudi Arabia bravely declared war on the Third Reich. It was a war the Saudis won without firing a single shot, but their nominal participation gained them the right to join the new United Nations as a founder-member.

In 1953 Ibn Saud died, to be succeeded by Saud, the eldest of no fewer than thirty-seven sons (and innumerable daughters) by a score

1 *The Arms Bazaar*, Hodder and Stoughton, London, 1977.

of wives. Saud tried to insulate himself from the growing conflict between traditionalists and modernists among his subjects, retiring into a world of private extravagance and public indifference. Under him, as under his father, there was no proper system of accounting, no national budget, indeed no regular government at all. Saud's predilection for elaborate palaces with a profusion of ornate fountains did little for Saudi Arabia — except reduce the water-table in the Riyadh area. More worrying to the United States and Britain, already heavily dependent on cheap Saudi oil, the king's fecklessness endangered an ally which was increasingly becoming the target of more modern and radical Arab states such as Nasser's Egypt and, after 1963, the revolutionary regime in the Yemen.

So on November 2, 1964, to the surprise of few, Saud was deposed and succeeded by his brother Faisal. A half-brother, Prince Sultan, took charge of the armed forces, with his brother, Prince Turki, as deputy. Another half-brother of Faisal's, Prince Abdullah, presided over the British-trained National Guard. Virtually every responsible post in Faisal's regime, as in his elder brother's and, before that, his father's, was occupied by one of Ibn Saud's numerous progeny.

A more travelled, less cloistered ruler than Saud or Ibn Saud, Faisal encouraged modernisation and trade, particularly in armaments. Riyadh turned almost overnight into something approaching a modern city, with roads, banks and hotels. To assist in the transformation, a host of middlemen flocked to the Saudi capital. One of the pioneers of this latter-day gold rush was St John Philby, father of double-agent Kim. But he regarded his business responsibilities as little more than a tolerably lucrative excuse for indulging in an Englishman's nostalgia for pure desert air and the romance of vanishing nomadic cultures. The time was ripe for more robust characters to dip their hands in the pot.

For a time, the most successful was another Englishman, a former RAF pilot and building contractor called Geoffrey Edwards. He first went to Saudi Arabia in 1960, astutely smelling out the opportunities and ingratiating himself with the royal princes while awaiting the big break. It came with Faisal's assumption of power and the arms bonanza that followed. Edwards was the beneficiary in what was then the largest military export sale in British history. For £120 million the British Aircraft Corporation (BAC) contracted to provide forty Lightning jets, twenty-five Provost trainers and an undisclosed number of air-to-air missiles. As part of the same package deal, Associated Electrical Industries (AEI) provided the Saudis with a new advanced radar system, and another firm, Airwork Services, provided 1,000 training personnel. It transpired, however, that Edwards's coup—it earned him some two million pounds in commission, some of which was promised to a royal prince, Abdul Rahman, and some to a Riyadh financier, Gaith Pharoan, whose father was one of the king's advisers—was not entirely the result of entrepreneurial genius. He in fact landed the contract as part of a complex diplomatic deal with the Americans, who secretly promised to back BAC and AEI rather than their own Lockheed and Northrop salesmen in return for a British decision to buy fifty F–111s from General Dynamics. (Economic crisis eighteen months later caused Britain to cancel the F–111 order, but by then the Saudi deal was done.) The immediate effect of these manoeuvres was that Northrop's Kim Roosevelt and Lockheed's Adnan Khashoggi fought a bitter battle for their respective firms, unaware that the spoils had been awarded in advance to the interests represented by Britain's Geoffrey Edwards. Northrop complained to King Faisal of Lockheed bribery, while Roosevelt sought the aid of 'my friends in the CIA'[1] to find out what was going on. For Khashoggi, who was pushing the Starfighter, it was an early and at the time inexplicable setback.

By birth and education Adnan Khashoggi was well suited to the role of middleman between the industrial west and the feudal desert kingdom. Like many of the men—the Saudi royal family apart—who came to play a prominent part in Saudi business and public affairs, his family were from Syria. His father was private physician to Ibn Saud, a post of enormous personal influence. Khashoggi senior had himself shown an entrepreneurial flair, cleverly arranging for the generator which powered his X-ray equipment to supply additional power for sale to the city of Riyadh. His important position enabled him to send young Adnan first to Victoria College, a British-run public school in King Farouk's Egypt, where he met the future King Hussein of Jordan, and later to Chico State University, California, where, somewhat incongruously, he studied 'typing and composition' before moving on to Stanford. Here, while still an eighteen-year-old student, he had a chance meeting with the director of a truck-manufacturing firm, Kenworth of Seattle, who sagaciously appreciated the value of the young man's connections and entrusted him with the firm's Saudi Arabian agency. Within months Khashoggi won a contract (against competition from Ley-

1 Letter, Roosevelt to Northrop, March 19, 1965.

land Motors in Britain) which netted him a profit of $200,000. The
pirate ship was launched.

Khashoggi returned to Saudi Arabia without taking a degree and
sank his newly-made small fortune first in the construction industry,
which was just beginning to boom, and then in a gypsum plant which
provided more modest but still substantial returns. It took the threat
of war arising from the Yemen revolution to get him into the big
time with a lucrative contract to supply the Saudi defence ministry
with trucks from his Seattle friends. Agency agreements followed
with the Chrysler corporation, British helicopter interests, Rolls-
Royce, Marconi, and a French tank manufacturer. This last contract
alone paid him a huge $45 million in commissions. Not entirely un-
connected to these spectacular successes were the close ties of friendship he cultivated with Prince Sultan, Faisal's minister of defence
(and half-brother), and Crown Prince Fahd, who was to become
Saudi Arabia's effective ruler after Faisal's assassination in 1975,
and Prince Khaled, the future king. Khashoggi introduced them and
their entourage to the delights of a less puritanical and more hedonis-
tic life than Riyadh offered. In a Beirut night club he himself met a
sixteen-year-old Leicestershire girl who became his wife six months
later and mother of his five children before they were divorced in 1974.

In the last months of Saud's reign, with the business-minded
Faisal already in virtual control of the kingdom's booming oil-rich
economy, Lockheed made their bid for a slice of the coming arms
and planes bonanza by proposing to the Saudi government a major
Hercules sale. Dan Haughton didn't have far to look for the middleman who could 'teach us the customs' of the country. With his track
record and proved connections, twenty-six-year-old Khashoggi was
invited back to the California he had left as a student only a few
short years before, to sign his first contract with Lockheed-Georgia
in October 1964. The agreement gave him 2 per cent of the sale price
plus $41,000 per plane 'incentive' money, candidly described in a
handwritten note in the margin of a Lockheed memo as 'requirement
for new players'.[1]

It is a common and much-fostered belief that bribery is and always
has been an accepted and acceptable business practice in the Middle
East in general and Third World countries in particular. It is 'the
custom'. Moralists may deplore it, runs the argument, but hard-
headed businessmen living in what Dan Haughton liked to call the

---

1 Undated and unsigned memo in Church Committee's Lockheed papers.

'real world' have an obligation, if not a downright duty, to respect the traditions of those who have not yet learned to live by the elevated standards of White Anglo-Saxon Protestants. Middlemen like Khashoggi build their fortunes by persuading foreigners to this view of their own people—and in the process do much to validate it. Corporations like Lockheed, where they can no longer deny corrupt practices, are glad to shift the blame to foreign custom and greed. The public in Britain, America and Western Europe fall easily for excuses which fit snugly into their stereotypes of greasy wogs and lesser breeds without the law. But, emphatically, this comfortable view does not bear close scrutiny. The fact is that in many Third World countries the acceptance by public officials of bribes is not only an offence but sometimes a capital one. A Saudi bribee, like his Anglo-Saxon or European counterpart, will go to considerable lengths to conceal his action, however 'customary' he may claim it to be.

Perhaps considerations of this sort were behind Khashoggi's insistence to Lockheed that he didn't want his commissions made public — 'however innocuous they might seem' — and in particular he 'begged that no mention' of them be made in Saudi Arabia or Beirut.[1] Possibly, and understandably, he simply feared a long procession of royal riders on his gravy train. In any case, he asked Lockheed to put his commissions through a Swiss representative, Gérard Boissier, who entrusted them to the safety of a numbered bank account.

The Saudis ordered five Hercules C-130s and more were to follow. Then Khashoggi turned his attention to the Starfighter campaign, unaware, of course, that the state department had sold out to the British Lightning. When his efforts failed, Khashoggi was left with 'obligations' but without any Starfighter commissions from which to fulfil them. Ingeniously, he found the money by successfully demanding from Lockheed an additional $50,000 on the fifth Hercules, suggesting that this 'surcharge' be invoiced to the Saudi government, where he promised to see that it would be 'pushed through'. 'In this particular case he has a great interest in pushing it through,' noted Lockheed's man in Geneva, Norman Otsea, 'since the money will really wind up in his pocket.'[2]

Lockheed's 1964 agreement was with Khashoggi's first company, the Alnasr Trading and Industrial Corporation. But in 1967, when the tension created by the Six Day War in June escalated the Middle

1 Memo, Gerard B. Juliani to Roger Williams and others, reporting Khashoggi's fears, July 5, 1965.
2 Otsea to Ed Hausman, September 4, 1967.

East arms race and released a further deluge of Saudi oil money for arms purchases, Khashoggi consolidated his interests in a new company, Triad, which he was later to describe, accurately enough, as the world's first Arab-owned multinational corporation. His two younger brothers, Adil and Essam, joined him as junior partners, but Adnan remained firmly in control, as absolute a monarch of Triad as Ibn Saud had been of Saudia Arabia. The new corporation was registered far from prying eyes in Liechtenstein, with a mailing address in Geneva. One result of all this corporate restructuring was a revised contract with Lockheed. On September 1 a consultancy agreement was exchanged granting Triad a 2 per cent commission on further Hercules sales in the pipeline—on the face of it a modest enough reward, and no improvement on the 1964 contract with Alnasr. But that wasn't the whole story. In addition to the open contract, three secret agreements were drawn up in 'side letters', raising Khashoggi's real commissions to a massive 15 per cent on selected items.

Khashoggi was now in the big time. His commissions from Lockheed alone over the next seven years would amount to a stupendous $106 million—though, as Dan Haughton put it, laconically, 'We think that some of the money went someplace else.'[1] Some of what Khashoggi kept for himself was re-invested in the United States, an ironic development which outraged Senator Frank Church, who fumed:

> Here is a case where over $100 million has been funnelled into one country by one corporation to grease the way for military sales contracts for the sale of military weapons. And the money is coming back and being invested in this country so that as a result of these extortionate practises American companies are really financing the purchases in the United States of Khashoggi and his associates. That is the way that these bribes are coming back, being re-cycled, as it were, and then take the form of foreign ownership of American assets.[2]

In fact Khashoggi's investments in America were not confined to the financial. More than any other Saudi middleman, he cultivated top-level political contacts in Washington hardly less assiduously than he cultivated royalty in Riyadh. His biggest prize was Richard Nixon, whom he first met in 1967 when Nixon's political fortunes

1 Church Committee, September 12, 1975.
2 Ibid.

were low and Khashoggi's financial fortunes still to be made. At a dinner in the Rasputin restaurant, Paris, Khashoggi offered himself to the former vice-president as his liaison with powerful figures in the Middle East. The two men continued to meet in the United States, in Washington and San Clemente, and by the time Nixon became President in 1969 they were firm friends. Arab newspapers suggested that Khashoggi was a major contributor to the notorious presidential campaign funds, when a sum of $10 million to $12 million — almost certainly an exaggeration — was said to have been made available to CREEP by anti-Jewish Arab interests. Khashoggi's personal subscription was alleged to be $1 million, though when the Watergate prosecutors questioned him he admitted only a $50,000 contribution to finance a record containing selected hits from Nixon's speeches.

Lockheed's relationship with Khashoggi was not without strains and upheavals. On August 15, 1968, within a year of the corporation's revised agreement with Triad, Harley Snyder of the Lockheed Aircraft Service division was reporting after a visit to Riyadh that an unnamed but apparently influential prince was 'completely disenchanted with Adnan Khashoggi', and had 'indicated that he never received the $150,000 that was agreed to last year'. As a result, all Lockheed programmes were 'in the deep freeze'. The angry prince had produced a set of accounts listing all Saudi payments to Lockheed. From this he had calculated Khashoggi's commission, from which he expected to be paid. Khashoggi had evidently told the prince that his commission was only 2 per cent and that he hadn't yet received it, which the prince described baldly as a lie. Snyder persuaded Khashoggi's brother Adil to meet the prince and try to reach agreement, but negotiations deadlocked on Adil's offer of 1 per cent and the prince's demand for 2 per cent. Snyder told Adil that 'no matter how it was worked out, and if it was worked out, the money would come out of Triad's commission' and not, as Khashoggi apparently expected, out of Lockheed's profits.[1]

The matter was evidently resolved — how is not clear — but it dramatically highlighted the weaknesses of Lockheed's method of doing business. Because the contract between the corporation and its agent had to withstand legal and audit scrutiny, no mention could be made of what the relationship was really about: the bribing of local officials. The agent thus had sole control, and Lockheed

1 Confidential memo by Alan Kaplan, August 15, 1968.

none, of who was bribed and by how much. Inevitably there were disputes: princes and generals clamouring to get in on the act whether or not they had real influence — and who could tell whether they had or not? Lockheed's intention, of course, was that Triad should handle all such disputes — that's what agents were for — but in practice the corporation frequently became embroiled. The pattern set by the case of the angry prince — a demand for a pay-off which left Lockheed and Khashoggi disputing who, if anyone, should pick up the tab — was to recur again and again over the next six years.

For a time, however, it looked as if such disputes might be ended summarily with a sudden mortal blow at the whole system of agents' commissions. In October 1969 the Saudi Arabian council of ministers published a decree requiring a clause in all contracts specifying that no agent was involved and that any agent fees already paid would not be added to the price paid by Saudi Arabia. This caused a flurry of interdepartmental memos at Lockheed (and no doubt in the offices of other corporations doing business with the Saudis) but it was soon clear that the corporation's resources of ingenuity were adequate to the emergency. Jim Davidson of Lockheed-Georgia, the division involved with C–130 and Jetstar sales, gave chief salesman Bill Cowden the legal department's view of what should be done, starting with a summary of how other divisions, Lockheed Aircraft Service (LAS) and Lockheed Aircraft International (LAI), were facing the problem:

> It is my understanding that LAS has accepted this as a necessary part of the risk in doing business in Saudi Arabia. They have signed, and are now negotiating to sign, contracts with such a statement included, but with full intention of paying our representative his usual fees. I have also been told that LAI is in process of negotiating a contract which will have the same clause, with the intention of paying our representative for his services and ignoring the subject clause.

Effective, but crude. The Georgia division's solution would have a trifle more subtlety:

> It is my recommendation that our initial contract submittal be patterned after GLX–160 and *not* include such a clause. Our failure to include the clause may possibly go unchallenged, with proper ground work, and at worst can be made to appear simply an oversight on our part. Should it become necessary during the

negotiations to include this clause, I recommend we do so and adopt the same position as now used by LAS and LAI.[1]

As it turned out, the council of ministers' decree was almost universally ignored and Khashoggi's commissions not only continued but increased. His progress from riches to greater riches was unimpeded. Soon there were more disputes with Lockheed. On September 16, 1970, Khashoggi wrote from Geneva to Max Helzel, international marketing director of LAS, requesting that Lockheed

> provide $400,000 of additional compensation to Triad under its present contracts with Lockheed. Such compensation is requested on the basis that Triad has incurred unforeseen additional direct costs and administrative overhead, all of which were required in connection with Triad's performance under existing contracts.

The 'unforeseen additional direct costs and administrative overhead' in fact covered another bribe to one of Khashoggi's royal contacts and the question again arose as to whether the bribe should be paid from Khashoggi's commission or be an additional charge on Lockheed. Early in 1970 the Saudis had contracted to buy two more C-130s for $7,072,956, which included – despite the council of ministers' decree – a huge commission of $752,000 for Khashoggi. But Lockheed, anticipating extra demands, had priced the planes to allow for total commissions of $824,956, which left $72,956 uncommitted. Lockheed proposed that this too should go to Khashoggi to help him meet the $400,000 'unforeseen additional direct cost'. Khashoggi's position seems to have been that, if there was additional commission available he was entitled to it anyway; and he still wanted the $400,000, over and above that. Eventually the dispute seems to have been resolved by an agreement to add the sum as a 'special adjustment' to commissions on future sales. Khashoggi 'reluctantly accepted the position',[2] according to Cowden, though his new American legal adviser, Morton MacLeod, made several attempts to speed the money through before any new sales had been agreed.

The months that followed saw a spate of similar disputes and irregular demands. Someone identified in Lockheed cables as 'minor consultant' demanded and was given 15 per cent commission on an $8 million contract for C-130 wing modifications, and then asked for

1 Davidson to Cowden, memo, November 25, 1969.
2 Cowden to Charles Valentine, memo, October 12, 1970.

an additional 5 per cent 'for negotiating room'.[1] An unnamed official asked for a Lockheed-Georgia contract to be routed through the corporation's Geneva office to facilitate payment of his commission into a secret bank account in Liechtenstein.[2] Another 'additional player' demanded what Lockheed's memos describe as a 'pay-off' direct from the corporation, whilst complaining that his 'payments have been delayed from Khashoggi'.[3] In May and June 1972 $600,000 was paid over to Triad 'for their subsequent disbursement to the parties concerned' in the purchase of more C–130s. This was 'over and above the normal fees and commitments' to Triad.[4] Yet even with all this activity business could meet sudden obstacles. 'RUSH RUSH RUSH', began an undated telegram from Lockheed's office in Jeddah, 'STRONGLY SUSPECT MACHINERY STALLED FOR LACK OF GREASE STOP IS FORMER AIR ATTACHE REALLY PUSHING QUERY URGE YOU INSIST AGENT MAKE MOVE NOW TO KEEP LOG ROLLING.' 'I take it "grease" in this context means pay-off, doesn't it?' asked Senator Frank Church. 'Yes sir,' acknowledged Dan Haughton, 'that is the interpretation that we have given it'.[5]

By the summer of 1973 the sums being paid out to Khashoggi and his friends had become so huge that alarmed senior executives commissioned a special report on Saudi sales arrangements, circulated only to a restricted few on a 'need to know' basis. The report began by explaining that Khashoggi's original 2 per cent commission had risen to 8 per cent plus $41,000 per plane on C–130 sales and 15 per cent on modifications 'due to more players getting involved and the necessity to satisfy their requirements in order to get our contracts signed'. In parenthesis it added: 'This is the Consultant's version.' The anonymous author continued with a revealing explanation of the corporation's strategy for absorbing additional demands over and above Khashoggi's:

> When pricing out a proposal to Saudi-Arabia, in addition to the commission that we are bound by our agreement to pay our Consultant, which is added to our 'net to Gelac' price, we also add an amount that we refer to as a marketing contingency. This marketing contingency fund has varied over different proposals anywhere from $100,000 to $200,000 per aircraft. This contingency fund has

1 Cable, Jay Walden to Ned Ridings, April 6, 1972.
2 Memo, Ridings to Cowden, March 9, 1971.
3 Memo, Davidson to Cowden, February 26, 1971.
4 Memo, J. E. Walden to J. C. Fogarty, November 7, 1972.
5 Church Committee, September 12, 1975.

in the past been used by us to give a price reduction during contract negotiations, but mostly has been used by the Consultant for so-called 'under the table' compensation to Saudi officials in order to get the contract signed. When we use this fund for an 'above the table' price reduction during negotiation, we know what has been done, but we really have no way of knowing if the so-called 'under the table' compensation is ever disbursed to Saudi officials or stops at our Consultant's bank account. The portion of the marketing contingency fund that is used for 'under the table' compensation is paid to our Consultant for disbursement and this accounts for some of the rather large sums of money that have been paid to our Consultant over and above his standard commission. Each one of these transactions necessitates a one-time amendment to his basic agreement.[1]

Sometimes a special company was formed to receive 'under the table' disbursements. One such was the 'Lauvier Establishment', registered in Geneva with an account (number 394124) at the Crédit Suisse Bank. The unknown principals of the Lauvier Establishment benefited handsomely from technical assistance, logistics support and aircraft maintenance contracts: a payment of $285,328 in November 1970, $490,959 in February 1971, $250,000 the same month, $58,939 and $287,519 in March and a final undisclosed payment later that year, making a grand total of around one and a half million dollars.[2] 'Charlie,' wrote LAS executive Mel Greene to Lockheed-Georgia's administrative director, Charles Valentine, 'I am sure that you understand completely the sensitivity of this thing.' Greene went on to explain that, though the contracts took the form of letters on Triad notepaper assigning the special commissions to the third-party recipient, he himself had written the letters, sent them to Khashoggi for his signature, and then acknowledged their receipt.[3] The point, of course, is not that Greene was deceiving Triad by—as he put it— 'creating sets of these letters', but that Lockheed themselves clearly controlled the process by which Khashoggi assigned parts of his commissions to Saudi officials. Greene's frankness—or his tidy passion for keeping the files in good order—disposes of any lingering notion that the Lockheed men considered bribery Khashoggi's private business and nothing to do with the corporation.

1 Report, 'Saudi Arabia Consultant', August 16, 1973.
2 Memo, Charles Valentine to M. H. Greene and others, January 16, 1973.
3 Memo, Greene to Valentine, April 7, 1971.

If the identity of Lauvier's principal or principals is known with certainty only to the Crédit Suisse Bank, we have a rather fuller picture with a similar Triad assignee, Cantona Establishment, registered in Vaduz, Liechtenstein. Cantona masked the identity of yet another royal sibling, Prince Khalid bin Abdullah, son of the head of the National Guard, whose striking talent for easing himself on to the payroll of his country's arms suppliers was beginning to make for him a sizeable fortune even by Saudi standards. On November 28, 1972, a coded cable from salesman Bob Conley to corporation marketing vice-president Duane O. Wood sought urgent advice on a demand from Khalid for a 1 per cent commission on all Hercules sales. When Wood had failed to respond a week later, Conley cabled again, requesting a reply the same day.

Wood cabled back instructing Conley to check with the Georgia division whether the quoted price included a contingency for extra payments, in which case 'you are authorised to offer it to party concerned, but only thru Consultant. You may be pressured to make direct arrangement but do not repeat do not do so.' Wood added the ominous information that 'code has been broken in Saudi Arabia so handle this accordingly'.[1]

Conley evidently made his checks and arranged for Khalid to be paid out of Khashoggi's commission. Khashoggi took the precaution of having another of his American lawyers, Lou Lauler, write to Wood making Triad's acceptance of the arrangement conditional on Lockheed's agreeing to reimburse Triad for Khalid's windfall.[2] And windfall it was. Lauvier had collected one and a half million dollars: Khalid's Cantona took no less than $6 million.[3] And that, as we shall see, was only the beginning of a lucrative if stormy partnership.

2

Khashoggi's commissions, fees, compensations and incentives from Lockheed totalled (it is worth repeating) a staggering $106 million. Even if half of that was committed to the grease machine, there was enough left to keep Khashoggi in the style to which he had got him-

---

1 Cables, Conley to Wood and Wood to Conley, December 6, 1972.
2 Lauler to Wood, January 11, 1973.
3 Memo, Valentine to Greene and others, January 16, 1973, which details one payment of $5,555,000, another of $287,519 and a third unspecified.

self accustomed. But, as we have seen, Lockheed was by no means Khashoggi's only account: his French, British and Belgian connections probably earned him almost as much again as Lockheed. And in June 1970 he was offered, and accepted, an agency agreement with Lockheed's arch-rivals, Northrop, now following Lockheed's trail in Saudi Arabia as they had done in Europe.

Northrop was keen to get in on the Saudi bonanza with a massive sale of F–5 Tigers. Khashoggi was recommended to Tom Jones by Kim Roosevelt, who suggested that as Lockheed lacked a fighter programme there would be no conflict of interest in the one agent working for both companies. The truth, of course, was that Lockheed's Hercules and Northrop's Tiger, though just about as different as two military aircraft could be, nevertheless competed for the same defence budget funds: but Roosevelt's was the argument that Jones and, above all, Khashoggi wanted to hear. Khashoggi was quick to teach Northrop the customs, starting with a Lockheed-type arrangement for both open contracts and secret side letters. There was one document, as Northrop's legal counsel R. B. Watts explained, 'which will be open and public to justify our relationship with Khashoggi in country', and others which were 'secret and under no circumstances ... to be disclosed or discussed outside of the key responsible people within Northrop'.[1] Not surprisingly, Northrop quickly ran into the critical problem which was bedevilling Lockheed's relationship with Khashoggi: who paid the 'additional players' scrambling for a share of the loot? First in the queue was our old friend Prince Khalid, who wanted a cool 10 per cent for his 'Cantona Establishment' in Liechtenstein. On January 11, 1971, Northrop's Bob Rogin met Khashoggi in the Mayfair Hotel, London, to discuss the Khalid problem.

Khashoggi's advice was simple. Khalid, in his opinion, didn't 'swing a big stick' and Northrop could afford to play tough. Rogin should tell Khalid that Northrop was 'annoyed' with his demands since commission was already high and 'we do not know how many more persons will be involved'. Rogin, advised Khashoggi, should then proceed with a threat and a promise: if Khalid tried to delay a Saudi order, Northrop would instantly shut down its F–5 production line, making sure in the process that Khalid was seen as the cause of the breakdown in negotiations. On the other hand, 'if Northrop sees some indication of seriousness by the Saudi government, we might

1 Memo, Watts to Gonzalez, October 6, 1970.

be able to work on an arrangement with the signing of an order, but not at 10 per cent'.

Khashoggi suggested 1 per cent was reasonable. If Khalid wouldn't play at that, he should be told that 'other members of the royal family have contacted Northrop in California re the sale and their demands are not so high'. To reinforce the point, Khashoggi casually mentioned to Rogin that he was expecting a new procurement official to be appointed, which 'could add one more player to the list'. The new official, unnamed, had happened to mention to Khashoggi that 'he wants 5 per cent and can handle the sale of the F–5s without the support of Prince Turki or Khalid'. The reference to Turki, deputy defence minister and yet another of the king's brothers, was significant: Northrop suspected Khalid was representing Turki, and the burden of Khashoggi's message to Rogin was that the unnamed about-to-be-appointed official would look after Turki at half Khalid's rate. Writing all this up in a memo for his boss, Robert Gates, the somewhat dazed Rogin added: 'I expect to see more players before we are through and especially when the F–5 sale looks like it's going to be approved, i.e. Minister of Finance, Chief of Armed Forces, etc. Adnan is of the same opinion.'[1]

Rogin had an appointment with Khalid at four the same afternoon in Khalid's suite at the Mayfair. He followed the strategy laid out for him by Khashoggi (except that he jibbed at mentioning demands from other members of the royal family) and made it clear that he had alternative and cheaper means of keeping Prince Turki happy. But Khalid took him somewhat aback by coolly assuring him that he wasn't representing Turki but himself alone. When Rogin protested that his 10 per cent commission on top of Khashoggi's 2 per cent was 'too much to hide' and might provoke an investigation, Khalid responded that he didn't believe Khashoggi was getting only 2 per cent (he was right) but he himself was in any case open to counter offers. 'He also said he would hold no hard feelings', reported Rogin to Gates, 'but that if he were going to represent us he was going to do it for more than one per cent … Khalid by this time was calling me by my first name. I did not reciprocate.'

Rogin left the prince with a promise to refer upwards. Next morning he flew to Paris to meet Samyr Souki, whose Middle East Business Services and Research Corporation, based in Beirut, was a crucial link in Northrop's labyrinthine network of agents, consul-

1 Memo, Rogin to Gates, January 28, 1971.

tants, listening-posts and bagmen. Souki said bluntly that Khalid should be Khashoggi's problem. Khashoggi 'should be advised he is our sole agent and Northrop is paying him a commission to get us the sale and not to have us negotiate with every Saudi who wants to get into the act'.[1] Next evening Khashoggi arrived in Paris and Rogin and Souki dined with him and what Rogin called his 'cast of thousands'. Khashoggi again put the view that Khalid was unimportant, particularly if he represented only himself and not Turki. Turki too would be no problem. He was 'a most reasonable individual, one or two per cent'. Rogin, somewhat bemused by it all, concluded his report: 'One of the more important things I'm going to have to do is call out who are the players that have to be considered in order to assure our getting the order, and soon.'

But before Rogin could call out the players, events inside Saudi Arabia complicated the matter further. King Faisal's attempts to clamp down hard on consultants' commissions were given a boost when the American ambassador in Riyadh, Nicholas Gilman Thacher, was recruited to the crusade. As an anonymous handwritten memo of June 26 in Northrop's files summarised it:

> Ambassador advised on June 24 that he had previously been approached by several of the high-level members of the Saudi government who asked him for the help of the US government in 'extricating themselves from the clutches of these agents.' He specifically mentioned Khashoggi by name. He indicated that high level people were beginning to realise that they had made a mistake in getting themselves indebted to these agents and were trying to change the age-old pattern here. The Ambassador advised them that it would be up to them to help themselves, that the US government couldn't do it for them.

There was one way for the Saudis to by-pass agents and consultants, however, and that was to 'go FMS'. Under an FMS or Foreign Military Sales agreement, the purchasing government buys not from the manufacturer, in this case Northrop, but from the US government, either on credit or as part of a reciprocal trade agreement. Because the buyer's contract is with the US government and not the manufacturer, the manufacturer's agents and consultants normally have no claim on commission. In the case of the Northrop F–5 sale and the 'support package' that went with it, it was clear by the end

1 Rogin to Gates, ibid.

of June 1971 that Prince Sultan and Prince Turki, despite the claims others were making to 'represent' them, genuinely wanted the sale to go FMS and avoid commission payments; and US ambassador Thacher was backing their request through the appropriate channels in Washington. Northrop were content to stand on the sidelines: it made little difference to them whether they were paid by the Saudi or the US government, and in any case they were not fussy about paying commissions whichever way it went. But Khashoggi was reported (in the same anonymous memo) to be 'working on the Saudis to get them to ask for the support package direct rather than FMS'. What Khashoggi apparently didn't realise, however, was that even if he succeeded in influencing a change of course, his own commission on 'support elements' was only 4 per cent compared with 6 per cent on aircraft sales. 'When this is fully understood by Khashoggi it will create some problems', mused the Northrop memo-writer, 'but I do not intend to review this in detail with him until after the sale is locked in, unless he brings it up. The entire area is extremely sensitive and potentially explosive.'

Khashoggi wasn't the only consultant with a direct interest in the matter. The Khalid problem had earlier been resolved by an assignment of part of Triad's commission to 'Cantona' (which Northrop memorandists curiously but persistently misspelt 'Contina'), but the assigned contract related only to direct sales and not FMS deals. On a government-to-government sale, Khalid would get nothing—and that would mean trouble.

Tuesday, July 27, was the appointed day for signing the contract, and as it approached, Northrop acted. First, Khashoggi was apparently squared with an assurance that he would still get his commission in the event of the sale going FMS, even, apparently, if it had to take the form of an under-the-table payment to avoid defense department or Saudi scrutiny. (He was still not told, however, that his percentage on the spares and maintenance 'support package' would be lower than he expected.)[1] Second, it was arranged that on the day of the signing, Khashoggi would stay in Beirut, over the Lebanon border, so that, if asked whether they had an agent in Saudi Arabia, Northrop could 'truthfully' answer no—a childish but effective piece of mendacity.[2]

Another memo, scrawled on a sheet of graph-paper (probably by

1 This seems clear from a handwritten memo, apparently from Watts to MacLeod, dated June 26, 1971.
2 Church Committee hearings, June 8, 1975.

area sales executive Manny Gonzalez) and headed 'Notes for Conversation with Adnan', gives a graphic account of what happened next. A top-brass delegation accompanied by ambassador Thacher made their way to the Moda Palace for the ceremonial signing, only to find themselves ushered into an anteroom. When they had been waiting some time, the head of the royal Saudi air force, General Hashim, appeared and announced: 'There will be no signing today. The contract will be signed at one o'clock tomorrow and His Royal Highness would like everyone to come since this will be a happy occasion.' The Gonzalez account continues: 'No reason was given as to why the contract could not be signed on Tuesday if it was ready for signing the next day. It appeared to be an unusual and unnecessary delay.'

Some hint of what had been going on behind the scenes came at eight o'clock that night when George Starling, leader of the Northrop delegation, took a telephone call at his hotel from Prince Khalid. Gonzalez's graph-paper memo takes up the story.

> He stated that he was calling from Prince Turki's house and wanted to come talk to us. About half an hour later Prince Khalid arrived at the hotel. He was very upset and stated that he had decided to go see Prince Sultan that evening to attempt to get him to delay the signing of the contract. He said that he had been asked by Adnan to return to Jeddah to make sure that everything went well on the F–5B program and that he discovered that it was going government to government and as a result he would get nothing out of the sale. He added that he had worked very hard — harder than Adnan — to bring the sale about and that he had even spent some of his own money on behalf of the program. He stated that he knew Adnan was getting paid by Northrop every month and would get a commission when the contract was signed. He added 'and I can prove it'. He indicated that he would tell Prince Sultan that his efforts to avoid a commission by going government to government had failed and he would ask him to either force Adnan to return any money he received from Northrop or delay signing the contract until he had worked out a deal with Adnan. He said 'If I get nothing then I will make sure that Adnan gets nothing. If he gets one dollar I want fifty cents. Otherwise I will take steps to make sure he never does any more business in this area.'

Gonzalez — assuming he was the author of this account — told Khalid he should be talking to Khashoggi: Northrop couldn't deal direct.

Khalid replied that Khashoggi had shown him his contract with Northrop which gave him a 5 per cent commission on direct sales and approximately 1 per cent on indirect, plus an expense account of $3,000 a month. If Northrop could do this for Khashoggi, why not for him? Gonzalez prevaricated, saying he didn't have a copy of Khashoggi's contract with him, but reminded Khalid that if the *maintenance* contract went direct instead of FMS he would benefit. Khalid retorted that that meant waiting for three years, which he wasn't inclined to do — unless Northrop would consider ending their agency agreement with Khashoggi and transferring it to 'Cantona'. Khashoggi was unreliable in any case, he suggested pointedly, since his real loyalty lay with Lockheed. Gonzalez replied that Northrop 'would have to live with any contracts we had already signed', but promised that he would go with Khalid to see Adnan 'to determine whether or not it would be possible for [Khalid] to share in any commission on a government-to-government sale of the aircraft'. The prince finally 'seemed less disturbed ... but was still obviously not happy'. He called General Hashim from the hotel and left without indicating whether or not he still intended to carry out his threats.

At one o'clock next day the ambassador, the defense department top brass and Northrop's executive team gathered again at the Moda for the postponed exchange of letters of agreement. 'Soon after one o'clock', runs the Gonzalez account, 'Prince Sultan and Prince Turki came into the conference room and were seated at the table. Sultan reviewed the contract.' Then came the expected question: 'Do you have any agent in Saudi Arabia?' to which Northrop gave the prepared answer, 'No, not in Saudi Arabia.' The ambassador chimed in to explain that since this was an FMS deal there was no middleman. No one from Northrop contradicted him. The prince then asked suspiciously whether there was a middleman back in the US between Northrop and the defense department. There was no agent at all, replied the ambassador unambiguously, and again no one from Northrop contradicted him. Prince Sultan said he would base his actions on his 'confidence in the US Government and the Ambassador', and signed. There is no evidence that ambassador Thacher knew otherwise.

Northrop's ordeal, however, was far from over. Gonzalez's account continues:

After most people had left the conference room and just as I was about to leave, General Hashim took me aside and said 'His Royal

Highness wants to see you'. I went downstairs with Hashim. He stated that Prince Turki had asked him to give me a message, but he thought it would be better if Prince Turki told me the message himself.

Hashim and I went into Turki's office. He chatted about meeting Tom Jones at the Paris Air Show and that he considered him a friend. He then stated that 'speaking as a friend, and not in any official capacity' he understood that 'there was a disagreement with Prince Khalid' and that he 'considered this to be most unfortunate' and that he 'hoped things would be worked out to his satisfaction'. Obviously Khalid had talked to Hashim, who acted as Turki's translator, Turki and Sultan. It is also obvious that they all expect Khalid to be taken care of in some way to his satisfaction or there could be a scandal. There would be no other reason for Sultan to have asked his question about an agent just before the signing except to set the stage for a pressure play if required.

Northrop cracked, and Khalid was eventually 'compensated', in accordance with the wishes of his royal relatives. The mechanism was characteristically devious. Khashoggi and his legal counsel, Morton MacLeod, were pressing Northrop for the full commission which would have been due had the sale been direct, instead of the reduced commission Northrop was proposing for the FMS deal. Northrop found it expedient to agree to Khashoggi's demand 'provided that Triad helped Northrop by compensating HRH Prince Khalid' by one eighth of their commission—a sum close to $1 million.[1] Khashoggi agreed and the deed was done. Northrop legal counsel Robert Watts described it ruefully as 'political dynamite'.[2]

But though the Khalid affair had ended without an immediate explosion, Northrop was still deep in the minefield. With Khalid's claim barely settled, Khashoggi soon came in with another player, Khalid's friend and Turki's right-hand man, the air force chief, General Hashim. An undated, unsigned and disjointed memo headed 'Notes for Discussion on Commission for General Hashim for Phase III' gives an outline of what was eventually to become Northrop's most public and notorious act of bribery:

1. Hashim would have participated ... on a direct sale ... would have been through Khashoggi ... Conversion to FMS commissions substantially reduced and apparently he received nothing from

1 Letter, Gonzalez to MacLeod, December 14, 1971.
2 Memo, Watts to Gonzalez, January 17, 1972.

Khashoggi; however Gates and Kuska indicated ... their understanding that Hashim would participate even in an FMS case. Khashoggi will receive somewhere between $1 and $1·6 million ... on Phase I and II. He has committed to pay Khalid approx. $150,000. In addition, Souki ½ of 1 per cent ... In any event there should be ample funds within what Khashoggi receives to make some payment to Hashim.

2. Khashoggi has stated it is necessary to make some payments to Hashim at this time in order to ensure his support on Phase III. His recommendation is, of course, that Northrop make such a payment and the amount he has recommended is between $200,000 and $250,000.

So once again what Northrop believed was Khashoggi's business was being presented by Khashoggi as a Northrop obligation, with the threat that unless Northrop paid up Hashim would throw his weight against a Phase III contract. The matter was considered important enough to be placed at the top of the agenda for a meeting in Riyadh on October 8 between Tom Jones himself, Gates, Souki and Khashoggi.

Precisely what was said or agreed at that meeting became a matter of bitter dispute between the Northrop men and Khashoggi. It seems (from notes taken of Gates's report, phoned back to California) that Khashoggi presented a clear demand for a down-payment to Hashim of $200,000 to $250,000, plus a 5 per cent commission on Phase III. Gates 'assumed that Khashoggi expects Northrop to make the first payment' and, crucially, the note adds: 'Gates indicated Jones had no objection to this arrangement; in fact, he appeared to be favourably inclined to it.'[1]

Jones's own recollection is very different. This is what he told the Church Committee of that meeting:

I went to Saudi Arabia on October 8 or 9 of 1971 for my first visit to see Faisal and the top people, and when I arrived the first evening, going to dinner to the home of the agent was the first time I ever met Khashoggi, by the way, and there was a debate going on between Mr Khashoggi and several others in our company, and the gist of it, as I recall it firsthand, was that Khashoggi thought he should be paid more money, and the predominant thing I heard was that ... there was some obligation to the other agents, and if we didn't meet that obligation our name would be very bad in Saudi Arabia ...

1 Typed memo of Gates's phone conversation, October 31, 1971.

Well I was very disturbed in coming into something I knew absolutely nothing about. I told Mr Khashoggi that I knew nothing of this problem. I assured him that Northrop was a company that met its obligations, met its commitments, if indeed they were commitments, and I would have it looked into.

At that same time, a mention was made about a problem with a general who was either standing in the way of or was a problem with respect to the sale of airplanes. And when this was brought to my attention, during this same meeting, I became really quite disturbed, and I said to our man, Mr Gates, who was there, look this is not the kind of subject that should be brought up this way, it is very delicate, very sensitive; we have an agent to keep us from getting into these kinds of problems. And I meant not that the agent should bribe him, but saying no to a general or getting disentangled from one who is on the take is as delicate or more delicate as otherwise. I said we have got an agent to straighten out these matters, use him. And I asked him will you please get this taken care of satisfactorily. That was the end of my involvement ...

It is very apparent that that statement on my part, Northrop meets its obligations, even though I left Saudi Arabia and went to Iran, reverberated through the company, obligations which either were felt had been made by some or might have been made were construed to be ... [1]

Jones left the sentence hanging, but his meaning was clear enough: he hadn't *intended* to authorise a pay-off, but both Khashoggi and Jones's own subordinates got the wrong message. Khashoggi interpreted Jones to mean that Northrop would look after Hashim. Gates assumed Jones had no principled objection to a pay-off but preferred to leave details of how it was done to Northrop's men in the field. The opportunities for continuing misunderstanding were endless: and most of them were taken.

Two weeks after Jones's catastrophic ambiguities, Gates's colleague, Manny Gonzalez, sent a coded telegram to Northrop's base at Hawthorne, California. For 'Wishbone' read Khashoggi, for 'Trumpet' Hashim, for 'Surf' Saudi Arabia and 'Hawthorne' USA.

MET WISHBONE 22 OCT IN BEIRUT STOP NO PROBLEM OUR NOT SEEING TRUMPET DURING MY VISIT TO SURF STOP APPARENTLY GATES BRIEF CONVERSATION WITH TRUMPET DURING TVJ TRIP

1 Church Committee, June 10, 1975.

ENOUGH TO KEEP HIM HAPPY UNTIL HE COMES TO HAWTHORNE STOP
WISHBONE PLANS TO BE IN HAWTHORNE SAME TIME TRUMPET STOP.

But there was a further complication.

WISHBONE CONFIRMS TRUMPET SOON TO BE KICKED UPSTAIRS AND
REPLACED BY GERANIUM STOP ADDITIONAL AMOUNT TO BE SPLIT
BETWEEN THOSE TWO TO AVOID ALL PROBLEMS STOP.[1]

'Geranium' was General Zuhayr, Hashim's deputy. According to
Khashoggi, he too was now getting in on the act. And the number of
minor players continued to grow. By April 1972 Khashoggi was asking Northrop for payments of commission in advance 'to commit to
necessary parties'.[2] And elbowing his way to the front of the queue
came Prince Khalid and his 'Cantona Establishment', now demanding an additional ½ per cent on Phase III. This time Manny Gonzalez
had a cunning answer. Northrop knew by now that Khalid was also
on the payroll of Lockheed (as was Hashim, but that was *not*
known), and there were plans afoot to involve Lockheed as sub-
contractors in some of the Phase III maintenance work. What neater
solution, therefore, than to arrange to make Khalid earn his Phase
III pay-off not at Northrop's but at Lockheed's expense? Gonzalez
accordingly rang Khalid, thanked him effusively for his assistance to
Northrop, and indicated that 'because of these services, if Cantona is
involved with other companies that supply services that Northrop
will need, Northrop will certainly consider placing orders with these
companies'.[3] But instead of taking the bait and recommending Lockheed as Gonzalez confidently expected, Khalid replied that, as it
happened, he owned a little electrical contracting company, Dyna-
Electron, which would be only too happy to take on the sub-contract
work. Gonzalez made his excuses and hung up—but Khalid eventually pocketed his extra ½ per cent.

Four months later, in August, the question of Hashim's $250,000
reared its head again. A year had passed since Khashoggi had first
raised it and nothing had been done, Khashoggi leaving it to Northrop and Northrop either leaving it to Khashoggi or just hoping the
whole question would go away. Now Northrop was chasing a Phase
IV contract. Khashoggi's Triad company promised Gates's 'full

1 Wire, Gonzalez to F. W. Lloyd and Milt Kuska, October 25, 1971.
2 Memo, Watts to Gates and Gonzalez, April 17, 1972.
3 Memo, Watts to file, recording Gonzalez's phone conversation, May 12,
1972.

support', but added that 'Adnan regrets Northrop has made the job more difficult' by not honouring its 'obligation' to Hashim.[1] Gates replied stiffly that 'Adnan must realize the difficulty and impracticability of meeting request' and suggested coolly that 'we all proceed with maximum effort on this large upcoming project'.[2] But nothing had been resolved two months later when Khashoggi once again repeated his demand for $250,000 for Hashim, adding a further $150,000 for Hashim's replacement, General 'Geranium' Zuhayr. On January 16, 1973, Gates replied patiently that the whole affair was an 'honest misunderstanding', reiterating Northrop's view that the payments should be booked to Khashoggi's own commission on Phase III. He added, in an apparent reference to Hashim's retirement, that since 'there is no longer a requirement to pay out ... Triad will be in a position to retain these funds'.[3]

But these wiles didn't wash with the wilier Khashoggi. He could see plainly that Northrop had not budged an inch from their contention that Hashim's bribe should come out of Triad's commission. All Gates was doing, in effect, was to encourage him to pocket what he regarded as already his, which he intended to do anyway. And he still wanted Northrop to make separate payments to Hashim and Zuhayr. To up the ante, he now hinted dramatically that Triad would withdraw altogether from its association with Northrop if 'commitments' were not honoured: and to emphasise that he meant business, he also upped Zuhayr's required pay-off from $150,000 to $200,000.

The unhappy Northrop team called in their Middle East experts Kim Roosevelt and Samyr Souki to advise them. Souki reported that Zuhayr was 'pleasant but distant'[4] and that Triad's co-operation was vital to the success of future programmes. Gates summarised their advice:

> the individual in question [Zuhayr] is not going to take a very positive attitude towards Northrop programs until this problem is settled. Hanging in abeyance is the NADC proposal on Cantonments, the follow and buy of F–5Es, plus perhaps a few other programs in which the RSAF would not have input to the decision. I am convinced that we are not going to get this positive input in the current environment.[5]

1 Wire, Lou Lauler of Triad to Gates, August 14, 1972.
2 Wire, Gates to Lauler, August 14, 1972.
3 Letter, Gates to Khashoggi, January 16, 1973.
4 Memo, Souki to Gates, March 16, 1973.
5 Memo, Gates to Gasich, April 3, 1973.

Inevitably, as Lockheed had done when similarly splayed out over the same barrel, Northrop decided the stakes were too high and caved in. Khashoggi was sent a cheque for $250,000 for the retired but still sounding Trumpet and another $200,000 for Geranium. There, no doubt, the matter would have rested had not the payments come to light when the Church Committee questioned Tom Jones. If the consequent publicity embarrassed Jones, it evidently troubled Khashoggi more. Although neither Hashim nor Zuhayr were named in the Congressional hearings,[1] Khashoggi was publicly branded a conduit for bribes to Saudi officials in circumstances which threatened to wreck his entire network of royal connections. His response demonstrated the resourcefulness which had made him one of the richest men in the world. He issued a statement coolly claiming that he had 'pocketed' the bribes rather than compromise the generals' integrity. Amplifying this in a television interview, filmed at his London home, Khashoggi told the author that Northrop had 'imagined these payments were necessary … so they came with this idea, thinking that I would respond favourably, which is against my principles'. To save embarrassment all round, he had generously left the two cheques in his own account where, he claimed, they were credited against future Northrop commissions.[2]

It is a tribute to Khashoggi's powers of persuasion that many have found his explanation plausible. But it does not square with the records. Northrop's memos and telexes, often obscure, sometimes coded and, like Lockheed's, intended for the decent oblivion of private files in locked filing cabinets, tell the familiar story in which bribery and extortion, seemingly opposites, merge and fuse into one.

3

Adnan Khashoggi's image had begun to tarnish some time before the 'bribes to the generals' affair. Early in 1973 Samyr Souki sent Bob Gates a clipping from the French satirical magazine *Le Canard Enchaîné*. It was a gossipy piece, speculating on what Khashoggi did for and with his money, describing his friendship with President Nixon and the alleged CREEP contributions of $1 million, and even

1 They are named, however, in the Northrop documents released by the Church Committee.
2 Khashoggi, interviewed for the TV documentary 'How To Sell An Airforce', Granada Television, January 1976.

hinting at a CIA connection. Souki, never slow to heap aspersions on his fellow Middle East agent and rival, told Gates the article had caused a lot of comment in Beirut. 'We have often discussed the possibility that we may have to reconsider the relationship with Khashoggi in the future', he wrote. 'I intend to look quite seriously into possible replacement in the event that developments make this necessary.'[1]

Warming to his task, Souki reported two months later that Khashoggi was working to 'project a new image of himself as an international businessman' and planned to move his base from the Middle East to either Geneva or London. This, suggested Souki, would mean less time spent on the ground for Northrop. Khashoggi's decision to build up an international profile, was 'due to mounting resentment against him in Saudi Arabia'. Although he retained influence with Prince Sultan, he was *persona non grata* with Prince Abdullah, Commander of the National Guard (and Khalid's father), and it was uncertain whether he had any influence on Crown Prince Fahd:

> AK's fortunes in the future as far as Saudi Arabia is concerned will depend to some extent on who emerges as the leading personality after King Faisal disappears. If Fahd becomes the real leader, there will be several other businessmen who will have as much if not more influence than AK. Should Sultan play in the leading role, then AK may become even stronger than he was in the past unless Sultan decides to cut him down to size. Sultan may well do this in order to appease many of the critics that AK has in the country and on whose support Sultan may want to rely.[2]

At the same time Northrop was receiving queries from the US Government, alerted both by the French article and by Khashoggi's immense commissions: one from the defense department enquiring after 'the qualifications of the bona fide established or selling agency' in Saudi Arabia,[3] another from Captain J. Gaston Kent, USAF, requesting 'full details and background of Northrop's agreement with Triad'.[4] Once again Northrop consulted the invaluable Kim Roosevelt who recommended a bold and theatrical gamble. Accordingly, Khashoggi was invited to Washington DC to justify himself not only to Northrop but, much more important, to the defense

1 Letter, Souki to Gates, January 8, 1973.
2 Memo, Souki to Gates, March 16, 1973.
3 Wire, ASD WPFB Ohio to AF PRO Northrop, March 5, 1973.
4 Letter, April 2, 1973.

department and USAF as well. The momentous meeting took place at the Pentagon on August 9, in the office of the defense department's director of international sales negotiations, David Alne. With Alne were Middle East expert Josef Hoenig, three USAF officers including Brigadier General Robert Trimble — a vociferous critic of high commissions — and two Northrop representatives, Jim Holcombe and Manny Gonzalez. Khashoggi was accompanied by one of his string of American lawyers, Dan Zurface. He must have known that in effect he was on trial. Ostensibly the meeting was merely considering the reasonableness or otherwise of his commissions on FMS sales. But what was really at stake was his entire reputation. Not only his relationship with Northrop but probably the Lockheed connection, too, depended on how he conducted himself before the Pentagon's top brass that afternoon.

The meeting, scheduled to last an hour but extended by Khashoggi's eloquence for a further ninety minutes, was vividly reported by Manny Gonzalez in a confidential blow-by-blow account which succeeds in casting more light on Khashoggi than any of his many public profiles have ever done.[1] Alne opened with a review of the procedures involved in FMS cases and summarised the provisions by which the defense department recognised agents' fees on such sales to the extent that they were 'reasonable'. Khashoggi was invited to 'shed some illumination' thereon.

He began with a review of his own career, starting with his first big truck sale after the Six Day War. He emphasised that 'the trucks were delivered on time, without red tape, and operated effectively and as represented. The Saudi Government was very pleased and as a result turned to [him] to render assistance in selecting a company to operate the Dhahran Airport. This was also a successful operation.' Thus the reason he had a good relationship with the Saudi defence ministry was that he had 'given sound advice and delivered excellent products'. He had never had to 'develop excuses for poor performances'.

Gonzalez noted in elucidatory parentheses:

(This first part of Khashoggi's story, was directed at the point that he did not reach a favoured position ... as a result of any personal friendship with Prince Sultan ... but as a result of good performance over the years. Most of the people in the meeting understood the point and after hearing the rest of Khashoggi's story, accepted it.)

1 Memo, Gonzalez to file, August 13, 1973.

Khashoggi next launched into an enthusiastic review of 'the economic infrastructure of Saudi Arabia', well tailored to the prejudices of his listeners. The country, he asserted blandly, was 'a welfare state in which the government is the only real purchaser or consumer', headed by a king who was 'a firm believer in the free enterprise system and concerned that the present economic infrastructure makes Saudi Arabia an easy target for a communist takeover'. The king

> ... could elect to distribute the government's wealth to the people, but to do so would be merely a temporary solution and an attempt to forestall communism by imitating it. Instead the king has elected to follow a slower, but hopefully more permanent solution of trying to foster a level of independent business within the economy.

Given Saudi Arabia's state of development, that meant the representation of foreign manufacturers. Such representation was 'very open and accepted' in all areas except defence. Defence equipment purchasers attracted unusual publicity everywhere. '(Everyone in the meeting readily accepted this point)', noted Gonzalez drily. The key government leaders were 'fully aware of the agency relationships in the military equipment field', continued Khashoggi, 'but publicly they cannot acknowledge them'. Khashoggi's point, added Gonzalez helpfully, was that the Saudis' apparent hostility to the use of agents in FMS sales was a public relations posture. It did *not* mean that agents were not permitted or even expected.

Khashoggi went on to tackle suspicions about the sheer size of his Northrop commissions. He summarised his earnings on other deals: $45 million on a $600 million sale of French tanks, $5·75 million on a $115 million sale of Belgian ordnance, $7·5 million on Chrysler sales totalling $50 million, at least $5 million on Raytheon sales of $100 million, an 8 per cent commission on an undisclosed value of Lockheed Hercules and Jetstar sales, and so on. Gonzalez noted that, 'rather obviously', Khashoggi was out to prove that his Northrop earnings, when seen alongside comparable relationships with other companies in the US and abroad, were 'reasonable' as required by the defense department, a measure of reasonableness being 'what the practice or experience is with respect to other non-government sales'. Again, everyone seemed to accept this with the exception of General Trimble, who 'made several comments to the effect that the common or usual practice still does not mean that the fee is "reasonable" if it is unrelated to cost'. Trimble, thought Gonzalez, 'was swayed but far from convinced by Khashoggi's statistics'. But the general had made detailed notes and, Gonzalez reasoned hopefully, could only become more convinced the more he studied the figures. Gonzalez himself was sure that Khashoggi's statistics were 'highly beneficial to Northrop's claim. If nothing else, they give full credibility to my personal statement that to my limited knowledge the business deal Northrop has worked out with Triad was on the low side of the commission spectrum. This supports our argument that we entered our agreement with Khashoggi based on our best business judgement at that time and when we were involved in a competition.'

Back to Khashoggi's presentation:

> The fourth and final point of Khashoggi's story was that, though the absolute dollar amounts of his commissions might lead people to believe that decisions in favor of the companies he represents were the result of pay-offs — undue influence or improper dealing by whatever name, such in fact was not the case. In support of this point, he stated that his annual operating expenses for his offices and personnel were in excess of $5 million. (He offered to submit his financial statements, audited by Price Waterhouse, in support of this comment, but no-one accepted.) He then pointed out that he represents many companies and several proposed sales for each of those companies. He stated that his batting average of success versus failure was maybe 2 out of 10 ... Khashoggi then stated that he works for many years on each transaction before it turns into a success or failure for him and that even when it is a success, his payoff is over the time period of performance which may be as much as 10 years. He concluded this area of his comment by stating that, as a 'free enterprise, in the American tradition', businessman, he must make his money on his successes, not his failures.

Anyone who thought the king and Prince Sultan could be reached by improper influence simply didn't understand the facts of life in Saudi Arabia, he told the Americans.

> 'Prince Sultan does not need an Adnan Khashoggi. If he wants $10 million, all he has to do is take it from the government since he is an essential part of the government and it is his to take. If Adnan Khashoggi, or anyone else, tried to buy a decision from Prince Sultan, they would insult him and to insult him is not only stupid, it is dangerous. Adnan Khashoggi will never offer Prince Sultan

money—that is like a beggar offering riches to a king. Adnan Khashoggi will only offer him truth, sound advice and good products.' (After these comments, even Gen. Trimble was impressed.)

Khashoggi's next slant was still more impressive, at least to the increasingly euphoric Manny Gonzalez:

He believes that the royal family in Saudi Arabia is a stabilizing influence not only in the country but in the entire Middle East. (Everyone nodded their concurrence). Khashoggi then added that loyalty to the royal family was in the best interest of such stability. (Once again, everyone nodded their concurrence.)

It was out of loyalty, and loyalty alone, that he performed favours for the royal family. He had once equipped a Bedouin school with textbooks—free of charge. On another occasion, when told that a Bedouin chief near the border with the Yemen needed twelve trucks to transport his goats between oases, he provided them—without compensation. 'Perhaps certain people might consider this to be improper influence, but in Saudi Arabia it is considered as loyalty to the royal family.' Added Gonzalez drily: '(Somewhat surprisingly, everyone appeared to understand and accept this comment.)'

Of course, Khashoggi acknowledged, improper influence did exist on direct sales at lower levels. They were even expected. But he, 'as a loyal Saudi, prefers that a sale goes FMS versus direct sale in order to prevent and avoid improper pay-offs'. Once again, Gonzalez interpolated, his main point was obvious. Even in FMS cases, a bona fide agent 'must make a commission adequate to pay for his operating expenses and loyalties to the royal family'.

As the presentation drew to a close, one of the USAF men, William Robinson, put a question: 'Mr Khashoggi, if all commissions are allowed and paid in this [Northrop] deal and the US Government doesn't disclose the fact, but Prince Sultan finds out about it, will everything blow sky high?' 'Certainly not, if it is handled with tact and diplomacy', Khashoggi replied. His $45 million commission on the French tank sale had been questioned by the king, he revealed, 'but the French Government handled the matter with tact and diplomacy and therefore no problem resulted'. Again, Gonzalez noted, 'the point was not lost, in fact Robbie seemed to have intentionally invited it. If the US Government was as astute in its diplomacy as the French, the question would be unnecessary.' Alne had already promised that the US would be 'true diplomats in this respect' and would use 'carefully selected and artful words'. The presentation was nearly over, and there was no doubt in Gonzalez's mind that Adnan Khashoggi had won the day.

Dave Alne concluded the meeting by saying that he was most appreciative of Mr. Khashoggi's coming to Washington and openly and honestly discussing the role and function of an agent in Saudi. Alne added that he was sure that as a result of this visit 'many people learned a great many things, not the least of which is that a commission agent can be an honest and an astute business-man, rather than an influence peddler who wears horns.' Robinson added that the USAF was most appreciative of Khashoggi's obvious professional approach and open disclosures.

As the meeting broke up, Alne took Gonzalez aside and said 'Manny, it was a stroke of genius to invite Khashoggi here today. We couldn't have arranged it for obvious reasons, but it's well that you did.' And Gonzalez's Northrop colleague Jim Holcombe added, 'Khashoggi sure as hell helped us as well as himself today.'

Only tough old General Trimble remained 'swayed but not fully convinced', and when the euphoria had died down Gonzalez had to concede that 'we will still encounter major difficulties in concluding a settlement with the USAF which covers us fully for all our com-missions to Triad'. But that apart, and second only to the insight it afforded into Khashoggi's *modus operandi*, the record of the meeting is invaluable for its picture of the cosy relationship between defence contractor and defense department. Alne and Robinson were not exactly resistant to the payment of huge commissions on govern-ment-to-government sales. They shared with Northrop an interest in maximising arms sales and not being too fussy how it was done.

The Pentagon's attitudes were encouraged no doubt by Northrop's big-spending and later notorious hospitality machine. This was the time when Northrop was lavishly entertaining selected defense department officials at its well-stocked, well-appointed and well-hostessed hunting lodge in the duck-country of Maryland. Alne was soon to retire from the Pentagon to become an arms company con-sultant, and Josef Hoenig, the assistant director of sales negotiations, Middle East, who had accompanied him to the meeting with Khash-oggi, later embarrassed his chiefs by an over-candid speech to the export committee of the Electronic Industry Association in which he stressed the necessary role of agents in buying influence:

Influence can range from normal friendship or family ties between local agent and procuring officer to the payment of substantial sums of money to individuals in high government positions with somewhat lesser amounts paid to lower echelon government officials ... Obviously the agent with the greatest margin of profit or percentage has a distinct advantage over those with a lesser fee in that greater 'influence' can be applied to all personnel in the government decision-making chain.

FMS deals did not eliminate 'exerting influence for a fee', Hoenig had added, since 'a distinction must be made between what top governmental officials say publicly and what they really mean'.[1] Khashoggi had clearly got his message across to the Pentagon.

Once again his star was in the ascendant. During his Washington trip he hired a public relations man and, soon after, Bob Gates was writing to Samyr Souki that Khashoggi was getting 'additional publicity in the US and some of it has been quite good'.[2] He cited in particular a flattering profile in the prestigious magazine *Business Week*, including a fulsome tribute from French banker Louis Dreyfus who described Khashoggi as 'the only man in the Middle East you can trust'. For their part, Northrop's relief at the new turn of events was such that no one demurred when Triad slipped in a request for consent to represent McDonnell-Douglas in a sale of F–4s, and the British Aircraft Corporation in a sale of Jaguars. (The Jaguars were intended for Egypt but Britain preferred to sell through the Saudis, for onward delivery to Cairo, to avoid the hostility of the Israelis and their supporters. Khashoggi also represented Marconi and Rolls-Royce in the same deal.)

Meanwhile, Triad continued as active as ever for Lockheed. In November 1973 a proposal for the sale of ten more Hercules aircraft was presented to General Zuhayr who by now had replaced Hashim

---

1 Speech on 'Agents Fees in the Middle East' given in Washington DC on June 11, 1974, and cleared for publication by the directorate for security review, defense department, on July 5, 1974. Hoenig also told his listeners that 'the French and British industries are masters in dealing through agents and generally have no compunction to agreeing to excessive fees, if, in the final analysis, the sale is consummated. In an on-going negotiation in the Middle East, one European aircraft contractor has a tidy 21 [per cent] for the local agent. On the basis of this $200 million contract, the agent had millions to use for influence and still retain a respectable profit for his effort.'
2 Letter, Gates to Souki, August 21, 1973.

as head of the air force. The price had now risen to a massive $6·3 million which, 'at the insistence of AK ... included the normal commissions plus $200,000 of "negotiating money"'. The $200,000 per plane — $2 million in all — was there either to be negotiated away for price reductions or used for 'under the table pay-offs'.[1]

Zuhayr, as expected, insisted that $6·3 million was too high, so Lockheed's negotiator, Temp Walker, obligingly dropped to $6·1 million. Next day, November 29, Khashoggi was told of the reduction and objected strongly, having 'taken the position that all negotiating money not negotiated away would go to Triad as a bonus'. The flexible Walker agreed to go back and renegotiate, and this time came out with a price of $6·2 million, which meant that $100,000 'negotiating money' remained in the kitty.

So far, so good. But a day or two later the ubiquitous Prince Khalid reappeared on the scene, summarily demanding Temp Walker's presence at his villa at 6.30 p.m. sharp on December 3. There Khalid told the bewildered Walker that he was most upset that Lockheed had given away $100,000 of 'his' negotiating money. It transpired that Khashoggi and Khalid had together formed a new company, Saveria Establishment (based, naturally, in Geneva), to which Triad was assigning its Hercules contract. The two men had agreed a commission split of 60 per cent for Khashoggi and 40 per cent for Khalid. The cause of Khalid's concern soon became apparent. He had committed $125,000 per plane of his share to a *fourth* party and was alarmed that Lockheed (which knew nothing of the arrangement) would leave him without a profit.

When Walker tried to sort out the tangle he uncovered yet more complications. It turned out that Khashoggi had told Khalid his 'normal commission' from Lockheed was 3 per cent (when in fact it was 8) and that the extra 'negotiating money' was $150,000, not $200,000. Khalid's share was thus a great deal less than the 40 per cent Khashoggi had promised.

Lockheed and Khashoggi finally did a deal at Khalid's expense. First, Lockheed agreed to support Khashoggi's deception by booking commission to 'Saveria' at 3 per cent instead of 8, the remaining 5 per cent going to Khashoggi alone. It was also agreed that Lockheed would restore the $100,000 'negotiating money' that Khalid was so concerned at losing, making it up to the $150,000 figure which Khashoggi had misrepresented as the true total. Khashoggi for his

1 Unsigned memo, January 22, 1974.

part, would go along with a 50–50 split of this bonus. As the Lockheed memo logging the deal put it, 'A story was developed to present to PK which would support the actual split AK intended to make with PK.'

The contract was signed on December 21 – ten planes for a total price of $62 million. 'Saveria' collected $2,610,000, of which Prince Khalid's 40 per cent share was $1,044,000 and Khashoggi's $1,566,000. In addition, of course, Khashoggi collected for Triad, behind Khalid's back, the 'extra' 5 per cent, $3·1 million.

It was a busy time for Khashoggi. The sudden onset of the Yom Kippur war in October gave the world's most artful middleman a new and more elevated role. In the aftermath of the fighting, his old friend Richard Nixon recruited him as a go-between in a highly secret negotiation with King Faisal in which the American President sought to persuade the king that the cause of stability in the Middle East would best be served by the diplomatic connivance of Saudi Arabia at the resupplying of Israel against the common enemy, radical Arabism. Khashoggi reportedly received and delivered these communications personally in the Watergate apartment of Nixon's secretary, Rose Mary Woods. What the President didn't know, according to the then Ambassador to Saudi Arabia, Thacher's successor James Akins, was that 'King Faisal had a strong distaste, dislike, for Mr Khashoggi' and was unlikely to welcome him as 'conduit for communication with the American President or with anyone else'.[1]

Others in Washington's high places were also embroiled in Khashoggi's affairs. In November 1973 secretary of state Henry Kissinger cabled ambassador Akins, asking him to smooth the way with Prince Sultan to avoid a damaging scandal over Triad's commissions.[2] (Kissinger was subsequently an active opponent of public disclosure of improper payments, fearing it would damage US state and business interests.) Akins, by his own account, thought the request unseemly and refused. When, shortly afterwards, he was relieved of his post and not offered another, Khashoggi told his friends that he was behind Akins's firing. As the ex-ambassador remembered it, 'I was told just before I left by Prince Sultan that Khashoggi had boasted that he had gotten me removed from Saudi Arabia because of my blocking agents' fees and bribes, and we both laughed. We thought

1 Akins to the Church Committee, May 4, 1976.
2 Memo to file from Gonzalez, December 3, 1973.

it was a big joke. I still think it's a joke but I don't think it's quite as funny as I did a few months ago.'[1]

Despite the doubts of the sceptical General Trimble, the Pentagon finally agreed Triad's FMS commissions on the Northrop programme. Not until his name first surfaced in the SEC and Church Committee hearings did Khashoggi's credit with Saudi royalty begin to collapse. By that time even a supportive letter to Prince Sultan from assistant secretary of defense Ellsworth[2] failed to uphold Khashoggi's crumbling reputation. The Saudis froze $68 million commission due from Northrop to Khashoggi, pending investigations of Triad's affairs.

But what was a mere $68 million to Adnan Khashoggi? If his homeland was barred to him, the rest of the world was not. He had his banks in California, his ranch in Arizona, his real estate interests in South America, his luxury homes all over the world, his palatial jumbo, his luxury yacht on the east coast of America (named the *Khalidia*), his pet project for a gold-plated pyramid in Egypt—and his place both in the history books and in Harold Robbins. 'The Pirate', not yet out of his thirties, continued his peripatetic existence, afraid to stop moving lest the whole adventure stop with him. As for Lockheed, which first made him a legend, they too had other worlds to conquer and other legends to create.

1 Akins to Church Committee, May 4, 1976.
2 Disclosed by Akins in Church Committee testimony, May 4, 1976.

10

The Great Jumbo War

Hang in there, baby!
Motto on Dan Haughton's office wall

1

To Saudi princes, Italian deputies and Indonesian widows and orphans, Lockheed in the late 1960s and early 1970s must have seemed a very rich company indeed, benevolently intent on spreading its wealth with appealing generosity. The truth, however, was very different. By 1970 the western world's biggest defence contractor was virtually bankrupt. The bribes and backhanders which had once been deployed to secure marginal advantages over competitors had become desperate stratagems for keeping a stricken company in business. The causes of this cataclysmic change in Lockheed's fortunes were complex, but they can be traced back to a single significant political decision

Ever since the creation of an independent US air force in 1947 the partnership between service chiefs and the contracting companies had been a close one. Cut loose from its army and navy contacts, the air force had deliberately bound itself more closely to its industrial partners, gaining powerful new allies in the business and banking communities, in local and state governments whose districts benefited from big air force contracts, and in labour unions. The civil arm of the partnership provided the political support necessary to sell the air chiefs' increasingly ambitious and expensive programmes to Congress and the taxpayer. In return the air force procurement departments in the Pentagon did their best to keep the contractors generously supplied with lucrative contracts.

But by the early 1960s the 'military-industrial complex' was under attack from liberal quarters, and President Kennedy charged his defense secretary, Robert McNamara, with the task of taming it. McNamara launched his attack by changing the rules of the procurement game.

Before the change it worked something like this. The Pentagon would make the opening move, inviting tenders for the research and development contract for a new plane, missile or other device. At this stage there would be genuine, keen competition among the contractors, which would tend to keep bids low. After much lobbying, the Pentagon would select a contractor to begin work on a programme for Pentagon approval. The Pentagon was free to reject the programme but that meant going back to square one and putting research and development out to tender again, so it was usually accepted, perhaps with modifications, and the contractor would be asked to quote for a prototype or a handful of test machines. At this stage there would be no competition, so the contractor would tend not only to quote on the high side but probably to overrun costs as well. On completion of the prototype, the contractor would again quote — without competition — for a full production run, on which there would almost inevitably be further cost overruns. Contracts for modifications, spares and maintenance would follow; and at each stage, in the absence of any competition, it would become progressively more difficult for the Pentagon to call a halt or regain control over costs. So the philosophy of deliberate cost overruns, of 'contract nourishment', became firmly established throughout the industry. The US treasury paid, the companies — particularly Lockheed — prospered.[1]

McNamara's answer was the fixed-price contract, or something very like it, which aimed to apply a brake to cost overruns by limiting the government's liability and requiring the contractor to pay most of any overrun out of his own pocket. But the reforms proved less effective than McNamara hoped. Contractors simply raised their quotes — estimating their overruns in advance, as it were, and thus legitimising them. A much more drastic revision of the rules was needed and it came with 'Total Package Procurement'.

TPP, as the industry called it, was the brainchild of Robert Charles, a poacher turned gamekeeper who had spent eighteen years with the McDonnell Aircraft Company before joining the Pentagon as assistant secretary to the air force. Under Charles's 'total package', the entire system of phased tendering was replaced by one in which competing manufacturers were required to submit one bid at the start, covering not only research and development but each subsequent stage too, right the way through to production. The winner got a contract that dictated total price (including the maximum profit the contractor was allowed to make on the deal), technical

---

1 See Ernest Fitzgerald, *High Priests of Waste*, for a detailed analysis of the weaknesses of the old procurement system.

specifications and delivery dates. In theory at least, 'contract nourishment' was killed stone dead.

Many contractors simply refused to believe that TPP could or would be enforced. The entire concept was widely dismissed as a public relations exercise designed to reassure anxious taxpayers that the defense department had at last gained a proper grip on the public purse. The first big test came in 1965 when the Pentagon invited tenders for the world's first wide-bodied jumbo, the C–5A Galaxy. Boeing, Douglas and Lockheed put in 'total package' bids – and Lockheed were the (as it turns out) unfortunate winners.

The C–5A was a revolutionary plane, far larger than any built before or since. The air force set out its requirement for a jumbo transporter that could carry the military equipment – including tanks and helicopters – of an entire army division within the compass of a single airframe. The plane had to be able to fly in the worst possible conditions, carry its 50-ton load 2,875 miles, land, unload, heave itself into the air from a 4,000 ft dirt strip and return to base without refuelling. So that tanks and helicopters could be driven aboard, the undercarriage had to be given 'knees' to allow the plane to lower its immense hatches to near-ground-level. In short, the manufacturer was required to explore new frontiers in aviation technology – and to do so at a fixed price.

The Pentagon itself had privately calculated that the C–5A would cost at least $2·2 billion for 115 planes. Boeing submitted a bid for $2·3 billion, Douglas for $2 billion. Lockheed, more optimistic or reckless than either, or perhaps more confident that TPP would never be enforced if estimates were exceeded, quoted $1·9 billion and collected the contract.

When Dan Haughton succeeded Courtlandt Gross as chairman nearly two years later, in 1967, there was little to suggest that the winning of the Galaxy contract was to prove a delayed-action bomb which would soon come close to blowing Lockheed out of business. On the contrary, Lockheed could and did boast that it was pioneering the jumbo age. And when the major American airlines began to show an interest in commercial jumbos, Lockheed seemed well placed to take up the challenge.

Haughton's Georgia division, home of the Galaxy, began design work on commercial jobs early in 1966. Boeing and Douglas were also in the field. Both had done preliminary research and development on the Galaxy while competing with Lockheed for the Pentagon contract, and both set out to put this to commercial use.

But Boeing chose to aim at the transcontinental and intercontinental routes with a 400-seater – the 747 – which would be too heavy and cumbersome to land at municipal airports. Lockheed and Douglas aimed at producing a medium-range, all-purpose jumbo airbus, one that would satisfy the big domestic airlines for a generation, and would also be capable of 'stretching' for long-range use.

The two rival contenders in what was to become known as the Great Airbus Race both faced difficulties before they even reached the starting line. Lockheed had been out of the commercial aircraft field since the Elektra débâcle, and had never built a jet airliner. Douglas was critically short of cash – so much so that they actually scratched from the race for a time, only to re-enter after being rescued by a merger with McDonnell. So Lockheed, though it had still to persuade the airlines that it understood the commercial as well as the military end of the business, was comfortably leading after the first lap. On September 11 Haughton announced publicly that he was ready to take orders for the three-engined L–1011, soon to be known as the TriStar.

Two months later McDonnell-Douglas pulled level by announcing they would start taking orders for the DC–10. To potential customers there seemed to be nothing between the rival planes, the interiors of which were almost identical. Both sales pitches were aimed at the domestic airline industry, some two hundred firms doing $15 billion worth of business a year, more than half of which was accounted for by the Big Four – American, Eastern, TWA and United. As TWA's Robert Rummel has recalled, 'There was hardly a day when there wasn't a McDonnell-Douglas man or a Lockheed man in this office discussing specifications. And whichever one *was* in here, the other guy was waiting outside for his turn.'[1] This lobbying had a victory-or-death quality. It was widely believed that the market could sustain only one jumbo airbus, that it would be a case of winner-takes-all.

On February 16, 1968, American, the first of the Big Four to make its choice, plumped for the DC–10, ordering twenty-five at a total price of $382 million – $15·3 million apiece. Lockheed, its lead wiped out at a stroke, reacted immediately. Within days, Haughton announced that, 'for a limited period', he would slash $1 million off

---

1 Quoted by Paul Eddy, Elaine Potter and Bruce Page in *Destination Disaster* (Hart-Davis, MacGibbon, London, 1976), to which excellent account of this phase of the Great Airbus Race I am indebted.

every TriStar sold, reducing the price to $14·4 million and under-cutting McDonnell-Douglas by $900,000. The move paid off. By the end of March Lockheed had orders for 118 TriStars from Eastern, TWA and Delta (one of the biggest airlines outside the Big Four). Even more significantly, the company announced the largest single order yet placed for jumbos: fifty to be bought by a mysterious British corporation called Air Holdings Ltd.

Air Holdings turned out to be a hastily assembled consortium launched by Lockheed itself in partnership with Rolls-Royce and the British government. Right at the start of the race, Lockheed and Douglas had both wanted to power their own airbus with Rolls-Royce RB–211 engines, first because lower labour costs in Britain made them cheaper than American rivals, and second because trans-atlantic partnership promised valuable business clout – a joint Anglo-American sales pitch. But Douglas had bowed to Congressional grumblings at the industry's lack of patriotism and left their more robust rivals to link up with the foreigner. Now Haughton was playing the British connection for all it was worth. If TriStar went down, the RB–211 would go down too. So Rolls and the British government were hustled into the Air Holdings arrangement, by which the company bought fifty TriStars for 'resale outside the USA'. The deal – criticised in the House of Commons as 'a bookkeeping transaction, and a dubious one at that' – accomplished two things for Lockheed. It topped up their order book to 168 against McDonnell-Douglas's 25, and it gave the British government a strong vested interest not only in buying TriStar for British Airways but in pushing sales to other friendly airlines.

So decisively had Lockheed re-established its lead by the end of March that McDonnell-Douglas were widely tipped to drop out of the race and leave their rival to go it alone. But Douglas division head David Lewis fought back, cutting half a million dollars off the DC–10 price and offering generous credit arrangements. On April 25, United, the biggest of the Big Four and the last to make up its mind, placed an order for 60 DC–10s.

That still left McDonnell-Douglas trailing behind Lockheed – 85 orders to 168 – but basic arithmetic now ceased to be of prime importance. What United's order did was to ensure that two almost identical jumbo airbuses would go into production when it was touch and go whether one alone, with the whole field to itself, could ever pay its way. McDonnell-Douglas needed 200 orders before its plane would begin to show a profit, Lockheed (because of its heavier price-cutting) 250. Ahead lay a catastrophic energy crisis which would make the thirsty jumbo an extravagance a declining number of airlines could afford; and in the wake of that, rampant world inflation and recession.

Added to all this, Lockheed had a handicap which was uniquely its own. It was lumbered with that fateful C–5A fixed-price contract. And by 1968 it was clear that the programme was heading for disaster—a disaster which threatened to drag TriStar down with it.

2

The Galaxy scandal is now a matter of record. Within months of production starting in Georgia it became clear that there was no chance whatever of Lockheed being able to build the plane for the fixed price quoted to and accepted by the Pentagon. In theory, and according to the letter of the TPP contract, that was exclusively Lockheed's problem: cost overruns were the company's responsibility, not the Pentagon's. But in practice both sides had an interest in working out some sort of compromise. The Pentagon was anxious that the much-publicised TPP concept was seen not to fall flat on its face. If Lockheed were allowed to bleed to death, not only would the Pentagon lose its biggest contractor (and its Galaxies) but industry critics who had all along claimed that the idea was unworkable would quickly force a return to the good old days of 'contract nourishment'. So Pentagon and Lockheed developed a common interest in bending the rules of TPP while giving every appearance to the taxpayer and the outside world of rigidly enforcing them.

This wasn't too difficult. In 1968, a Congressional investigation established later, Lockheed had no fewer than 210 retired military officers of the rank of colonel or above on its payroll. McNamara and Charles notwithstanding, the military-industrial complex was still alive and well, if discreetly maintaining a low profile. What happened, in essence, was that the Pentagon agreed to make progress payments to Lockheed *before completion of the stage at which the payments were properly due*, where necessary falsifying the records accordingly. It was a crude strategy which by its nature could not be sustained indefinitely. Sooner or later, if it were continued, the final instalment would have to be paid on a plane which was only half completed. The air force would then either have to take delivery of the unfinished giants, presumably hoping nobody noticed the gaps, or go to Congress for further funds to enable Lockheed to finish the job — which would be to admit the failure of TPP.

In fact it never got that far. Ernest Fitzgerald, a civilian cost-control expert working for the air force department in the Pentagon, saw what was going on and tried to put a stop to it. When he repeatedly failed to interest his superiors in the matter, he put his information in the hands of a powerful critic of profligate public spending, Senator William Proxmire, who opened Congressional hearings to investigate the charges. The Pentagon clumsily tried to prevent Fitzgerald from testifying, failed, and promptly discovered that his appointment as a permanent civil servant was the result of a unique computer error. Reprogrammed, the computer conveniently pronounced Fitzgerald redundant. Only the intervention of the Civil Service Commission won him back a job at the Pentagon.

Within Lockheed, too, there was one man who wouldn't keep quiet. Henry Durham had been with the company since 1951 and had risen to become a departmental manager in charge of production and testing at the Marietta factory building the Galaxy. 'Among his many qualifications', testified his superiors prior to the Galaxy affair, 'are unquestioned loyalty, energy, initiative, product and corporate knowledge, ambition, and an insistence on a job well done — first of all by himself, and secondly by all reporting to him.'

It transpired, however, that in some eyes it was possible to take 'insistence on a job well done' a little too far. In July 1969, Durham later told Proxmire's Committee, he began to notice 'serious deficiencies' in C–5A planes when they were being moved from assembly areas to test positions. In particular:

thousands upon thousands of parts and assemblies which Lockheed inspection records showed to be installed were in fact missing from the aircraft and had not been installed. Aircraft which according to company records were complete except for planned flight line installations and a few engineering jobs were in fact virtual shells.

After monitoring these deficiences for two months, Durham told his superiors of his worries. 'I expected everyone to be shocked and come to the rescue,' he told Proxmire. But the response was negative, so he went to higher management with a series of written reports. 'I was told to shut up and even hide the reports.' When he tried to make an appointment with the president of the Georgia company, Robert A. Fuhrman, hostility turned into intimidation. 'I was ostracised, criticised, pushed in a corner and even warned by my immediate superior that I would never get up on the right side of the bed if I went to see Fuhrman and continued to persist in seeking reforms.'

Durham nevertheless got to see his boss in April 1970 – and was told his job was abolished in May. He says he was 'literally run out of the plant'. A long letter to Dan Haughton produced a promise of an investigation (which Durham claims never materialised), followed by an invitation to return to Lockheed in a more junior capacity and at a much lower rate of pay. Durham swallowed his pride, accepted the offer – and continued his campaign. At one point he was called to see the director of manufacturing, W. P. Frech.

> Frech asked if I knew what had happened to Mr. Fitzgerald who had gone to Washington with some Lockheed problems. When I said I did not, Mr. Frech said that Mr. Fitzgerald was now the Chief Shithouse Inspector for the Civil Service and that he would never be able to get a good job. I consider this to be intimidation. The inference was that anyone who bucks the Lockheed Company or the Air Force is in trouble for the rest of his life.[1]

Durham's response to these ugly threats was to resign from the company and follow Fitzgerald's path to Proxmire and public disclosure.

Going public only increased the intimidation. Threats against Durham's life became so widespread that Haughton himself found it necessary to write an open letter 'to the men and women of Lockheed'.

> There have been reports that apparently some Lockheed employees are threatening Lockheed critics in various ways ... It is understandable that we would become emotional about others' threats to our jobs and our futures but it is not acceptable for anyone to make threats of any type to our critics ... In spite of our strong feelings, I hope you will join me in expressing those feelings in a calm and considered manner worthy of the tradition of the men and women of Lockheed.[2]

Lockheed found it hard to live down the uglier aspects of the Durham affair, and what the company conspicuously failed to do was provide a convincing answer to Durham's specific charges of Lockheed–

1 Durham to Proxmire's Sub-committee on Priorities and Economy in Government of the Joint Economic Committee, September 29, 1971.
2 Evidence to the Proxmire Committee, September 29, 1971.

Pentagon collusion to buck the TPP system. The company's sliding reputation was not helped by two technical embarrassments at Marietta. First a C–5A test flight, arranged with much ballyhoo to demonstrate to VIPs and TV cameras that the plane's troubles were finally over, came to an undignified end when a wheel dropped off during landing and preceded the mutilated giant up the runway at Charleston SC air base. Soon after, a wing parted from its mountings and crashed to the ground, revealing a structural weakness in all models which eventually cost an incredible $1 billion to patch up. Even then, the huge, flapping wings threatened to break off again after a mere 8,000 flight-hours, compared with the 30,000 flight-hours for which they were designed, and in March 1978 the air force prepared to ask Congress for another $1·3 billion to finance further repairs (which were expected, somewhat ironically, to be contracted out to lucky Lockheed). But long before this, in November 1969, with the programme already more than $1 billion over budget, the air force cut its losses and reduced its order from 115 planes to 81, leaving Lockheed with losses of $200 million and the Treasury — despite the supposed safeguards of TPP — with a deficit of more than $800 million.

As if all this were not enough, the corporation also faced new and terrifying difficulties on other fronts. A TPP contract for an army rigid-rotor helicopter, the Cheyenne, ran far over budget and was abruptly cancelled by the army after a prototype crashed, killing the pilot. Yet another TPP contract for the propulsion system of a new short-range air-to-air missile, SRAM, ran into seemingly insoluble technical difficulties; and on top of all that, Lockheed's shipbuilding subsidiary lost no less than $100 million on a huge fixed-price contract with the navy. By the end of 1969 the corporation had written off a gigantic $290 million on these programmes, as a result of which it reported a loss of $32 million for the year, compared with a profit in 1968 of $44 million.

The results in 1970 were even worse. On March 2, Haughton wrote to the defense department requesting a hand-out of $640 million to keep the company's military contracts afloat. The request was refused, and Lockheed had to turn to the banks. By the end of the year the company's overdraft, spread over 24 banks, was $350 million. Even when the Senate grudgingly sanctioned a further $200 million advance for the crippled C–5A programme, that still left the company nearly $100 million short of the $640 million Haughton estimated he needed to stay in business. Lockheed's relations with the Pentagon were hardly improved when government accountants revealed that although the C-5A was being built by Lockheed-Georgia, $181 million of the Pentagon's progress payments had found their way to Lockheed-California, home of the TriStar. The corporation strenuously denied the insinuation that Pentagon cash was being used to fund one of its non-military projects, but not everyone was convinced by Lockheed's explanation that the Georgia company had innocently subcontracted C-5A development work to the TriStar's home base without thought of commercial advantage.

Ironically, it took an apparent disaster to save Lockheed from sudden death. In January 1971 Rolls-Royce, makers of the TriStar's engines, went bankrupt. The TriStar programme was halted overnight and 9,000 workers at Burbank were laid off. But the sudden collapse of one of Britain's most prestigious companies, threatening as it did to drag one of America's largest and most labour-intensive corporations with it, prompted a frenzy of diplomatic activity between the Heath government and the Nixon administration, both ideologically resistant to state aid for lame ducks but pragmatically alive to the dangerous social and political consequences of leaving such giant birds to collapse and die. After three months of hard bargaining the British government offered a deal. They would provide $240 million to complete development of the RB-211 engine provided Washington guaranteed the future of the TriStar. Lockheed and the Nixon administration together persuaded the long-suffering banks to advance a further $250 million, which they did on condition that Congress itself guaranteed the company's survival. On July 30 the House agreed to the loan-guarantee by just three votes. In the Senate, three days later, Lockheed's survival was finally endorsed by an even finer margin — 49 votes to 48.

TriStar lived — but only just. Everything now depended on Lockheed's ability to beat the world slump and outsell its rivals.

3

The natural starting point for a high-pressure overseas sales drive was western Europe. First there was keen interest in the jumbo airbus concept among a growing number of European airlines. Second, Lockheed's undercover connections there were particularly strong.

Throughout 1968 Lockheed's crack sales-inducement team, starring Carl Kotchian and Roger Bixby Smith, were in regular touch with

Prince Bernhard, meeting him in Paris, Annecy and on a golf course at Utrecht. While a prime purpose of these meetings was pursuit of the Orion contract—the campaign which culminated in the $100,000 payment to the fictitious 'Victor Baarn'—Kotchian has testified that the meetings and the payment were also 'intended to create the right atmosphere' for other Lockheed products, specifically TriStar.[1]

The Dutch airline KLM, of which Bernhard was still an active director, had entered into a loose consortium arrangement with Swissair, Scandinavian Airline System (SAS) and the French Union de Transports Aériens (UTA). By the end of 1968 the consortium, later formalised as KSSU, had set up a joint working party to study a projected purchase of thirty-six airbuses. The only candidates in which they were interested were the TriStar and the DC-10.

Thirty-six was in itself a substantial and welcome order, the more so since there was every chance it would trigger further overseas orders for the fortunate winner. But the wide spread of procurement responsibility within the consortium left little scope for fruitful hanky-panky. The Lockheed men no doubt learned from their top-level Dutch contacts that some 300 officials would be involved in the whole evaluation process and that the KLM board's preference would not necessarily prevail. What Bernhard no doubt omitted to tell the Lockheed team was that he had already made up his own mind—in favour of the DC-10.[2]

Kotchian knew that what he most needed was intelligence—information on the criteria to be applied to the evaluation by each member of the consortium. Such intelligence could come only from within the small and select KSSU working party. And it was made clear to Kotchian that he would have to pay for it.

The man who told him so and proceeded, on Kotchian's instructions, to make the necessary arrangements, was Edward Fife, an old Lockheed salesman from Elektra and Constellation days. Fife was a veteran of a golden age of aviation salesmanship when it was accepted practice for the sales agent to split his commission with officials of the buying airline without Congressional investigators, probing journalists or nit-picking auditors asking questions or so much as whispering the ugly word 'bribe'. Now based in Geneva, but still very much in touch both with his old employers and his contacts in the major European airlines, Fife advised Kotchian and his number

1 'Commissie van Drie', chapter 5, page 1.
2 The 'Commissie van Drie' noted that the prince privately expressed satisfaction at the eventual choice of the DC-10.

two, Bob Mitchell, that they could buy their way into the KSSU working party for the modest outlay of $25,000.

Accordingly, Fife was authorised to call at the Crédit Suisse bank at Geneva and pick up the money in $1,000 bills, drawn on Lockheed's secret 'off-the-books' account organised by Roger Bixby Smith and Coudert Frères in Paris. The cash was delivered to Mitchell in Amsterdam.[1] Mitchell, by his own account, then met 'a high KLM official' in the Amsterdam Hilton and placed the $25,000 'within his reach'. The cash disappeared and, as Mitchell put it later, 'in view of what happened during that meeting it seemed unlikely that anyone other than that official could have taken the money'.[1]

Mitchell declined to name his man but Kotchian and Fife were less reticent, both telling secret sessions of the Church Committee that he was Fritz Besançon, a director of KLM and a member of the KSSU working group. Besançon, who left KLM in 1974, vigorously denied ever receiving the money, which prompted Senator Symington of the Church Committee to ask Fife, 'How do you know Mitchell did not put [the money] in his pocket?' Fife replied, 'I don't know what he did.' Such were the hazards to the corporation of an 'off-the-books' strategy designed with in-built non-accountability.

Whatever intelligence Kotchian did manage to glean from within the KSSU didn't help him much. At the Paris air show in June 1969, while he was hosting a lunch for Prince Bernhard and other dignitaries, the news came through that the consortium had turned down the TriStar and opted for the DC-10. Thereafter, as we shall see, Kotchian concentrated all his energies on the Japanese market. But Europe, though left to Haughton's less elevated henchmen, was not entirely abandoned. A new strategy was developed which in effect meant concentrating on military sales in the hope of opening doors through which TriStar might be pushed at the opportune moment.

Thus in West Germany Lockheed appointed a new agent, Christian Steinrucke. 'Steinrucke has a rather magnificent home in Neuss on the outskirts of Düsseldorf', wrote salesman Norman Orwat to his chief, Maurice Egan, 'and entertains in what might moderately be termed the grand old style'. A dinner for sixteen guests, including the breathless Orwat, was 'as splendidly presented and served as any I have attended in Europe. Mrs Steinrucke is a charming and highly experienced hostess, as well as a lovely lady. I am told — and I can

1 Fife's testimony to Church Committee in secret executive session, March 4, 1976.
2 Mitchell to the Dutch 'Commissie van Drie'.

believe it! — that Germans seldom turn down a dinner invitation from the Steinruckes.' Orwat declared himself no less impressed by 'the political, military, financial and industrial associations that Steinrucke has in high circles. It seems to me,' his letter concluded, 'that he possesses many of the assets that we seek when we arrange for effective local representation in a foreign country ... I am confident that Steinrucke could be helpful to us by putting us in touch — under favourable circumstances — with the type of people to whom we would wish to communicate.'

Steinrucke was indeed signed up, though Orwat thought it prudent to warn Burbank that 'an agreement of this kind may be illegal in Germany', making it necessary that 'copies be limited only to those with a strict need to know'. Orwat added: 'You may wish the legal people to give it some careful scrutiny. Although, since Roger Smith helped to prepare it, I am sure it is legally sound.'[1] Steinrucke's contract was drawn up primarily with S–3A anti-submarine aircraft sales in mind and gave him a handsome $100,000 for each plane sold. But he was also paid a $1,000-a-month 'advance against any commissions earned' on other types of plane. Soon he was asking for an additional $8,000 to cover gifts 'distributed equally between the two political parties in Germany' and $43,000 'to meet certain other obligations for which there will be no receipts',[2] to be paid into a numbered account at the Schweizerische Kredit Anstalt bank, Zürich. When Burbank seemed to be unduly delaying its response to these requests, Orwat wrote from London urging a decision — otherwise 'Steinrucke's deportment is likely to be that of an offended bear whose wounded paw has just been stepped on'.[3]

Lockheed did pay up the $8,000 which Steinrucke claimed he had spent on bribing political parties, only to learn a year later, when privately informed of the conclusions of a secret Bonn government investigation, that the genial host of Düsseldorf had in fact kept the money for himself.[4] Once again Lockheed had been taken for a ride and there was no sale to show for it, and certainly no opening for the TriStar.

The corporation continued to seek intelligence of European airline requirements, at one point parting company with $10,000 to two

---

1 Letter, Orwat to R. R. Witte, April 1, 1974.
2 Coded cable dated August 30, 1972.
3 Memo, Orwat to Dale Daniels, January 24, 1975.
4 *International Herald Tribune*, Feb. 12, 1976, confirmed by the leaked version of the investigation which appeared in the *Süddeutsche Zeitung*, May 9, 1978.

self-styled private investigators in London who claimed to be in a position to use CIA connections to provide accurate inside information on each airline's procurement plans for the next ten years. The report, when it was delivered, told Lockheed nothing they couldn't guess for themselves or glean from the newspapers. British Airways was 'revealed' as one line which could be expected to go for the TriStar rather than the DC–10, which was hardly news to Kotchian and Haughton. The Italian magazine *Panorama* was later to speculate suggestively on the discovery in Lockheed's codebook of the names of former premier Harold Wilson ('Pointer') and former foreign secretary George Brown ('Powder'), alongside such world statesmen as Georges Pompidou ('Cosmos') and Ludwig Erhard ('Halibut'). But the British attachment to TriStar clearly owed nothing to hanky-panky and everything to the Rolls-Royce connection.

Apart from Germany there were also major sales campaigns in Spain and Turkey. In Spain the loss-leader was the ever-youthful Hercules. Lockheed set up a front in Madrid called Avionica, and proceeded to pay sums of more than $300,000 each to a former chief of air defence command, General Luis Rey Rodriguez, and the former military aircraft procurement chief, Col. Carlos Grandal Segado.[1] The Hercules sale went through, but failed to open up any prospects for the TriStar.

In Turkey, Lockheed pitched simultaneously for a TriStar sale to the Turkish state airline THY and a sale of Italian-built Starfighters — the last of a long line — to the Turkish air force. Lockheed's agent for the Starfighter deal was an Ankara businessman, Nezih M. Dural, who was paid $30,000 for 'quote extraordinary unquote expenses' and 'gifts'. The chief worry of sales executive Allen Meyer, however, as expressed in a memo to Don Wilder and Duane Wood, was that 'there is little indication that Dural is offering really significant inducement at decision-making levels'. A reworded agreement was prepared to 'assure Nezih of a thoroughly adequate amount with which to buy real influence'.[2] An indication of where that influence may have been exerted was provided in April 1977 when a Turkish parliamentary committee ruled for an investigation against the prime

---

1 Report of the chief prosecutor fiscal, Spanish Supreme Court, November 1976. The report confirmed these payments to the two military men and further payments to three wealthy businessmen, but concluded that the 'irregularities' did not amount to bribery or corruption.

2 Memo, September 5, 1973.

minister, Suleyman Demirel, and the defence minister, Ferit Melen, both charged by the committee with accepting bribes and authorising 'great irregularities and illegal activities' in connection with the purchase of 40 Starfighters.[1]

THY looked at first to be no less persuaded than the air force to buy Lockheed. Its requirement for six jumbos was small, but every sale counted to Lockheed and McDonnell-Douglas and both companies lavished disproportionate effort on winning the contract. But just as it seemed certain that Lockheed's more reckless price-cutting would win the day for TriStar, six ready-made DC–10s originally destined for the Japanese All Nippon line came on the market for immediate delivery. Faced with a choice between six gleaming jumbos at the ready and Lockheed's promise of delivery 'within twelve months', THY went for the DC–10s. It was the second order Lockheed had lost in Europe.

As it happened, however, Haughton and Kotchian had cause to celebrate rather than mourn their defeat in Turkey, since the six DC–10s bought by THY had been turned down by All Nippon as the direct result of a breathtaking power-play by Lockheed's secret agents in Japan. For it was back in the 'black mists' of Tokyo and the murky underworld of Yoshio Kodama and his friends that the fate of TriStar, and of Lockheed's commercial business, was to be finally decided.

4

Kotchian had long been a frequent visitor to Japan, making the journey three or four times a year from 1961 onwards. But not until 1969, when the TriStar campaign began, did he trouble to make contact with Yoshio Kodama who had been the company's secret agent since 1959. Kotchian confessed later:

> I was not much concerned about Mr Kodama's political ideas or behaviour. It was enough to be told that he had an excellent record as an agent ... including the last-minute reversal of Lockheed's unfavourable position in selling F–104 fighters to Japan in the late 1950s and early 1960s ... It may be that Mr Kodama had undesirable aspects, but for us who had to win in a difficult inter-

---

1 Demirel successfully blocked the investigation, which he described as an opposition plot.

national sales campaign, the most important point was how useful an agent could be in pushing our sales.[1]

Kotchian's first move was to arrange for a renewal of Kodama's contract on substantially improved terms.

Japan's two principal airlines had both let it be known that they were interested in buying jumbo airbuses and all three American jumbo-makers were chasing the contracts. Of the three, Lockheed were the outsiders. Japan Air Lines (JAL) had long-standing relationships both with Boeing and McDonnell-Douglas. All Nippon (ANA) seemed similarly yoked to Boeing. Lockheed was starting from scratch and Kotchian quickly concluded that 'ordinary methods were not likely to achieve our aim'.

Of the two extraordinary methods on which Kotchian came to rely, the first was centred on a smooth public relations man named Al Elliot who had come to Japan with the American forces after Hiroshima and Nagasaki and had stayed to promote his own business and, eventually, to join Lockheed's sales team. Elliot ingeniously spread the word among Japanese journalists that President Nixon himself was rooting for Lockheed. 'Fortunately for us,' recalled Kotchian, 'President Nixon came from the State of California where the Lockheed Corporation has its headquarters.' Most of Lockheed's employees were his constituents. He had backed the $250 million loan guarantee. And he was on record as pointing out the value of Japanese purchases of US hardware in easing the US balance of trade deficit. Said Kotchian:

> If US products were to be imported by Japan, the Nixon administration would be happiest if Japan purchased Lockheed planes. These were the plausible rumors which we were going to circulate. It was the main feature of our strategy. In fact, unless we adopted such a strategy our company had practically no chance in Japan at all. That our strategy ... hit the mark is shown by the fact that the rumors were much discussed among the Japanese at the time. It even got back to the United States where magazines like *Time* and *Fortune* ran articles containing this information.

Having got into the game, Kotchian, in his own words, 'switched to a more sophisticated strategy'. He didn't need advisers like

1 Kotchian gave his version of events in a revealing interview with Yoshio Murakami of the *Asahi Evening News*, Tokyo, published in five instalments, August 23–27, 1976, on which much of the account that follows is based, and from which subsequent quotations from Kotchian are drawn.

Kodama to tell him that Japanese airlines' procurement decisions would be made not in the boardroom but at government level. A tiny group of officials — perhaps one man — would decide which line bought what plane. And in the nature of things there would probably be some sort of shareout. Elliot's brilliant rumour-making had boosted Lockheed's chances of participating in the spoils. But how would the split be decided? Who would get what?

On the surface it seemed uncomplicated. JAL wanted six planes for its domestic routes and another six for its short international flights, while ANA wanted six for domestic routes. Three orders of six, for three competing manufacturers: one each for Boeing, McDonnell and Lockheed. But for Kotchian it wasn't as simple as that. To him the All Nippon order was by far the most attractive because, unlike the others, it had huge potential for expansion. The first order of six would almost certainly be followed by more, up to a likely fifteen and a possible total of twenty-one. That represented a billion-dollar order, beside which the JAL requirement of six seemed peanuts. So Kotchian set out to obtain a division of the contract in which Boeing would get JAL's domestic routes and McDonnell-Douglas its short international routes, leaving the big ANA prize to Lockheed. It 'could be made to look fair', Kotchian reckoned.

It was an ambitious aim, the more so since ANA had already taken out an option on six DC–10s. But Kotchian proceeded to deal with that. In a manner which remains obscure but which is believed to have involved Kodama's good offices, he managed to dissuade ANA from converting its option into a hard order. (These were the six unwanted DC–10s which, once cancelled by ANA, found their way to Turkish Airlines.) That done, he arrived at Tokyo International Airport on August 20, 1972, to begin what was to turn into a seventy-day blitz on 'the core of the decision-making process'. He checked into suite 1070 on the tenth floor of the Hotel Okuru which Kissinger had vacated earlier the same day. 'I thought the coincidence was convenient to sell aircraft', Kotchian mused later, 'because it gave the impression that there was some relationship between Lockheed and the US Government.'

In the next three days he had crucial meetings with his three principal contacts. His recollection of those meetings, given in somewhat piecemeal fashion to the Church Committee and the SEC three years later and eventually published in a Tokyo newspaper, would provoke a political crisis even more profound than the one Lockheed had planted in Italy.

First, on the morning of August 21, Kotchian called on Hiro Hiyama, president of Lockheed's official representatives in Japan, the Marubeni Corporation — grown, since its inauspicious beginnings during the Starfighter campaign more than a decade earlier, into Japan's third biggest trading company. Over lunch, Kotchian boldly suggested that Hiyama should arrange to meet the prime minister 'by all means, and explain the good points of the TriStar'. The prime minister was Kakuei Tanaka, elected only the previous month after fending off criticism of shady financial dealings and a bribery conviction back in 1948 which had gone to the highest appeal court in the land before being quashed. On the face of it Tanaka looked a likely friend of Lockheed (or of Boeing or McDonnell-Douglas if they reached him first). But Kotchian insists: 'Nothing about money was talked about' at the meeting with Hiyama. 'I had no thought of making payments.'

That was soon to change. Next day he was invited by Hiyama's Marubeni colleague, managing director Toshiharu Okubo, to discuss the matter further. They met in Okubo's office and the portly businessman came to the point at once. As Kotchian recalls it, 'Mr Okubo advised me to make a pledge to pay money to prime minister Tanaka.' Kotchian asked, 'How much?' to which, he says, Okubo replied: 'The customary amount to ask for a favor in connection with a major transaction is 500 million yen. It can be smaller. But if you wish to succeed in selling aircraft, you would do well to promise 500 million.'

Couldn't Marubeni pay the money out of their commissions, asked Kotchian? No, said Okubo, 'Commissions Marubeni receives for the TriStar are small. Besides, the payment must be made in Japanese yen cash. It is impossible for Marubeni to pay it.' Would Marubeni lend the cash? 'That can't be done. The money must be readied by Lockheed.' Mindful of the practical difficulties involved in raising and transporting so vast a sum (nearly $1·7 m, or not much short of £1 m), Kotchian asked, 'Will you then keep sums of cash as we get hold of them little by little?' No, again: 'You must come up with all of the 500 million yen when we give the signal.' Okubo added that his fellow-director, Hiroshi Itoh, would look after arrangements for transferring the cash, since he was 'very close to Mr. Enomoto' (Tanaka's secretary). 'It was at this point,' says Kotchian, 'that I was convinced that the money was going to the office of Japan's Prime Minister.'

Kotchian still claims, unconvincingly, that this was the first he knew of the need to make pay-offs in Japan. The veteran of Italy and the Netherlands had not lost his ability to be surprised and shocked by human greed. His sensibilities were to suffer further shock that same afternoon.

From Okubo's office, says Kotchian, he and his Lockheed colleague, John Clutter, made for Kodama's headquarters in the red-light Ginza district. Kodama had acquired the Lockheed code-name 'Tomodachi', or Friend, and was sometimes referred to in Lockheed papers as 'Mr. T.' (The Japanese press later misconstrued these entries as referring to Tanaka.) In Kodama's office Kotchian had arranged to meet the man who happened not only to be the biggest single private shareholder in both the Japanese airlines but also a long-time crony and confidant of the prime minister – Kenji Osano.

Osano was the one man who could challenge Kodama himself for the title of most influential kuromaku in Japan. Like Kodama, he had been an ultra-nationalist, had been jailed by the Americans (for black-market trading) and had made himself a billionaire by organising supplies to US forces during the Korean war. Kotchian had bumped into him once before at a TriStar demonstration flight and, learning of his connections, had 'kept watch on him as a person I wished to enlist co-operation for Lockheed ... I wanted to have him join in the sales operation at all costs, so I asked Mr Kodama to do something about it.' Mr Kodama had responded by arranging the meeting on August 22.

Formal introductions over, Kodama proved no more a slouch than Okubo in coming to the point. Lockheed needed Mr Osano: it would cost 500 million yen. Kotchian was to reflect drily: 'In the morning I was made by Mr Okubo to promise 500 million yen intended for Mr Tanaka and in the afternoon I was asked by Mr Kodama to pay an additional 500 million to Mr Osano. It occurred to me that 500 million yen seemed to be a figure frequently used in Japan.'

In the course of a single day Lockheed's president had committed the corporation to pay-offs totalling $3·5 million dollars – approaching £2 million. Even for Lockheed, so huge a total committed so readily was without precedent. Moreover, the two 500 million yen promises were made without either recipient party knowing anything of the other: Marubeni at this stage knew nothing of Kodama's and Osano's involvement, and Kodama and Osano (who was perversely code-named 'Curly' by Kotchian because of his bald head) were ignorant of Kotchian's promise, through Okubo, of the pay-off destined for Tanaka. Since Osano's 500 million was also intended to smooth the way to Tanaka, the prime minister's stake in a Lockheed victory was huge. And that, for Kotchian, was very much the object of the exercise.

At seven o'clock the next morning, August 23, Marubeni's two chief executives, Hiyama and Okubo, called on prime minister Tanaka at his private residence in the opulent Mejiro section of Tokyo. There are two versions of what happened at that meeting: Hiyama's and Tanaka's. According to Hiyama, in his evidence at Tanaka's subsequent trial, he began by introducing Okubo as the grandson of a high-ranking aristocrat of the Meiji-restoration period of a century ago, sure that this would impress the self-made country-boy prime minister. This done, and fulsome congratulations on his accession to the premiership having been offered, Hiyama asked Okubo to wait outside while he talked serious business. Alone with the prime minister, Hiyama launched into a detailed account of Lockheed's efforts to sell TriStars to ANA, ending by offering 500 million yen if Tanaka would use his influence to swing the deal. According to Hiyama, Tanaka replied 'Yossha, yossha', or 'OK, OK', and went on to nominate Toshio Enomoto as his courier.

Tanaka has told the Tokyo court a quite different story. Hiyama's visit, he says, was sandwiched between several others during 'a busy clinic' in which he received several deputations, each lasting only two or three minutes. He couldn't possibly have had time to meet Hiyama's colleague Okubo, listen to congratulations, hear about the excellence of the TriStar and discuss influence for cash. 'I cannot recall anything about the conversation,' he has stated. Whatever did happen at the meeting, Kotchian recalls that immediately afterwards Okubo telephoned him to say 'the promise' had been conveyed to the prime minister. Kotchian was 'surprised at the peculiar Japanese way of doing things. As I have not had the experience of being present at such a meeting, I can't even imagine how the matter of money was brought up.'

A week later, Tanaka was due to fly to Honolulu for a trade summit with Nixon. On the eve of his departure, according to his prosecutors, he took the first step towards earning the half-billion yen promised by Hiyama. He telephoned ANA president Tokuji Wakasa and asked if he had decided to buy TriStars. Wakasa indicated that he was still evaluating all three (Lockheed, McDonnell-Douglas and

Boeing) competitors. Tanaka, say the prosecutors, replied, 'It will be convenient if you decide for Lockheed.' Tanaka denies the conversation.

The same night, according to Kotchian, Tanaka met Hiyama and Okubo at a private party. Hiyama seized the opportunity to impress on Tanaka the political advantages of buying an American plane fitted with British engines, since British prime minister Edward Heath was due to visit Tokyo shortly for trade talks. Tanaka reportedly told them he was 'exerting great efforts' on Lockheed's behalf. Kotchian, given a blow-by-blow account of all this, declared himself 'greatly encouraged' by the way things were going.

At Honolulu Nixon and Tanaka got down to some hard bargaining. It later became known that at Nixon's urging Tanaka agreed to spend about $720 million on US manufactured goods to reduce the trade imbalance, including $320 million on jumbo airbuses. Tanaka subsequently vigorously denied that he and the US President had engaged in any collusion to buy Lockheed. He did not, however, deny the prosecutors' claim that, on his return to Tokyo, he had *claimed* that Nixon had spoken in favour of the TriStar. In particular, he told Lockheed's reserve kuromaku, 'Curly' Osano, 'Nixon said to me he would appreciate it if the plane that Japan is going to purchase would be Lockheed's.'

If Nixon did state his preference in this fashion – and, though politically questionable, there wouldn't necessarily be anything corrupt about doing so – it raises the intriguing question of whether all those bribes were necessary. But be that as it may, two weeks passed after Honolulu and Kotchian heard nothing. By mid-September he was growing decidedly restless. ANA was due to announce its decision by the end of the month, but the announcement would normally be preceded by friendly signals, and of such there was no sign. Inevitably, Kotchian wondered if despite his promises the final round of discussions which he was eagerly awaiting were not already taking place with McDonnell-Douglas or Boeing. Perhaps they had promised more?

On September 14 he called on ANA president Tokuji Wakasa. Did he have any news? Wakasa made non-committal noises and Kotchian noted that he was 'unable to grasp any clear-cut outlook'. Two days later, buttressed this time by Kodama and his interpreter, Taro Fukuda, he paid a call on Osano, whom he found – as he put it somewhat quaintly – 'amid a busy-ness as if he were making decisions on scores and hundreds of things at once'. Osano promised to find time to check on the situation. A week later, on September 22, Kodama told Kotchian that Osano had met the chief secretary of the cabinet, Susumu Nikaido, and had reported back that 'everything was going well'. Kotchian by this time 'had realised that Mr Osano might be contacting top Government officials through Mr Nikaido, and I had figured out that the Osano route led to the Prime Minister via Mr Nikaido.'

Another tense two weeks passed and the end-of-the-month deadline came and went without a decision. Then came October 5 – 'memorable', says Kotchian, 'as the most painful day in my long aircraft company career'.

The drama began at 6 o'clock in the morning when Kotchian was awoken by a telephone call from interpreter Fukuda. Late the night before, said Fukuda, Osano had called him with the information that Lockheed had indeed secured a contract – but with JAL. 'What?' screamed Kotchian down the line. 'This is fatal! It will mean complete failure!'

Fukuda was astonished. He had clearly expected the Lockheed president to be delighted. Quickly the appalled Kotchian pieced together the full extent of Osano's message. ANA was to order twenty-one DC–10s, leaving JAL to divide its much smaller order between Lockheed's TriStars and Boeing's 747s – precisely the opposite of Kotchian's strategic plan. The JAL order was virtually worthless, even as a consolation prize. For a start, the airline didn't like Rolls-Royce and was likely to demand an expensive refit with American Pratt and Whitney engines. And since JAL's need was much less urgent than ANA's, there was a real risk that, in eighteen months or so, the airline would discover the advantages of compatibility with ANA and cancel its TriStars in favour of DC–10s. There was also the added nightmare that failure to win the ANA contract could lead to the cancellation of at least one American airline order: Pacific Southwest, for instance, trained ANA's pilots and would doubtless find it impracticable to buy TriStars for themselves while training the Japanese for DC–10s.

Most stunning of all to Kotchian, however, was the realisation that he had committed three and a half million dollars to men who had evidently understood nothing of his carefully devised strategy. Osano, Okubo, Kodama, probably Tanaka himself had all apparently assumed Lockheed would be happy with JAL's meagre share of the market. The alternative explanation was a plot by Lockheed's competitors. Kotchian talked it over with Fukuda and they decided 'there was a conspiracy purposely aimed at destroying the Lockheed sales campaign'. Subsequent disclosures that McDonnell-Douglas and Boeing were also making 'questionable payments' in Japan no doubt fortified this conviction, to which Kotchian still passionately holds.

Kotchian was not a man to accept defeat so easily. Back in Burbank Dan Haughton had hung on his office wall a poster showing a cat clinging by one paw to the top branch of a tree. It was captioned 'Hang in there, baby!' The philosophy had rubbed off on his chief lieutenant. Kotchian told Fukuda to arrange an immediate meeting with Osano, then tried to eat some breakfast but found he had lost his appetite. Fukuda rang back to say Osano was scheduled to leave Tokyo that day for Hawaii (where he had extensive business interests) but he would grudgingly make a few minutes available at 10 a.m. Kotchian wanted Kodama to accompany him but couldn't locate him in time. 'Then I thought that if John Clutter, who is stout of build, were with me, I would feel more confident.' But Clutter — president of Lockheed's Asia subsidiary — was in Taiwan. 'The thought of meeting Japan's most influential person alone made me feel helpless', confessed Kotchian.

As he feared, the awesome Osano 'looked very displeased and spoke harshly'. He couldn't understand why Kotchian wasn't grateful for the JAL order, and told the harassed American bluntly that he was 'an odd person'. Kotchian tried to explain his conspiracy theory but Osano said that nothing could be done to change the situation, then terminated the conversation.

Kotchian's last chance now was Kodama. Fukuda was sent scurrying around to find him, and Kotchian at last got a message to meet his secret agent in the Ginza district after dark. Fukuda collected him from his hotel, drove him to the rendezvous, led him up an emergency staircase and showed him to a back-room office where Kodama was waiting. After listening to Kotchian's explanation, Kodama volunteered the view that the decision must have been made by 'some people in the higher echelons of the Government who had not grasped the whole situation'. Then he turned to the telephone and began to dial. Fukuda told the astonished Kotchian that his master was calling Yasuhiro Nakasone, minister of international trade and industry and a key figure in the decision-making process.

The conversation was in Japanese and Fukuda did not offer to translate it. But when it ended, Kodama told Kotchian that Nakasone had 'pledged to try to do something early the following morning'.

Kotchian left Kodama's office at 9.30 p.m. It had been 'a long and painful day'.

Early next morning, at 7.30 a.m., Kotchian arrived at the Marubeni office for an 8 o'clock meeting with Okubo. He outlined the situation and told him he had 'taken measures to reverse the plot'. He did not mention Kodama or Osano, but got the impression that Okubo now guessed at his connection with Kodama. The meeting over, he returned to the Hotel Okura to find a message from Fukuda: 'Mr Nakasone has succeeded in reversing the plot and the situation has reverted to its previous state.' Back hurried Kotchian to Marubeni to ask Okubo to seek confirmation. 'He called director Hiroshi Itoh and telephoned to Mr Toshio Enomoto, a Secretary to Prime Minister Tanaka, and as a result it was confirmed that the dreadful plot had been reversed.'

A few days later Marubeni president Hiyama confirmed to Kotchian that Tanaka himself had promised him that 'everything was going all right'. Osano too, back from Hawaii and now magically transformed to as genial a mood as he was capable of, told Kotchian that he too had secured the prime minister's ear. Everyone suddenly seemed anxious to claim responsibility for turning the tide in Lockheed's favour.

But once again the days slipped by without definite news. On October 26 Kotchian fell ill with feverish prostatitis and took to his bed, tended by the broad-shouldered John Clutter. Three days later he was again woken early by a frantic phone call from Fukuda who told him to switch on his TV set immediately and tune to the NHK news bulletin. Kotchian did so, just in time to hear the announcement he had been waiting for: the government had decided JAL would purchase DC–10s and 747s, and ANA would buy TriStar.

That afternoon there was a small, select champagne party in Kotchian's suite. Kotchian presided in his pyjamas. 'There had been so many different informations and so many changes in the situation,' he was to recall later, 'I could not bring myself to believe this news.'

He was right. That night, about 10.30 p.m., there was another phone call, this time from Okubo. For the managing director of Lockheed's official representatives, his tone seemed distinctly menacing. 'You will succeed in selling TriStars', he told Kotchian, 'if you do three things. First, freeze the costs of maintenance and fuel; second, station 20 Lockheed technical experts at each of the five airports where ANA is scheduled to fly TriStars; and third, ready 120 million yen in cash as soon as you can.'

Kotchian thought the demand 'preposterous' — he was later to blame his uncharacteristic feeling of disgust on his prostatitis — and summoned Okubo to his hotel. There, at midnight, the still feverish and bedridden master-salesman was told that Okubo had entered into commitments of $300,000 'secret money' for ANA president Wakasa and a further $100,000 split between six Japanese politicians: Tomisaburo Hashimoto, secretary-general of the ruling Liberal-Democratic Party; Susumu Nikaido, chief cabinet secretary; Hideyo Sasaki, transport minister; Kazuomi Fukunaga, chairman of the LDP's aviation committee, Mutsuki Kato, parliamentary vice-minister of transport; and Takayuki Sato, former parliamentary vice-minister of transport. 'If you ready the money first thing tomorrow morning,' said Okubo, 'we can formally get the ANA order during tomorrow without fail. I would like you to have the whole sum ready by 10 a.m.'

Kotchian told him he was asking the impossible. The money could be found, but not in the time. 'The 30 million yen for politicians is highly important,' replied Okubo, 'couldn't you have that much ready at least?' Kotchian wearily agreed to do his best — and to meet the other two demands about maintenance costs and stationing Lockheed experts at ANA airports. Okubo left at 2 a.m. and Kotchian fell asleep exhausted.

Four hours later, at the crack of dawn, he was calling Jack Clutter and summoning him to a 7 a.m. meeting. Clutter, who clearly had experience of such problems, said it was possible to get the 30 million yen before 10 a.m. and he would arrange delivery of the remaining 90 million within a week. Recalling Clutter's unquestioning co-operation, Kotchian said later:

> Few members of Lockheed Aircraft Corporation were so loyal to the company and worked so hard for it, not shrinking from difficult assignments. He responded to my summons quickly at any time, carried large sums of money in cash in compliance with the requests from the Japanese side, and worked in defiance of personal danger. In some quarters it seems to be rumoured that he might have embezzled part of the money, but there was no possibility of embezzlement, because most of the sums had been promised between myself and Mr Okubo or Mr Kodama and the amounts had been fixed beforehand.'

Six hours after Clutter's 10 a.m. delivery, Kotchian received a call inviting him to ANA's head office at 6 p.m. There, with deadpan formality, Wakasa told him: 'Congratulations Mr Kotchian, your company has got our company's contract.' Three days later, with the formal letter of intent in his pocket, Kotchian flew home to Burbank 'after 70 straight days of battle as the President of Lockheed, at the head of our forces and literally running about in the great city of Tokyo'. He was met at Los Angeles international airport by Dan Haughton, who told him: 'Carl, you've saved the company.'

The commitments Kotchian left behind him in Tokyo took months, even years, for Lockheed's finance department to unravel fully. And as ANA's initial order was extended, as expected, to twenty-one, the commitments continued to grow.

First there were the official commissions to Marubeni which totalled $2·9 m. Then there were the payments made to Kodama. These included $1,024,000 in commissions earned from 1969 to July 1972, a further $1,733,333 on the first six TriStars ordered by ANA, and $1,140,000 on the repeat orders. In addition, there was the 500 million yen ($1,666,667) paid to Kodama and intended for Osano, and a further $150,000 intended for Fukuda. Total for Kodama on the TriStar campaigns: $5,714,000. From 1973–5 he was to pick up a further $560,000 in contract fees, though not all for TriStar. Grand total $6,274,000.[1]

Then there was the Okubo route. It was not until after delivery of the first six TriStars to ANA in 1973 that Kotchian was reminded of his promise to make 500 million yen available for Tanaka through Okubo. Kotchian claims, implausibly, that he had 'completely forgotten' this promise, but it was nevertheless thought politic to honour it. The sum was paid in two instalments, one of $850,000 in June 1973 and another of $900,000 in January 1974, a total of $1,750,000, which a changed exchange rate and bank charges brought up to $1,831,000. On top of that was the $100,000 intended for Hashimoto and the other five politicians. Then there was the $300,000 demanded for president Wakasa of ANA—followed by a further $400,000 extracted from Kotchian for the same purpose when ANA ordered the next 15 planes.[2] Grand total through Okubo: $2,631,000.

1 Even this figure excludes the commissions and other commitments paid by Lockheed on earlier deals, such as the Starfighter, which add at least $1 million.

2 The first $300,000 was described to Kotchian by Okubo as a $50,000 'secret commission' on each of the first six planes, but Kotchian was 'so nonplussed at the time that I didn't even think of finding out if similar payments to ANA would have to be made in the future'. Similar payments were indeed demanded

Finally, there was yet another pay-off to be made direct to ANA, when the airline demanded a concealed payment of $179,000 in cash as the price of lending Lockheed a TriStar for a demonstration flight to Australia; and on top of that, a $75,000 fee to a dummy corporation called I.D. That brought Lockheed's total commitment to $12,059,000. Kotchian was to dismiss this as 'a rather small amount of money', arguing that it 'accounted for little less than three per cent of the total sales value'. But such a judgment was absurd. Certainly the odd assortment of bit-part players who had the job of carting the cash into and around Tokyo in orange boxes and attaché cases didn't act as if they were on routine assignments.

The physical transportation of these huge sums was not the least ingenious aspect of Lockheed's resourcefulness. The corporation made use of what Japanese police officials described as an 'underground bank', Deak and Company, which specialised in discreet currency transactions for the CIA as well as multinational corporations. Lockheed bought the Japanese currency it needed at Deak's headquarters in Los Angeles, then wired it to the Deak office in Hong Kong, where Clutter or Al Elliot arranged for its collection, sometimes in corrugated cardboard orange boxes and sometimes in airline flight bags holding upwards of 9,300 10,000-yen notes—weighing 27·5 pounds. The bags and boxes were then hand-carried to Tokyo by an agent of Deak's, a Spanish-born priest who had become a naturalised Japanese, and changed his name from José Gardeano to Hoze Aramiya. Father Hoze had forsaken the church to dedicate himself to the life of a high-flying cash courier. He brought the money to Clutter in fifteen deliveries (the last on the day Americans went to the polls to re-elect Richard Nixon) and they passed it on to Kodama. Kodama insisted on being paid in cash after an attaché case containing more than $1 million in Swiss cheques was stolen from his home. (Lockheed invalidated the cheques and made good the loss.)

Kodama receipted his regular commissions in his own handwriting:

---

and made, on the next eight, but this time Kotchian told Clutter to tell Okubo that Lockheed wouldn't make any more payments on the seven remaining orders. 'Immediately after that,' says Kotchian, 'I received a report from Mr Clutter to the effect that ANA had bluntly said to Mr Okubo: "In that case we'll switch to an aircraft of a different make from now on."' The remaining seven were duly delivered but, as Kotchian puts it, 'Fortunately or unfortunately, now that the affair has come into the open, it seems certain that Lockheed will not have to make secret payments' on them.

Amount Seventy Five Million Yen Only
Have duly received the above.
Showa 47th Year Nov. 6
Kodama Yoshio

But more puzzling to Lockheed's auditors, when they eventually surfaced, were a string of receipts reading:

I received One Hundred Peanuts.
Hiroshi Itoh.

These turned out to be Okubo's quaintly coded receipts to Clutter. Hiroshi Itoh was one of Okubo's fellow directors at Marubeni, and a peanut was a million yen.

Okubo's peanuts did not travel the same route as Kodama's orange-boxes and duffel-bags. They were laundered through what Kotchian called an 'arm's length' firm called ID Corporation, set up in the tax-lax Cayman Islands in the Caribbean. ID's sole owner was a Japanese-American named Shig Katayama, former intelligence officer with the American forces of occupation, scrap iron dealer, drug-squad policeman, Lockheed agent in Indonesia (before Dasaad), and eventually the owner of Japan's largest coffee-vending machine business. More to the point, he was a friend of Clutter and Elliot. When Lockheed needed cash for Okubo, Katayama provided the funds from ID's Hong Kong office and issued Lockheed with false receipts for their auditors, for which service he was paid $75,000.

Whether through Kodama or Okubo, Tanaka or Nakasone, Wakasa or Hashimoto, Richard Nixon or Edward Heath, Kotchian won the great jumbo war in Japan. ANA's cancelled DC-10s were diverted, some to Turkish Airlines, some to Laker. 'Somebody Up There Likes Lockheed!' commented *Time* magazine wryly. But only Carl Kotchian knew the whole story, and he had no qualms of conscience. He asked:

If, in a situation where high government officials have influence on matters pertinent to a private company, money is requested as pay-offs for those officials, can that private foreign company, which wants its products to be bought at all costs, realistically decline the request on the grounds that it is not a good thing from the ethical point of view?

For Kotchian, the question was rhetorical. In his own eyes he was the victim, not the malefactor; the corrupted perhaps, but not the corruptor.

11

The Grease Machine Exposed

There is not a crime, there is not a dodge, there is not a trick, there is not a swindle, there is not a vice which does not live by secrecy. Get these things out in the open, describe them, attack them, ridicule them in the press, and sooner or later public opinion will sweep them away. Publicity may not be the only thing that is needed, but it is the one thing without which all other agencies will fail.

Joseph Pulitzer

1

Watergate did much more for America than rid the country of a crooked President. It inspired an explosion of righteous wrath directed at all forms of non-accountable power, with a razor-sharp focus on corporate corruption. It produced a new lexicography, a Newspeak of the 1970s: 'slush fund', 'conduit', 'off-the-books', 'bag-man'.

The slow slide towards discovery began on the afternoon of February 18, 1972, when Northrop chief Tom Jones received three powerful and persuasive visitors. Herbert Kalmbach was President Nixon's personal lawyer, Maurice Stans chairman of the finance committee to re-elect the President, and Leonard Firestone a Nixon fund-raiser in California. Kalmbach put his arm round Jones's shoulders and told him: 'Tom, the President needs you. Like $100,000 he needs you.'

Being solicited for political contributions was all par for the course for Jones, but the size of CREEP's demand was unprecedented. He could have refused, or stalled, even though that meant risking Nixon's disfavour. Instead, as the chairmen of Braniff, Gulf and Goodyear had secretly done before him, and as others were secretly to do later, he told Kalmbach the money would be found. As the three white-collar protection racketeers left, he instructed his trusty lieutenant Jimmy Allen to see to the payments.

Allen's usual course on such occasions was to collect the money in cash from his French bag-man, Bill Savy, who of course operated Northrop's slush fund for just such purposes. But on this occasion, with the amount so high, Allen instructed Savy to write out twenty $5,000 cheques on his Wilco Holding account at the Banque International, Luxembourg, payable direct to CREEP. It was a costly mistake.

Jones, meanwhile, had so far demonstrated his worldly-wise lack of concern as to tell Kalmbach not to hesitate about asking for more should the need arise. On August 1 Kalmbach was back in Jones's offices to say the need had indeed arisen. He did not explain that he was now collecting for a special secret fund with which the White House hoped to buy the silence of the Watergate burglars. But Jones took from his desk a package of hundred-dollar bills, a total sum of $50,000 or $75,000 — it's not clear which — and handed them over.

Two months later, only days before the Presidential election and Nixon's landslide victory, the House Banking and Currency Committee chaired by Congressman Wright Patman announced that it had stumbled across secret receipts of the Nixon campaign, including $30,000 in cheques written on Savy's Luxembourg bank. It wasn't long before the money was traced back to Northrop. Jones tried to get some of the money back from CREEP, pretended some came (legally) from his personal account, not (illegally) from the corporation's, and tried to backdate the last cheque to make it appear to have been written out before the date on which a new law tightening up the rules for disclosure of corporate contributions became operative.

His cover-up, which involved misleading statements to his own outside directors and lies, later 'corrected', to a federal grand jury, only made matters worse. Patman's Committee had hit on evidence which, in the months ahead, was zealously pursued by the fashionable new breed of investigative reporters, by such consumer bodies as Common Cause and the Ralph Nader organisation, and before long by Sam Irvin's Senate Watergate Committee, the Watergate Special Prosecutor, the Justice Department and the SEC. Gradually the real scandal of Watergate was unearthed by the indefatigable diggers for truth and a good story: not only the burglary, not only Nixon's lies, but the secret, illegal links between some of America's biggest corporations and the Nixon White House, culminating in the million-dollar big-business fund to buy the conspirators' silence and finance the cover-up.

Through 1974 a score of America's top executives and tycoons trooped before the courts. On May 1 it was Tom Jones's turn. He pleaded guilty to wilful violation of federal law — a felony — and Allen and Northrop pleaded guilty to non-wilful violation — a misdemeanour. Jones and the company were fined $5,000 each and Allen $1,000. Jones, whose personal earnings were in excess of $286,000 a year, reimbursed Northrop both for its fine and the $50,000 he admitted having given to Kalmbach in August. The Northrop board subsequently deprived him, temporarily, of his title as chairman but kept him securely at the helm as chief executive. By the summer he must have assumed that he had ridden the worst of the storm. He was wrong.

Among the watchdogs who needed to be heard barking in such circumstances was Stanley Sporkin, a Yale law school graduate, son of a hawkish judge and head of the enforcement division of the SEC. Sporkin's job was to police big business: to prevent or prosecute the very tricks, dodges and swindles Watergate had flushed into the open. His staff was adequate to deal with the occasional corporate offender but far too small to investigate the huge number of companies on CREEP's register of illegal contributors. Sporkin's ingenious way round his lack of manpower was to obtain consent decrees in the Washington district court under which each company in effect agreed to investigate itself and deliver its detailed findings to the SEC and the court. If the report appeared to tell all, the SEC would consider what further action should be taken; if not, Sporkin would concentrate all his available resources to turn over the offending corporation.

In Northrop's case, the directors got in first. They commissioned the Los Angeles auditors, Ernst and Ernst, and the international accountancy firm of Price Waterhouse, to investigate and report on 'the extent of the misconduct'. Thus it was that the history of Jones's Savy fund began to emerge, along with the baffling but suggestive De Francis arrangement. Meanwhile, after three new members had been added following a shareholders' suit, the board organised its own investigation into the conduct of its chief executive. This brought to light the EDC front, the Stehlin connection, Khashoggi and all. Even so, the board merely slapped Jones's wrist with accusations of 'poor business judgement' and 'the appearance of impropriety', and kept him on as chief executive. Within a year, after Northrop had announced its best-ever trading year, with net income up by a fat 37 per cent to $25 million and sales up to nearly a billion dollars, Jones, the great survivor, was quietly reinstated as chairman.

Meanwhile, most of what the auditors' and the board's investigators had learned they kept to themselves. In this course they had the powerful support of Henry Kissinger and the state department, already alarmed at the harm the Watergate revelations were doing to America's image abroad and anxious to reverse the growing passion for washing seemingly endless piles of dirty linen in public. The state department successfully pressured the SEC to withhold from publication the meatier sections of the Ernst and Ernst report detailing Northrop's questionable overseas payments. So the full dimensions of the scandal remained, for a little longer, under wraps.

Certainly there was no hint, late in 1974, of a Lockheed connection. Which is why, in total ignorance of the time-bomb on which his American friends were sitting, Prince Bernhard of the Netherlands felt confident enough in September to write to Burbank asking for a new commission arrangement. The sum involved this time: anything up to six million dollars.

2

Early in 1973 the Dutch government had begun to consider a long-term replacement for the navy's obsolete Lockheed P–2V Neptune patrol and anti-submarine planes. By June the admiralty council had three candidates under consideration: the British Nimrod from Hawker Siddeley, the French Breguet Atlantique Mark 1A and II, and Lockheed's P–3C Orion.

The Dutch deliberations soon came to the notice of Fred C. Meuser in his mountain retreat at St Moritz. Meuser was by now something of an elder-statesman among the master-salesmen of the aerospace industry. He had served Lockheed, Northrop, and Lockheed again. His loyalty to Prince Bernhard, meanwhile, had never wavered. Now, with an immense new order in the offing (the Dutch admiralty were talking of spending up to 148 million guilders on thirteen planes between 1974 and 1978, and a further 452 million in the 1979–83 period) his eye for the main chance did not fail him.

Meuser contacted the prince and put to him a simple proposition. If the Orion were selected, and if a consultant's contract were concluded with Lockheed on the basis of commission for aircraft supplied to the Dutch navy and for the supply of spare parts, a large sum of money would be at the prince's disposal. He might wish to pass it, for instance, to his very own prestige charity, the World Wildlife Fund.

Bernhard didn't turn down the idea and Meuser was encouraged to take it a step further. In April 1974 he gave the prince a draft note and suggested he send it to Lockheed. It read:

Last time around it would have been of no use to accept Lockheed's offer to appoint Dr. H. Weisbrod agent for the re-equipping of the Navy's ASW aircraft fleet with Orions, as European pressures required a European solution. This time around the situation may be more favourable for the Orion, in part due to Dr. Weisbrod's efforts, and it would now seem appropriate for Lockheed to appoint him their 'sub silentio' agent for a prospective Orion program. This could be done on the basis of an agent's agreement between Lockheed and Dr. Weisbrod, calling for a 4 per cent commission on all Lockheed billings for complete aircraft and 8 per cent for parts, services, etc., for the life of the program. As and when payments are received by Lockheed, corresponding commission payments to be made in a manner to be indicated by Dr. Weisbrod.[1]

It was the same old formula that had proved so successful in the past: The Meuser–Weisbrod connection, with Bernhard as the intended principal beneficiary. When Meuser wrote that the Orion's prospects were good 'in part due to Weisbrod's effort,' he was unmistakably signalling to Lockheed that the prince himself had been, and could continue to be, active on Lockheed's behalf. In fact there is no evidence whatever that Bernhard really did involve himself in any way with the admiralty's evaluations. But what mattered was that Lockheed should *believe* he was rooting for them, and that this could be decisive.

Bernhard accepted Meuser's draft but did not send it to Lockheed immediately. Possibly he was shaken by the much-publicised conviction of his friend Tom Jones on May 1 and fearful of further revelations: but if so, he had overcome such fears by September. On the ninth of that month he sent the note to Roger Bixby Smith, the intermediary with Lockheed on the abortive Orion deal in 1968 when $100,000 had ended up in the pocket of 'Victor Baarn'. With it he sent a covering letter in his own handwriting. It was one of two letters which, when unexpectedly made public, would finally destroy his good name.

It was short and to the point. He recalled the talks of 'a few years ago', evidently meaning 1968, and said that 'after a hell of a lot of pushing and pulling' it now looked as if something positive might develop and that it therefore might be a good idea to 'process the enclosed idea personally'. Neither the letter nor enclosure referred to the World Wildlife Fund, which seems by now to have dropped from Bernhard's mind.

Bixby Smith passed the letter and note on to Burbank, probably

1 This account follows the report of the Dutch 'Commissie van Drie' and Carl Kotchian's testimony to the SEC.

direct to Haughton or Kotchian, but when they calculated that commission at the rate suggested would add up to between $4 million and $6 million they decided the prince's price was altogether too high. Smith was asked to convey as much to Bernhard, and to explain that in any case commission wasn't allowed on a government-to-government contract—though this prohibition hadn't always inhibited the company in the past.

Accordingly, Bixby Smith arranged to meet the prince on October 30 on one of his frequent visits to Paris in the elegant company of Miss Helen 'Pussy' Grinda. The prince expressed surprise that the commission rate he was asking had checked out at so high a total. He had in mind, he told Smith, 'only about $1 million'. But he was angry at Lockheed's flat rejection of his proposal, and as the evening wore on he became angrier.

Three days later the prince despatched a second handwritten letter to Burbank. He was to claim later that he based it on a draft suggested by Smith. It seemed incredible, he wrote, that his approach had been rejected without discussion and without consideration of other possibilities. And he added bitterly: 'It would never have happened in the days of Bob or Courtlandt Gross.' He had 'spent a great deal of time and effort' since 1968 'to turn things in the right direction and to prevent wrong decisions influenced by political considerations'—meaning a French or British purchase in the interests of European unity (of which he was a professed champion). He had done this because of his old friendship for Lockheed 'and based on its past actions'. He now felt 'a little bitter' and would do nothing more for the company. What's more, he would make his attitude clear if he were consulted on the procurement decision by the admiralty or government. Finally, he was considering writing to or phoning Courtlandt Gross, who was still on Lockheed's board with the title 'Senior Adviser', and—at least in Bernhard's view—not without influence.

The letter evidently made a strong impression on Haughton and Kotchian. Whether moved by Bernhard's recollections of old and productive friendships, or by the implied threat to throw his influence decisively against the Orion, Lockheed came up with a new offer. Presumably Bixby Smith had conveyed to them the prince's expectation of 'about $1 million', because that is exactly what was now proposed: a fixed commission of $1 million provided at least four aircraft were bought. The prohibition of commission on a government-to-government sale was conveniently forgotten. Bixby

Smith conveyed the offer to the prince on December 2 during a visit to the royal palace at Soestdijk, and he accepted immediately. Weisbrod, however, was to be cut out of the reduced sum. The prince, for reasons which are not clear, told Smith he did not wish the money to be paid through the Weisbrod route and would prefer it to be paid into a numbered account in Geneva specially opened for the purpose.

As it turned out, Bernhard never received his million dollars. The Dutch Government opted for defence cuts and postponed its purchase of a successor to the Neptunes. The prince's fateful, tell-tale letter lay forgotten in Haughton's files. And meanwhile the time-bomb in Washington ticked away on an ever-shortening fuse.

3

Concurrent with all the Watergate investigations and quite independent of them was another which had quite separate origins. In 1972 the Democratic Senator from Idaho, Frank Church, had set up a Sub-committee on Multinational Corporations of the powerful Senate Committee on Foreign Relations, to follow up disclosures of ITT's interventions in Chile and to investigate how far big companies were influencing or forming foreign policy. From ITT Church and his Sub-committee moved on to the oil giants, opening public hearings on Gulf, Exxon and Mobil on May 16, 1975.

'What we are concerned with', Church told a huge array of press, radio and television reporters who would soon become very familiar with the dark-panelled Hearings Room, No. 4221, in the Dirksen Senate Building, 'is not a question of private or public morality. What concerns us here is a major issue of foreign policy for the United States.' Watergate had shown how domestic corruption could weaken democratic government. The multinationals' investigation would show that corruption abroad subverted the free world and weakened America's international standing.

The Senate's revelations of huge, systematic bribery by the oil companies caused a sensation. Suddenly it was Church rather than Sam Irvin, Archibald Cox or Stanley Sporkin who held the limelight; and now the Sub-committee decided to expand its reach and go after Northrop.

Jones had so far managed to hold the lid down on most of his company's scandals. The convictions and fines in the CREEP affair were public knowledge, of course, but the incriminating, tell-tale documents subpoena'd by the SEC—including the most sensitive sections of the Ernst and Ernst report—had still not been made public. Church's decision to investigate Northrop would end all that for the Sub-committee was armed with the same subpoena powers as the SEC; and having duly demanded, received and read the documents, Church decided to publish first and ask questions later.

Public hearings on what Church and the press called 'the Northrop case' began on June 9, 1975. Church set the tone, castigating the company's 'sordid' behaviour and 'deliberate deception', but insisting that more than corporate morality was at issue.

Arms sales are supposedly related to the legitimate defense needs of friendly governments. So there is an element of trust involved, a trust which on the basis of the record before us, has been abundantly abused.

The competition is out of control. We and the Europeans are in an unprincipled race to arm to the teeth the newly rich nations of the Persian Gulf. It is obvious that the United States alone cannot reform the methods now being employed. But if the NATO alliance is not to be ruptured by greed run amok, the United States should press for fundamental reforms in Western military sales practices.

If we do not, we will end up corrupting ourselves and those who deal with us. Instead of meeting legitimate defense requirements, we will find that we have sown the seeds of new wars. At present, we are on a treadmill with no end in sight.

This was high politics, and much was at stake for Northrop when Tom Jones faced the Sub-committee on the second day of the hearings. The papers were full of the 'Northrop case' and Northrop, it seemed, was to be made a scapegoat for the sins of big business in general and of the none-too-popular armaments industry in particular. Yet when Jones stepped down after a three-hour grilling, the 'Northrop case' was dead. A few deft words had converted it into what it would remain forever after: the 'Lockheed scandal'.

It has been generally assumed that Jones's deliberate, planned intention that day was to divert attention to his rivals. A careful reading of the transcripts hardly supports this natural, if uncharitable, supposition. What is clear from the record is that it was Church and his colleagues who were determined to pick up and explore the references to Lockheed scattered through the Northrop documents. Far from helping them, Jones seemed uncomfortable when this line of questioning was pursued, and often stalled. The reason is perhaps not hard to fathom: a searchlight on Lockheed might leave Northrop less exposed in the short run but it might also unearth Lockheed's relationship with Bernhard, which in turn would almost certainly expose Northrop's own dealings with the prince. And Bernhard, a pillar of the global Tiger strategy, was still crucial to Northrop's global influence.

So when, at the outset, Senator Church acknowledged that 'the particular problem we are inquiring into was not confined to Northrop alone', then paused to ask leadingly, 'Would you agree with that statement?' Jones declined the implied invitation and replied that he couldn't speak for other corporations. Church then took him through the meeting with German procurement officials when, according to his own statement to his auditors, Jones was warned that 'Northrop was put to a disadvantage over other American competitors through illegal activities and influence on the part of others'. Did he infer from this that he was being advised to emulate these competitors in the field of illegal activities and influences? 'Not at all', replied Jones, stiffly. But his denial clearly failed to convince his questioners, who had already drawn their own conclusions.

The Sub-committee turned to Northrop's dummy corporation, the EDC. Jones attempted to justify the arrangement, for which he seemed ready to accept sole responsibility. Eventually Church asked him outright: 'Was this whole arrangement not patterned after the Lockheed arrangement?' Even then Jones replied at first that he 'could not vouch for' the connection, and was driven to acknowledge it finally only under persistent questioning.

The rest was gradually drawn out of him: The Meuser–Weisbrod connection, the Khashoggi connection, the Gerritsen connection. This last was the most sensitive, for properly pursued it led straight to Bernhard. But—like many other tantalising leads—it wasn't effectively followed through. Only in a series of written questions— the Sub-committee's afterthoughts—was Jones asked to name the 'highest levels in the Dutch Government' who had recommended Gerritsen's appointment. Jones replied that he 'didn't recall'. The written questions and answers continued:

Question 26. What is your relationship with Prince Bernhard? *Answer:* We are friends of long standing ...
Question 28. Do you feel it appropriate to discuss business with the Prince*: Answer:* I do not feel it appropriate to discuss Dutch procurement business with the prince.

Question 29. Has the prince been of any help to Northrop? *Answer:* The prince has been of help to me in my gaining a better understanding of Europe.
Question 30. Did the prince give you any advice in selling the YF–17 Cobra? *Answer:* He did not give me any advice in selling the YF–17 Cobra.
Question 31. Did he receive payments or favors of any kind for his involvement? *Answer:* No.

The potentially explosive thrust of these questions went unnoticed, not least because they were not published for three months, by which time Northrop was no longer in the limelight. But what did emerge clearly from Tom Jones's testimony was that there were bigger fish behind the small fry. All eyes were now on Lockheed.

In Burbank, the company's hard-pressed vice-president in charge of public relations, Bill Perreault, issued indignant denials of any wrong-doing. 'I cannot figure out why Northrop keeps comparing its foreign operations with Lockheed's', he complained to the *Washington Post,* and his ignorance was no doubt real enough. The few in Lockheed who knew very well what the Church Committee was on about were not disposed to share such guilty knowledge with their public relations man. Mr Perreault had a lot to learn, and he would learn it fast.

The Northrop hearings were scarcely over before the Church Committee subpoena'd Lockheed to supply all documents relating to overseas sales and commission payments from 1970 on. The SEC did the same. Lockheed's outside auditors, Arthur Young, leaped into action and announced they would not sign the corporation's annual report unless its principal officers, including Carl Kotchian, were willing to sign a declaration that they knew of no questionable commission payments. To have signed, just as the dirty deeds of the past were marching on Burbank like a plague of cockroaches, would have been suicide. Kotchian and company declined to sacrifice themselves, the auditors refused to budge, and the shareholders' meeting, called to approve an annual report the auditors wouldn't certify, had to be cancelled. Lockheed was clearly in deep, deep trouble.

At this point the company's old arch-enemy, Senator William Proxmire, re-entered the fray. He had led the Senate investigation into the Galaxy fiasco and had organised Congressional opposition to the government loan guarantee which had barely saved Lockheed from bankruptcy in 1971. Now his Senate Banking Committee announced its intention to hold public hearings on Lockheed's overseas commission payments. Church was furious: his thunder had been stolen just as the storm was breaking. But for Lockheed Proxmire's intervention merely brought forward the date of execution. On the eve of the Proxmire hearings Bill Perreault was made to eat all his previous denials and issue a press release blandly acknowledging that the corporation had made 'questionable payments' totalling $22 million.

The Banking Committee's hearings were fixed for Monday, August 25. So too, as it happened, was a routine meeting of the Emergency Loan Guarantee Board, which was due to release a further instalment of $30 million in debt payments to the company. But, not surprisingly, some members of the Board made it known that they opposed further assistance to a company which appeared to be bribing its way to survival on public funds. The consequence of such a decision for Lockheed would have been instant bankruptcy — and, ironically, a sudden end to the planned Congressional hearings, since Lockheed would technically cease to exist once the receiver had been called in. But in the event, the Board voted the $30 million and the emergency passed.

All this was too much for corporate treasurer Robert N. Waters, a moody bachelor who had been with the company twenty-one years. Only weeks before the Lockheed scandal broke, Eli Black, chairman of the huge fruit and meat-packaging conglomerate United Fruit, under investigation for a $1·25 million bribe in Honduras, had smashed a window in his Manhattan office and plunged forty-four floors to his death. Waters was not in quite the same league: he was never a member of Haughton's inner cabinet, and though he had been involved in administering some of Lockheed's 'off-the-books' payments, his overall responsibility was small. Nevertheless, on the eve of the Proxmire hearings and the Emergency Loan Guarantee Board meeting, Waters cocked his hunting rifle and shot himself dead through the temple. His death was hushed up. Lockheed ascribed the tragedy to 'personal difficulties', but a suicide note referred to business problems.

As it turned out, Proxmire failed to get much out of Dan Haughton. Testifying before the Committee, the Lockheed chairman declined to go beyond the guarded admissions in his press release of a few days earlier. The high-spot of the hearings came when Haughton was pressed to concede that questionable payments meant bribes. He paused, then held a whispered consultation with his lawyer, Roger

Clark, a partner in Rodgers and Wells, the prestigious law firm run by former attorney general and secretary of state William P. Rodgers. Then to laughter, in which he joined but Clark did not, he told Proxmire: 'My counsel says he'd prefer to characterise it as a kickback, but, you know, if you want to call it bribes, I guess it's all right.'

Haughton also set a pattern which he and his colleagues were to follow rigorously in the months ahead: persistent refusal to name individuals, and often even countries, to whom 'kickbacks' had been paid. Batting blind, without benefit of the clues scattered through the much wider range of documents subpoena'd by Church's more thorough and experienced staffmen, Proxmire failed to dent Haughton's wall of silence on this score.

Thus significant revelations had to await the opening on September 12 of the long series of Church's hearings which were to run on, sometimes public, sometimes closed and secret, until well into the following year (though often with intervals of several weeks between sessions). As with Northrop, Church punctuated each hearing with the prior release of masses of the subpoena'd documents. The press tables drowned in them. Often the duplicated copies were left behind, unread and certainly not unravelled, to be shovelled into the janitors' waste-bins as the session adjourned. More attention was paid to the set-piece speeches, clearly directed at the television news cameras as much as at the witnesses. Thus Senator Church in his opening statement:

> The bribes and the payoffs associated with doing business abroad represent a pattern of crookedness that would make, in terms of its scope and magnitude, crookedness in politics look like a Sunday school picnic by comparison ...
>
> What was merely implicit in the Northrop documents ... is most explicit in the Lockheed documents; that is, that foreign agents or consultants are hired not for their local expertise or their technical knowledge but for their connections in influential Government circles, and they are paid huge fees on this not for services rendered, but so that a part or most of these fees can be passed on as bribes or kickbacks to foreign officials.

One reason—apart from sheer volume and density—why the vital documents tended to be ignored by the press was that some of the most sensitive sections had been doctored by the committee staff before release. That was because the still tough and combatant

Haughton won a vital behind-the-scenes battle over the suppression of the names of bribe recipients. His argument with Church and the SEC was that disclosure would be unfair to the officials involved and could finish Lockheed in the overseas market. Faced with the prospect of a lengthy battle with Lockheed's lawyers and with indefinite stone-walling by the corporation's executives, Church caved in, as the SEC was soon to do during protracted consent decree negotiations.

To Lockheed's critics and outright enemies, the Church Committee's attitude amounted to craven capitulation. One who professed to think so was Ernest Hauser, former friend and confidant of Franz Josef Strauss and Lockheed customer-relations executive in Germany. From his home in Phoenix, Arizona, where he had retired to run his own aircraft spare parts business, Hauser wrote to the *Wall Street Journal* recalling the Starfighter saga of the early 1960s and the parts played – according to his story – by Strauss and Bernhard. Hauser also talked to the Church Committee. After Levinson and his staff had satisfied themselves that Hauser's diary was genuine, a secret session of the Committee was convened to hear his testimony and place it on record. Days later, on December 4, the *Journal* published a portion of Hauser's diary, naming Bernhard and Strauss for the first time.

Now the air was thick with denials from Burbank, Bonn and Amsterdam. Church was embarrassed. The leak brought into question his private promise to Haughton not to publicise names. And politically, his embarrassment ran even deeper.

Months earlier, Church had made a private decision to toss his hat in the ring for the Democratic nomination in the 1976 Presidential election. His zeal in pursuing both the multinationals and, in another Senate Committee under his chairmanship, the CIA, had made him a national figure, not much less well known than Hubert Humphrey and far more familiar at the time than a rank outsider named Jimmy Carter. But by the end of 1975 Church's plans were beginning to go awry. First, both the multinationals and the CIA hearings were going on seemingly forever, involving a huge volume of work which left little time for campaigning. But second, and more important, his own sensitive political antennae had begun to detect the first rumblings of a nation-wide backlash against the post-Watergate frenzy of public disclosure and exposure. And Frank Church, fearless crusader against the sins of Exxon, Lockheed and the CIA, looked the likeliest target of those who complained that investigative journalism and investigative politics were America's new blood sports. By the end of November Church had decided to steer the Lockheed hearings towards an early end.

His decision baffled and infuriated the zealous staffmen whose backroom detective work had given the Committee its punch. They saw it as a surrender to Haughton, whose latest ploy was to promise detailed revelations of Lockheed's dirty work in Italy (which in any case could not long be hidden) in return for an 'understanding' that the Committee would not investigate the company's deals in Japan, where a billion-dollar sale of 44 Orions, negotiated in part through Yoshio Kodama, was at that moment hanging in the balance.

The staffmen would have been angrier still had they known all that was going on behind the scenes. At Carl Kotchian's instigation, his Washington attorneys, Rodgers and Wells, were quietly soliciting the help of the state department. On November 28, 1975 Henry Kissinger himself wrote a letter to attorney general Edward Levi in which, while condemning corporate bribery overseas, he argued that the disclosure of the names of officials and politicians paid by Lockheed and its agents 'can have grave consequences for significant foreign-relations interests of the United States'. He requested a 'protective order' to prevent such disclosures, which, at the attorney generals' behest, the Washington District Court promptly issued. But the whole heavy-handed manoeuvre proved counter-productive. It seems to have galvanised Church into a determination that the Senate would not be muzzled, least of all by the Nixon administration, and this was almost certainly a critical factor in his decision to continue the investigation and even to press for limited disclosures of names, at least in secret sessions where the court order could not be enforced. Kotchian learned of the failure of his attorney's ploy when he received a subpoena to testify before the Church Committee. A year later he was telling the Japanese papers, 'I still believe today that there must have been some reason in the United States for reopening the Lockheed investigation.'

The truth is that what also effectively ditched Church's plan to call an early halt was the new surge of world-wide interest which followed the back-door entry of Bernhard and Strauss. Hauser was flown to London for a lengthy interview with Granada Television in which the stories cryptically covered in the austere *Wall Street Journal* were recounted in unambiguous detail, with copious references to the now famous and damning diaries. Transmitted in prime time, the interview was seen by some twelve million British viewers; and over the next few weeks it was shown in a score of countries around the world, including the Netherlands, Germany and the United States. Like it or not, Church now had little choice but to arrange further hearings, which would carry the Committee's investigations on to March 1976. In the Presidential stakes he was an early drop-out.

Meanwhile ever-increasing delegations of foreign officials and pressmen were beating a path to Church's door, and to Stanley Sporkin's at the SEC, seeking documentary evidence for new investigations sprouting up all over Europe and in Japan. Air freight companies did a roaring trade shipping cartons of xeroxed memos and bills, as they had once shipped cartons of currency. The Spanish came to dip their documents in whitewash. The Turks came too, to produce a report that was later suppressed by the Demirel government but continued to be wielded as a political weapon by the social democrat opposition. In Italy and Japan, the scandals were to lead to major trials, and to 'Lockheed elections' where the ruling parties suffered unprecedented losses.

Most thorough of all was the investigation of the Dutch 'Commissie van Drie' headed by Judge Donner of the European Communities Court of Justice, which concluded that Prince Bernhard's continuing denials that he had ever received Lockheed money 'cannot be reconciled with established facts'. After noting that its enquiries were 'repeatedly hampered by H.R.H.'s poor memory', the commission concluded that the prince,

> in the conviction that his position was unassailable and his judgment was not to be influenced, originally entered much too lightly into transactions which were bound to create the impression that he was susceptible to favours. Later he showed himself open to dishonourable requests and offers. Finally, he allowed himself to be tempted to take initiatives which were completely unacceptable and which were bound to place himself and the Netherlands' procurement policy in the eyes of others in a dubious light.

Thus disgraced, the prince resigned all his public posts. His wife was with difficulty dissuaded from abdication by assurances that he would not be prosecuted.

In Japan, the long and always highly coloured saga climaxed in a manner no less bizarre than anything that had gone before. On March 25, 1976 three young Japanese wearing red headbands emblazoned with the crest of the Imperial army ran through the regional

airport building at Chofu shouting the samurai warcry 'Banzai!'
Then one of them, Mitsuyasu Maeno, climbed into a Piper Cherokee,
taxied out to the runway and took off in the direction of
Tokyo.

Five years earlier, Maeno, then 24, had been one of a select band
of ultra-nationalists who had gathered in the plush Okura Hotel to
hear the premier performance of a proposed new national anthem,
'Song of the Race', which called for a kamikaze coup d'état to restore
the glories of Imperial Japan. The composer of the anthem was none
other than Yoshio Kodama.

Maeno was then an actor with Nikkatsu, a leading film company
in Tokyo. But the parts he played were small and so were his earnings. Soon Maeno found he could make much more money starring
in crude porno films. By 1976 he could be seen nightly in scores of
back-street movie-houses, thrusting away on the flickering screen.
It was a sad and speedy decline for a young man who had sworn to
devote his life to the Divine Emperor and rid his land of foreign,
corrupting influences.

Now he was embarked on an act intended to atone not only for
his own sins but for those of his fallen idol, Kodama, who was confined to his home by a stroke which had swiftly followed the first
news of his role in the Lockheed affair. So Mitsuyasu Maeno flew
his tiny hijacked plane to the closely guarded suburban house of the
man who had supplied the wartime Imperial air force with its kamikaze planes, circled twice, then pointed the nose at Kodama's roof
and began his dive to ritual, redemptive suicide.

The plane smashed through a veranda and started a fire. Maeno
was burned to death, but Yoshio Kodama was unhurt. He survived
to face trial in June 1977 for tax evasion and violating foreign exchange laws, to which he pleaded not guilty. In separate trials, Osano
has denied charges of perjury in his testimony to the Japanese Diet in
February 1976, when he disclaimed using influence on Lockheed's
behalf; and eight Japanese government officials and corporate
officers of ANA have pleaded not guilty to perjury and bribery
charges. In the most important trial of them all, Tanaka and four
co-defendants—Enomoto, Hiyama, Okubo and Itoh—have denied
charges of accepting or giving bribes. All four trials are expected to
last until 1979 and, with appeals, to run on into the 1980s. Meanwhile
they have inspired a cottage industry based on what the Japanese call
Rokkiedo Jiken, the 'Lockheed incident'. A spate of books on leading
figures in the scandal—some fifty on Kodama alone—have briefly

hit the best-seller lists. The Japanese feature-film industry has turned out a spectacular on the Starfighter deal, and even the traditional kabuki theatre has got in on the act with a play about a group of samurai involved in bribery. Other enterprising manufacturers have produced such items as a 'commuter pass' enabling subway passengers to travel from 'Peanuts Station', to 'High Government Officials Station' via 'Cover-up Station', and white handkerchiefs bearing the inscription 'I Received One Hundred Peanuts'. A pop record, 'I Also Would Like Peanuts', made the charts. And in the back-street porn cinemas, the pathetic Mitsuyasu Maeno became something of a cult object: the naked, thrashing figure who aptly summed up the obscenity of it all.

4

In the new world into which we are stumbling, 56 of the 100 largest economic entities are nation-states. The other 44 are multinational companies, like Lockheed.[1] By 1980 there will be more multinationals than nation-states in the top hundred.

That perhaps goes a long way towards explaining why corporate corruption as an issue has dominated the politics of the 1970s. And neither American-based nor large-scale companies have patents on the processes of bribery. Many of the 200 companies which have voluntarily disclosed questionable payments to the SEC are relatively small. And British no less than American businessmen have been caught at the same greasy game. British Petroleum would appear to have spent £9 million over four years in special payments; Shell £2·5 million over five years in Italy; ICI £1·2 million in four years (through four subsidiaries): and British Leyland an undisclosed sum in slush fund 'commissions'. A BBC poll of twenty of Britain's top exporting companies, carried out in September 1977, disclosed that ten admitted in confidence to having special payments built into foreign contracts, while four of the ten admitted paying bribes. It seems not at all unlikely that Britain, a much less open society than the United States, with more restrictive libel laws and virtually no effective

1 Strictly speaking, Lockheed, being wholly American-owned, is not a multinational. But its overseas subsidiaries and participation in multinational projects make it virtually so except by the most academic of definitions. Certainly no one thought to challenge the jurisdiction of the Senate Sub-committee on Multinational Corporations in Lockheed's case.

investigative mechanism or tradition in the legislature, has in its boardrooms more concealed corporate corruption than its much-maligned Atlantic neighbour.

In Washington the Lockheed scandal prompted a rash of draft legislation designed to remedy the clearly anomalous situation that, while it was illegal under applicable law in Japan or Italy for nationals of those countries to *take* bribes, it was not illegal under American federal or state law for Americans to *give* them. Lockheed's own response to any reform was at first unashamedly negative, a statement shortly before the first Proxmire hearing in August 1975 claiming defiantly that the company's 'future inability to conform to local business practices could seriously prejudice its ability to operate in certain foreign markets'.

But by the time the Church hearings began in September this view had undergone considerable modification – at least for public consumption. Dan Haughton told the Church Committee:

> At the present time there is great confusion over what is legal under US law and what is not, over what has to be reported in financial statements and what does not. Certainly there is a great need to have the laws and regulations clarified at the earliest possible time. It is my hope that this can be done without causing undue harm to American companies, American workers, and American shareholders. As far as Lockheed is concerned, it is my hope that the actions of our Government in this regard can be accomplished without causing the maximum amount of damage to my company.

To virtually all the legislators who applied themselves to the problem in the immediate aftermath of the scandal – and they included Hubert Humphrey as well as Proxmire and Church – the answer was to make all commissions and consultancy payments illegal unless declared openly: and even this modest reform, of highly questionable efficacy, was opposed by the Ford administration as an intolerable interference in the process of private enterprise and the rights of the business community. A more sophisticated blocking tactic was to argue that any regulatory legislation should await world agreement, perhaps achieved through the United Nations, in order to avoid unfair discrimination against American companies: a policy that would guarantee no effective change for decades.

But in all the talk of global bribery and how to stop it, few attacked the heart of the matter with the clear-witted incisiveness of a long-dead sociologist named Edward Alsworth Ross. In a book called

Sin and Society,[1] published back in 1907, Ross had written of the business corporation:

> It feels not the restraints that conscience and public sentiment lay on the business man. It fears the law no more, and public indignation far less, than does the individual. You can hiss the bad man, egg him, lampoon him, caricature him, ostracise him and his. Not so with the bad corporation. The corporation, moreover, is not in dread of hell fire. You cannot Christianize it. You may convert its stockholders, animate them with patriotism or public spirit or love of social service; but this will have little or no effect on the tenor of their corporation. In short, it is an entity that transmits the greed of investors, but not their conscience; that returns them profits but not unpopularity.

Corporations, complained Ross, were marvellously adroit at diffusing and hiding responsibility. This kept public opinion impotent, since

> it allows itself to be kept guessing which shell the pea is under, whether the accountability is with the foreman, or the local manager, or the general manager, or the directors. How easily the public wrath is lost in the maze! Public indignation meets a cuirass of divided responsibility that scatters a shock that would have stretched iniquity prone.

How then should corporate iniquity be dealt with? Fines and financial sanctions would not be enough, wrote Ross.

> Fine the corporation, and, if its sinning is lucrative, it heeds the fine no more than a flea-bite ... Fine the law-breaking officers, and the board of directors by indemnifying them encourages them to do it again.

What then? Ross had the answer:

> Never will the brake of the law grip these slippery wheels until prison doors yawn for the convicted officers of lawless corporations ... The directors of a company ought to be individually accountable for every case of misconduct of which the company

---

1 The credit for re-discovering and recognising the appositeness of Ross's neglected work belongs not to me but to Morton Mintz and Jerry S. Cohen who quote from *Sin and Society* in their book *Power, Inc.* (Viking Press, New York, 1976).

receives the benefit, for every preventable deficiency or abuse that regularly goes on in the course of the business. Hold them blameless if they prove the inefficiency or disobedience of underlings, but not if they plead ignorance.

That went far beyond the recommendations of Humphrey, Proxmire, Church and the reformers of seventy years later. Not until Carter succeeded Ford were Ross's remedies taken seriously and translated into a bill imposing stiff penalties for those convicted of bribery: up to five years in prison for individuals, and fines of up to $1 million for companies. The impact of the bill, signed by the President in December 1977, is uncertain. Britain, it should be noted, shows no sign whatever of following suit. The Confederation of British Industries announced in April 1978 its opposition to reforms mooted by the International Chamber of Commerce, and its implacable hostility to unilateral action by the British government. As the CBI's president, John Greenborough, put it: 'We are anxious that there should be no question of British industry being put at a disadvantage.'

It is unlikely that, by itself, even the fear of yawning prison doors will deter undercover bribery, veiled as it is in the secret mysteries of front-companies, third, fourth and fifth parties, local custom and numbered accounts. 'I'm not sure that the ingenuity of man's mind is so limited that he couldn't get around it', said Hubert Humphrey of his own proposed legislation when interviewed by the author on ITV's 'World in Action' programme, but he argued that the real brake would be 'the spotlight of public attention, what we call "operating in the sunshine"'. The same thought had occurred to the prescient Edward Ross. He assigned a role to the media – in his day the press – which, he said, ought as a matter of routine

> to print along with the news of the exposure of corporation misconduct the names of the directors, in order that the public indignation may not explode without result, but find rather a proper target; for just indignation is altogether too precious a thing to be wasted. Consider the salutary effects of such severity. When an avalanche of wrath hangs over the head of a sinning corporation, no one will accept a directorship who is not prepared to give a good deal of time and serious attention to its business. Strict accountability will send flying the figurehead directors who, when the misdeeds of their protégés come to light, protest they 'didn't know'.

Lockheed had many 'don't know' directors. If Ross had been heeded in 1907 there would have been no corporate scandals in the 1970s.

5

Lockheed survived. Indeed, by the end of 1977 business was booming. The company whose name had become a universal byword for the big bribe was again boasting annual sales well over $3 billion — almost entirely in the defence field — and profits looking to exceed $50 million. The government's loan guarantees were no longer needed, stock had doubled in value in twelve months, and the banks looked set to waive their dividend prohibition some time in the not-too-distant future. Even the TriStar looked set for an unexpected late recovery, with a substantial Pan-American World Airways order announced in April 1978 promising to put the programme on course in the 1980s. Dan Haughton's chickens, which had come home to roost in the 1970s, seemed set to lay golden eggs for his successors.

Could it be that bribery had paid off? That all publicity had proved good publicity? Or was the upturn the fruit of a much-publicised internal clean-up? Probably neither. The easing of the oil famine and more favourable economic trends clearly had much to do with the company's revived fortunes.

But there was a clean-up. Lockheed publicly dismantled its grease machine. In March 1976, with the Church hearings still unfinished, Haughton and Kotchian were ousted from their top posts, given golden handshakes and eased into premature retirement. Robert Haack, a former president of the New York Stock Exchange, was brought in as caretaker chairman. A little more than a year later, the company completed and published the report of its Special Review Committee, set up under the terms of the self-policing consent decree negotiated with the SEC. The report followed Haughton's refusal to name names, but otherwise pulled few punches. The blame for what had happened was laid squarely at the door of Haughton and Kotchian, who had 'been willing to distort such a primary principle as integrity for short-term expediency' and were 'obviously responsible'. The rest of the board, it was implied (shades of Ross!), didn't know what was going on.

Ignorance was the plea in particular of former vice-chairman and chief financial officer Roy Anderson. The Review Committee — seven Lockheed directors — acknowledged that Anderson had been 'informed by Kotchian of certain questionable commitments shortly after they were made', and noted that 'large questionable payments were made by or through the company's financial organisation', for which Anderson was responsible. But the Committee decided that 'he was to a certain extent the victim of a plan by Haughton and Kotchian to keep him uninformed', and 'in balancing both sides of the matter' it was felt that 'the circumstances are not such as to bar him from continuing to serve the company under its now applicable ethical standards'. Five months later, in October 1977, Roy Anderson succeeded Haack to the top job: chairman of the board.

By then, Lockheed had a new code of business conduct, distributed in the May 1977 issue of the company magazine *Lockheed Life* to all employees. Just as each of the Watergate conspirators in turn seemed, in the end, to find religion, so what Haack called 'the New Lockheed' became perhaps the world's first born-again corporation. The code seeks to bury the grease machine and gives it a fitting epitaph:

LOCKHEED PRINCIPLES OF BUSINESS CONDUCT

High principles of business conduct must underlie the policies of any corporation. We believe the management of Lockheed has an obligation to articulate the general principles which should guide and motivate the people of Lockheed. We are clearly stating them now as a mark of our determination to conduct the company's business on an ethical basis and as an imperative signal to every man and woman in the corporation that they must share these principles.

Lockheed will comply with the laws of the United States and will comply with foreign law in those countries in which we do business, making all reasonable effort to determine what laws are applicable to our operations in those countries. Beyond legal compliance, we will strive for integrity in every aspect of our work.

Lockheed's business will be fully recorded in the corporate records, and open to appropriate inspection. Our people not only must scrupulously avoid any conflict of interest, but must avoid even the appearance of such conflict.

Lockheed recognizes that beyond the responsibilities common to all American corporations, we have a special obligation as a major contractor to government to operate in a manner that is in concert with the objectives of the U.S. Government and consistent with U.S. foreign policy.

Ethical conduct is the highest form of loyalty to Lockheed. For that reason, it is the responsibility of every man and woman in the corporation to know and accept these principles. It is the obligation of every manager, from the chief executive officer to all ranks of supervision, to understand the principles and the specific policies which govern the corporation and to see that they are understood by every person within his or her responsibility.

Principles governing ethical conduct require continuing attention, guidance and enforcement by management. Lockheed's management will insure that there are management policy statements governing aspects of corporate ethical practice. These policies will be continually reviewed and expanded as the need arises.

Index